THE INTERPERSONAL NEUROBIOLOGY OF GROUP PSYCHOTHERAPY AND GROUP PROCESS

NEW INTERNATIONAL LIBRARY OF GROUP ANALYSIS

Series Editor: Earl Hopper

Other titles in the Series

Contributions of Self Psychology to Group Psychotherapy: Selected Papers
Walter N. Stone

Difficult Topics in Group Psychotherapy: My Journey from Shame to Courage
Jerome S. Gans

Resistance, Rebellion and Refusal in Groups: The 3 Rs
Richard M. Billow

The Social Unconscious in Persons, Groups, and Societies.
Volume 1: Mainly Theory
edited by Earl Hopper and Haim Weinberg

The Social Nature of Persons: One Person is No Person
A. P. Tom Ormay

Trauma and Organizations
edited by Earl Hopper

Small, Large, and Median Groups: The Work of Patrick de Maré
edited by Rachel Lenn and Karen Stefano

The Dialogues In and Of the Group: Lacanian Perspectives on the
Psychoanalytic Group
Macario Giraldo

From Psychoanalysis to Group Analysis: The Pioneering
Work of Trigant Burrow
edited by Edi Gatti Pertegato and Giorgio Orghe Pertegato

The One and the Many: Relational Psychoanalysis and Group Analysis
Juan Tubert-Oklander

Listening with the Fourth Ear: Unconscious Dynamics in Analytic
Group Psychotherapy
Leonard Horwitz

Forensic Group Psychotherapy: The Portman Clinic Approach
edited by John Woods and Andrew Williams
(joint publication with The Portman Papers)

Nationalism and the Body Politic: Psychoanalysis and the Rise of
Ethnocentrism and Xenophobia
edited by Lene Auestad

The Paradox of Internet Groups: Alone in the Presence of Virtual Others
Haim Weinberg

The Art of Group Analysis in Organisations: The Use of Intuitive and
Experiential Knowledge
Gerhard Wilke

The World within the Group: Developing Theory for Group Analysis
Martin Weegman

Developing Nuclear Ideas: Relational Group Psychotherapy
Richard M. Billow

THE INTERPERSONAL NEUROBIOLOGY OF GROUP PSYCHOTHERAPY AND GROUP PROCESS

Edited by

Susan P. Gantt and Bonnie Badenoch

LONDON AND NEW YORK

First published 2013 by Karnac Books Ltd.

Published 2019 by Routledge
2 Park Square, Milton Park, Abingdon, Oxon OX14 4RN
52 Vanderbilt Avenue, New York, NY 10017

Routledge is an imprint of the Taylor & Francis Group, an informa business

British Library Cataloguing in Publication Data

A C.I.P. for this book is available from the British Library

ISBN 978-1-78049-177-6 (pbk)

Edited, designed and produced by The Studio Publishing Services Ltd
www.publishingservicesuk.co.uk
e-mail: studio@publishingservicesuk.co.uk

CONTENTS

ACKNOWLEDGEMENTS   vii

ABOUT THE EDITORS AND CONTRIBUTORS   ix

NEW INTERNATIONAL LIBRARY OF GROUP ANALYSIS   xiv
FOREWORD by Earl Hopper

INTRODUCTION   xix
Susan P. Gantt and Bonnie Badenoch

CHAPTER ONE
Integrating interpersonal neurobiology with group
psychotherapy   1
Bonnie Badenoch and Paul Cox

Commentary: Reflections on mind, brain, and relationships
in group psychotherapy   19
Daniel J. Siegel

CHAPTER TWO
Mirror neurons: their implications for group psychotherapy   25
Victor L. Schermer

CHAPTER THREE
Group psychotherapy and neuro-plasticity: an attachment
theory perspective   51
Philip J. Flores

CHAPTER FOUR
Developing the group mind through functional subgrouping:
linking systems-centred training (SCT) and interpersonal
neurobiology   73
Susan P. Gantt and Yvonne M. Agazarian

CHAPTER FIVE
Introducing couples to group therapy: pursuing passion
through the neo-cortex   103
Don Ferguson

CHAPTER SIX
Sensorimotor psychotherapy as a foundation of group therapy
with younger clients   123
Bonnie Mark-Goldstein and Pat Ogden

CHAPTER SEVEN
Hunger and longing: a developmental regulation model for
exploring core relational needs   147
Mitchel Adler

CHAPTER EIGHT
Relationship-focused group therapy (RFGT) to mitigate marital
instability and neuropsychophysiological dysregulation   171
Gloria Batkin Kuhn and Darryl B. Feldman

CHAPTER NINE
A transformational learning group: inviting the implicit   189
Bonnie Badenoch

INDEX   203

ACKNOWLEDGEMENTS

Susan: Much appreciation for Kirk's support to do what I care about, for Kathy's support and help which enables me to have time for writing, for the support of my friends, Carol, Fran, Claudia, Yvonne, and my mentors, most especially Yvonne. And in celebration of Mary Ellen, may she flourish. Also much appreciation to Rich for helping incubate my learning and to the American Group Psychotherapy Association and its *International Journal of Group Psychotherapy* for supporting the special issue on which this book builds.

Bonnie: So grateful for the support of family—Kate, Patti, and Riley—and friends—particularly Coease, Kate, Sarah, Kirke, and Sher—as I seek to foster the application of the principles of interpersonal neurobiology in all walks of life. They provide the nest in which these ways of being and knowing hatch, and are there to celebrate the often-surprising new life that results. I am especially thankful for the groups who are shaping my experience as much as I am shaping theirs—two IPNB study groups here in Vancouver, one in Salem, and especially the group of twenty-four dedicated therapists in Portland, Maine whose story unfolds in the last chapter of this book. You have taught me so much.

viii   ACKNOWLEDGEMENTS

Six of the chapters in this book are reprinted here with the permission of the publisher. Chapters One and its commentary, Two, Three, Four, and Five were originally printed in the *International Journal of Group Psychotherapy* as part of a special issue on "Neurobiology and interpersonal systems: groups, couples and beyond" as follows:

Badenoch, B., & Cox, P. (2010). Integrating interpersonal neurobiology with group psychotherapy. *International Journal of Group Psychotherapy, 60*(4); 462–431.

Siegel, D. J. (2010). Commentary on "Integrating interpersonal neurobiology with group psychotherapy: reflections on mind, brain, and relationships in group psychotherapy". *International Journal of Group Psychotherapy, 60*(4): 483–485.

Schermer, V. L. (2010). Mirror neurons: their implications for group psychotherapy. *International Journal of Group Psychotherapy, 60*(4): 486–513.

Flores, P. I. (2010). Group psychotherapy and neuro-plasticity: an attachment theory perspective. *International Journal of Group Psychotherapy, 60*(4): 546–570.

Gantt, S. P., & Agazarian, Y. M. (2010). Developing the group mind through functional subgrouping: linking Systems-Centered Training (SCT) and interpersonal neurobiology. *International Journal of Group Psychotherapy, 60*(4): 514–544.

Ferguson, D. (2010). Introducing couples to group therapy: pursuing passion through the neo-cortex. *International Journal of Group Psychotherapy, 60*(4): 572–594.

In Chapter Six, *Self Portrait*, by David Whyte is reprinted with permission of the author.

Chapter Eight was originally published as:

Kahn, G. B., & Feldman, D. B. (2011). Relationship-Focused Group Therapy (RFGT) to mitigate marital instability and neuropsychophysiological dysregulation. *International Journal of Group Psychotherapy, 61*(4): 518–536.

Mitchel Adler, PsyD, is a clinical psychologist, certified group psychotherapist, and the Director of MindBody Intelligence (MBI) Consulting where he provides leadership training in emotional intelligence. He has served on the faculty of the UC Davis School of Medicine and he is co-author of the book *Promoting Emotional Intelligence in Organizations*. He received his doctoral degree in clinical psychology from Rutgers University and his BA from the University of Michigan, Ann Arbor, where he graduated with Distinction. Dr Adler has a private psychotherapy practice in Davis, California where he lives with his wife and two daughters.

Yvonne M. Agazarian, EdD, CGP, DFAGPA, FAPA, is the developer of a theory of living human systems and its systems-centred practice and the founder of the Systems-Centered Training and Research Institute. She lives in Philadelphia, Pennsylvania and teaches and consults internationally. She has published numerous books and articles, and in 1997 she received the Group Psychologist of the Year award from the American Psychological Association "for her involvement in research, publication, teaching and training. She exemplifies the finest in scholarship in the discipline of psychology. She has contributed to expanding our knowledge of the boundaries between clinical and social psychology . . . Her considerable body of work illustrates the highest blend of creativity and learning.

Bonnie Badenoch, PhD, LMFT, is a marriage and family therapist, supervisor, teacher, and author who is integrating the discoveries of relational neuroscience into the art of therapy. She co-founded the non-profit agency, Nurturing the Heart with the Brain in Mind in Portland, Oregon. As a mentor/supervisor of marriage and family therapist interns, she supports their developing mental health while helping them internalise the principles of interpersonal neurobiology. Bonnie currently teaches at Portland State University, and speaks internationally about applying IPNB principles both personally and professionally. She is the author of *Being a Brain-wise Therapist* (2008) and *The Brain-sawy Therapist's Workbook* (2011).

Paul Damian Cox, MD, is a board certified psychiatrist and Associate Professor of Psychiatry, UC Davis School of Medicine, Department of Psychiatry and Behavioral Neuroscience, Davis, California. His professional areas of expertise and interest include comprehensive management combining medication and therapy, as well as mindfulness based stress reduction (MBSR). He was recently awarded the Alonso Award for Excellence in Psychodynamic Group Psychotherapy by the Group Psychotherapy Foundation for co-editing with Susan Gantt, the special issue of the *International Journal of Group Psychotherapy* on "Neurobiology and interpersonal systems: groups, couples and beyond". Dr Cox is an experienced teacher drawing from interpersonal neurobiology and social cognitive learning theory.

Darryl B. Feldman, PhD, ABPP, CGP, is a clinical psychologist and psychoanalyst. He has served on the American Board of Professional Psychology for group psychology, as President of the American Academy of Group Psychology as well as the Group Division of the New York Psychological Association and the Suffolk County Psychological Association. He was formerly the Director of the Pederson Krag Institute for Psychotherapy and Director of Psychological Services at both Adelphi University's Institute of Advanced Psychological Studies and the State University of New York at Farmingdale. He is a certified Imago Relationship Therapist.

He lectures nationally and internationally, teaches and publishes on the utilisation of group techniques to improve communication and lessen tension in relationships.

Don Ferguson, PhD, is a psychologist and marriage counsellor in private practice in Verona, Wisconsin. Dr Ferguson has worked with couples and organisations for over twenty-five years. His book, *Reptiles in Love*, provides an organised approach for couples wanting to improve their relationship. He has presented extensively on relationships and on group and organisational dynamics.

Philip J. Flores, PhD, ABPP, CGP, FAGPA, is a clinical psychologist who specialises in the area of addictive disorders and group psychotherapy. Dr Flores is also Adjunct Faculty at Georgia State University, the Georgia School of Professional Psychology at Argosy University, and is supervisor of group psychotherapy at Emory University in Atlanta. In addition to his two books, *Group Psychotherapy with Addiction Population*, and *Addiction as an Attachment Disorder*, he is the winner of the 2005 Gradiva Award issued by The National Association for the Advancement of Psychoanalysis. He has also presented numerous workshops nationally and internationally on these two subjects.

Susan P. Gantt, PhD, ABPP, CGP, FAGPA, FAPA, is a psychologist in private practice in Atlanta, Georgia and works for Emory University School of Medicine where she coordinates group psychotherapy training. She is the Director of the Systems-Centered Training and Research Institute, and trains, supervises, and consults in the practice of SCT in the USA and Europe. She has co-authored three books with Yvonne Agazarian and was recently awarded the Alonso Award for Excellence in Psychodynamic Group Psychotherapy by the Group Psychotherapy Foundation for her work with Paul Cox on the special issue of the *International Journal of Group Psychotherapy* on "Neurobiology and interpersonal systems: groups, couples and beyond".

Bonnie Mark-Goldstein, LCSW, PhD, works through the lens of attachment theory, sensorirnotor psychotherapy, and the dynamic interaction of group psychotherapy. Her work also integrates traditional psychodynamic psychotherapy with progressive psychotherapeutic interventions such as hypnosis, mindfulness exercises, and EMDR. In 1989 Dr Goldstein founded and has continued to direct the Center for Psychological Services, offering a training opportunity for clinical interns, school-search assistance, and ongoing weekly therapy groups helping children and adolescents transition to the next stage of life, as well as two groups for young-adults.

Gloria Batkin Kahn, PhD, ABPP, CGP, is the Immediate Past President of the American Board of Group Psychology and a Past President of both the Westchester County Psychological Association and the Westchester Group Psychotherapy Society. She received the American Group Psychotherapy Association's Affiliate Assembly Award for contributions to the development of Group Therapy and the Westchester County Psychological Association's Distinguished Service Award. She frequently presents workshops both nationally and internationally and is the author of a number of journal articles and book chapters. Dr Kahn is in private practice in White Plains, New York, where she works with groups, couples, individual adults, and adolescents.

Pat Ogden, PhD, is a pioneer in somatic psychology and the founder/director of the Sensorimotor Psychotherapy Institute, an internationally recognised school specialising in somatic-cognitive approaches for the treatment of post-traumatic stress disorder and attachment disturbances. She is a clinician, consultant, international lecturer, and trainer, and first author of *Trauma and the Body: A Sensorimotor Approach to Psychotherapy* and is currently working on her second book, *Wisdom of the Body, Lost and Found: Sensorimotor Interventions for the Treatment of Trauma and Attachment*.

Daniel J. Siegel, MD, is clinical professor of psychiatry at the UCLA School of Medicine where he is on the faculty of the Center for Culture, Brain, and Development; Co-Director of the Mindful Awareness Research Center, and Executive Director of the Mindsight Institute. He is the Founding Editor of the *Norton Professional Series on Interpersonal Neurobiology* which contains over two dozen textbooks, and author of seven books on interpersonal neurobiology. His book *The Developing Mind*, originally published in 1999, introduced the field of interpersonal neurobiology.

Victor L. Schermer, MA, LPC, CAC, FAGPA, is a psychologist in private practice and clinic settings in Philadelphia, Pennsylvania. He is executive director of the Study Group for Contemporary Psychoanalytic Process and a Fellow of the American Group Psychotherapy Association. He has co-authored/co-edited seven books, been guest editor for six special editions of group psychotherapy journals, and written over forty articles and reviews in group psychotherapy and other subjects. He is a frequent presenter of lectures, workshops, and panels internationally. In 2006, he gave the Annual S. H. Foulkes Lecture for the Group Analytic Society in London.

I am pleased to include *The Interpersonal Neurobiology of Group Psychotherapy and Group Process* edited by Susan P. Gantt and Bonnie Badenoch in the New International Library of Group Analysis (NILGA). Based mostly on articles in a Special Issue of the *International Journal of Group Psychotherapy, 60*(4), 2010) entitled "Neurobiology and Interpersonal Systems: Groups, Couples and Beyond", the chapters in this book are very well written and carefully edited. The bibliographies remain timely and comprehensive. Several of the authors are well known to group analysts in England and Europe, and to those of us who participate in the annual conferences of the American Group Psychotherapy Association. Information about the qualifications and backgrounds of the authors is provided in the Introduction.

My Foreword to this second printing of a highly regarded book about a very important topic offers a sceptical appreciation of the importance and value of the study of IPNB for the practice of psychotherapy in its various forms. No one should doubt the value of the ideas and the findings that have been spawned by the new discipline of "interpersonal neurobiology" and the study of the so-called "social brain", especially when applied to the study of relationality and the development and maintenance of human groupings. The nature of the comparatively brief gestation of human beings within the body of the mother, followed by the lengthy period of maturation during which they are highly dependent on the (O)ther for their survival and development, has always suggested that we are "hard-wired" for participation in relationships and groupings of various kinds, sizes, and complexities. Equally, the problem with this perspective is that it has tended towards reductionist conceptualisations and explanations of properties of higher order systems in terms of properties of lower order systems, based on confusing analogies with homologies. Although organisms and societies are each living human systems, and each part of the environment of the other, they are not the same "thing".

I am reminded of debates that I have had with those psychoanalysts who have become preoccupied with the effects of the life of the foetus in relationship to the pregnant mother (almost always outside the context of family and community dynamics—no matter how permeable the boundaries of the uterus might be) on the later personality of the adult. Whereas I have valued the discoveries of research into antenatal life, I have also wondered whether the energy with which such research has been pursued might be defensive against the anxieties associated with the full appreciation of the vicissitudes of the Oedipus complex. Is the search for neurological "beginnings" connected with a retreat from the slings and arrows of later phases of the life trajectory, not to mention the sheer complexities of the multi-disciplinary study of them?

Recent decades have been characterised by the march of high technology medicine and science, seen most clearly in the development of the brain scan. There has been a virtual return to the search for the Holy Grail of organismic materiality as the foundation of mental and emotional life, the structure and functions of personality, and of the "life" of social systems, ranging from dyadic relationships to societies rooted in territory. At the same time, less importance has been given to the study of social systems, as manifest in the organisation of university departments, journal and book publications, research grants, etc.; sociology has been absorbed within the social sciences in general, associated with a highly suspicious use of the term "science". Might these developments be traced, at least in England and in the US, to the policies of the Thatcher and the Reagan governments, with their respective emphases on "individualism" as opposed to "socialism"? The observation that we all have brains and that our brains are attuned to the brains of others through our various senses, leads to an appreciation of sameness rather than to an appreciation of differences, and, thus, to the exploration of possibilities for the resolution of conflicts based on them.

In many of our conferences in the US it has become easier to have a good discussion about the social brain than about variations in family structure in terms of social class and ethnicity. I would suggest that this is a function of the massification of our profession, which is in so many ways a traumatised one (Hopper, 2012). These developments are also related to the increased importance of so-called "evidence-based" psychotherapy, which, on the one hand, is to be entirely welcomed and encouraged, but which, on the other, depends on what is being measured and on the validity and reliability of the measurement of it. After all, it is easier to measure the body and the brain than the "mind", and the "matrix" and the "mentality" of a social system, or the intensity of psychic conflict and the denial of social reality, the ultimate acknowledgement of which is always negotiable. This accords with the "relational egoism" that underpins the practice of those forms of psychotherapy that are coloured by the assumptions that the mind is rooted in the brain, whether monadic or social in nature.

The rediscovery of interpersonal neurobiology and an apprecia-tion of the social nature of the brain should not be used to divert our attention from the essential axioms of group analysis. The individual and his or her groupings are two sides of the same coin, both in the beginning and forever. This is why we think about human beings as "persons", and why we are preoccupied with the study of the field theory of the social unconscious, with its emphasis on processes of socialisation, relationality, transpersonality, and collectivity within a transgenerational context (Hopper & Weinberg, 2011). Actually, the rediscovery of interpersonal neurobiology and the social brain should strengthen our appreciation of the sociality of human nature. Biology is an essential element in, and dimension of, the foundation matrix, not to mention individual persons. Communication in general, and especially language, is a bridge in this project. However, our growing appreciation of the socio-biology of "musical communicality" in the infant's relationship with the (O)ther, and vice versa, (Wotton, in press) is an important step forward, as is the exploration of the dynamics of music in connection with cohesion and incohesion of societal social systems (Klimova, in press).

Susan Gantt and Yvonne Agazarian, the co-authors of a chapter about the "group mind", have begun to redefine the boundaries of group analysis through their emphasis on systemic thinking and on the use of what they call "functional sub-grouping". This is an important contribution to the conceptualisation of the mental and emotional life of groups and group-like social systems. Nonetheless, it must be remembered that whereas Bion and his followers neglected the study of building effective and efficient workgroups (which has become a preoccupation in recent OPUS conferences), Foulkes, de Maré, Pines, and other group analysts have focused on processes of translation, dialogue, and discourse as ways of increasing the coherence of communication as a dimension of the dynamic matrix of a group, which Foulkes considered to be its "collective mind". The continuing resolution of focal conflicts, as conceptualised by Stock-Whitaker (1985), should also be acknowledged as a contribution to the study of the collective mind. These scholars have each attempted to conceptualise the "mind" of a social system on the basis of models of the brain that were available to them, each of which carries its own difficulties.

Similarly, studies of interpersonal neurobiology and the social brain have refined our thinking about attachment and affect regulation, especially, but not only, in connection with trauma. These are essential considerations in the study of the transgenerational transmission of social trauma. However, whereas words alone are rarely "enough", words that are used within the context of appropriately attuned affect between and among people are likely to be all that will ever be available to us. We might yet develop an enhanced appreciation of the poetry of interpretation, which is not to suggest that this is the only therapeutic factor within our clinical repertoire.

I very much look forward to a second edition of this important book. I hope that it will generate creative dialogue and productive discourse. I also hope that it will contain contributions from group analysts that convey how much they have absorbed from the study of it.

References

Hopper, E. (Ed.) (2012). *Trauma and Organizations*. London: Karnac.
Hopper, E., & Weinberg, H. (Eds.) (2011). *The Social Unconscious in Persons, Groups and Societies: Volume 1: Mainly Theory*. London: Karnac.

Klimova, H. (In press). The unbearable appeal of totalitarianism and the collective self: an inquiry into the social nature of non-verbal communication. In: E. Hopper & H. Weinberg (Eds.), *The Social Unconscious in Persons, Groups and Societies: Volume 3*. London: Karnac.

Stock-Whitaker, D. (1985). *Using Groups to Help People*. London: Routledge & Kegan Paul.

Wotton, L. (in press). The musical foundation matrix. In: E. Hopper & H. Weinberg (Eds.), *The Social Unconscious in Persons, Groups and Societies: Volume 3*. London: Karnac.

Earl Hopper, PhD
Series Editor
London, 2015

Introduction

Susan P. Gantt and Bonnie Badenoch

Might it be possible that neuroscience, in particular interpersonal neurobiology, can illuminate the unique ways that group processes collaborate with and enhance the brain's natural developmental and repairing processes? This book brings together the work of twelve contemporary group therapists and practitioners who are exploring this possibility through applying the principles of interpersonal neurobiology (IPNB) to a variety of approaches to group therapy and experiential learning groups. IPNB's focus on how human beings shape one another's brains throughout the lifespan makes it a natural fit for those of us who are involved in bringing people together so that, through their interactions, they may better understand and transform their own deeper mind and relational patterns. Group is a unique context that can trigger, amplify, contain, and provide resonance for a broad range of human experiences, creating robust conditions for changing the brain.

Group psychotherapy has been an important treatment modality for many years, with its long history extending back to Bion (1959) and Freud. The great need for psychological support during the Second World War led to an increased focus on group treatment. Surprisingly, that interest and focus has actually decreased somewhat today in spite of studies showing that group psychotherapy is as effective as individual therapy (Burlingame, MacKenzie, & Strauss, 2004), and in spite of the shortage of resources in the mental health field. It is possible that an awareness of IPNB principles might put a firmer foundation underneath us as group leaders so that we can approach our groups with a greater awareness of how to contain the group and develop the group's capacity to support the neurobiological changes that underlie richer relationships. It is our hope that this book will support this kind of shift. In our experience, deepening awareness of the brain's processes increases the felt sense of *stability*, of knowing where we and the members of our groups are, while broadening our capacity for ***non-judgmental containing and holding***—two key components in group leadership.

While group therapy has a lengthy history, IPNB is a relatively new scientifically-grounded paradigm emerging from the seminal work of Daniel Siegel (1999, 2012), Allan Schore (1994, 2012), Louis Cozolino (2006, 2010), and others. Building on the vast research into the workings of the brain, these integrators have linked the research to the realm of the interpersonal, looking at how relationships affect our brain's function and structure. In this book, we take the next step to see how these processes actually unfold within our groups.

We can think of the benefit of interpersonal neurobiology from two perspectives. First, gaining knowledge of IPNB allows group therapists to offer brief explanations to patients about aspects of brain functioning that relate to the patients' challenges or symptoms in a way that can relieve shame and normalise their experience. This can provide additional "holding" while the longer processes involved in therapy take root. Understanding the important differences between treatments directed at changing "chemicals" (e.g., medication) *vs.* psychotherapies, directed at altering brain circuits, can be of great assistance in framing how therapy is different from and often synergistic with other treatments. Similarly, understanding the interpersonal nature of brain development and its role in illness, healing, and recovery also helps discriminate how group therapy is different from individual therapy, and, in many instances, may be a more powerful and logical choice from a brain-based perspective.

In addition to the psycho-educational support IPNB offers, it also points us toward the most efficacious ways to be with our groups. As We understand more deeply the interpersonal nature of change and ongoing development from a brain perspective, we can use what we now understand about mirror neurons and resonance circuitry (Iacoboni, 2008), the autonomic nervous system (Porges, 2009a,b), the social brain (Badenoch, 2008; Cozolino, 2006; Siegel, 2007), and the power of right-brain to right-brain communication in developing the circuits of emotion regulation (Schore, 2012) to guide our ways of taking leadership and being present within the group.

Briefly, the social brain consists of the limbic region and its interface with the middle prefrontal cortex. The limbic region is often referred to as the emotional brain and its most basic components are the amygdala (the locus of implicit memory and quick assessments of safety or danger), hippocampus (site of the creation of explicit memory and important in some memory retrieval tasks), and hypothalamus (regulator of the neuroendocrine system in conjunction with pituitary). The middle prefrontal cortex refers to the medial, ventral, and orbitofrontal cortices (circuits involved in attachment, regulation, the felt sense of ourselves in our history, and overall brain integration), working with the anterior cingulate (attentional focus central in regulation and in drawing cognitive and affective experience into coherence with each other). In brief, when these two regions are strongly connected, we develop many capacities including emotion regulation, attuned communication, response flexibility, empathy, autonomic regulation, and even the greater likelihood of moral behaviour. Without these connections, these capacities are diminished, profoundly affecting our ability to find and maintain warm, stable relationships. Our early attachment history provides the initial wiring of all these regions, both separately and in relation to each other. When we have sustained significant difficulties in these early relationships, group can provide a rich interpersonal context that may be uniquely able to offer the conditions in which implicit memory and early attachments can be repaired, bringing these two regions into sustained neural connection.

The illustration below (Figure 1) shows the contiguous relationship of many of these brain components and serves as a visual reference for the discussion of these brain systems in the chapters that follow.

The chapters included here introduce and highlight the theoretical and research literatures from an IPNB perspective, especially the newer understandings of brain plasticity, mirror neurons, the autonomic nervous system, implicit and explicit memory, affect regulation, and the relation between attachment and brain development. Building on these understandings, the authors elaborate on work with varying

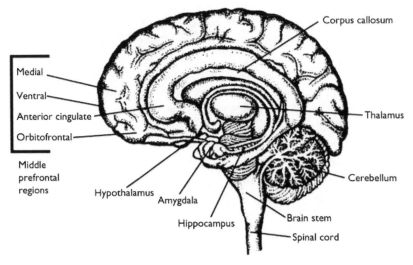

Art by Ron Estrine

Figure 1. Brain subsystems important in social and emotional functioning. Adapted from *Being a Brain-wise Therapist: A Practical Guide to Interpersonal Neurobiology*, by Badenoch, 2008, New York: Norton. Reprinted with permission of artist.

types of groups as seen through an IPNB lens, for example; how systems-centred therapy creates a rich neurobiological climate that supports integration; how children's groups can help with sensori-motor, psychological, and interpersonal development; how using an IPNB frame enables couples' groups to attain more solid interpersonal regulation; and how experiential learning groups can transform implicit memory.

Our first chapter highlights IPNB and its relevance for group therapy with Bonnie Badenoch and Paul Cox's chapter "Integrating interpersonal neurobiology with group psychotherapy". Their chapter describes key understandings of the brain, including the nature of implicit, explicit, and autobiographical memory; group as a source of regulation (with a brief mention of mirror neurons); and four of the domains of neural integration. They offer clinical examples from group therapy where these understandings have influenced both the group therapist as well as the group process.

This is followed by a brief commentary on the Badenoch and Cox article by Daniel Siegel, "Reflections on mind, brain and relationships in group psychotherapy". Here he highlights mind, brain, and behaviour as major aspects of human experience that are central to the process of change. He emphasises using the process of focusing attention to stimulate new neural activity that leads the group towards here and now experiences that foster transformation by increasing neural integration. This is one process by which IPNB can work to support the natural drive in group members toward increasing coherence and harmony among their neural circuits

Next is Victor Schermer's "Mirror neurons: their implications for group psychotherapy". He summarises the research on mirror neurons and discusses potential implications of this research for group psychotherapy. importantly, he proposes that mirror neurons provide support for the centrality of relationships, a belief long-emphasised by group therapists, and links this to understandings of the group-as-a-whole. From this confirmation of the social nature of perception, he then discusses and explores the implications for group therapists and training of group leaders.

Philip Flores, in Chapter Three, "Group psychotherapy and neuroplasticity: an attachment theory perspective", highlights some of the brain imaging studies that have identified changes in the brains of patients receiving psychotherapy, and identifies central premises of an attachment viewpoint for group therapists. On this foundation, Flores then highlights key neurobiological research and postulates five major factors for influencing brain plasticity in group therapy.

In Chapter Four, "Developing the group mind through functional subgrouping: linking systems-centred training (SCT) and interpersonal neurobiology," Susan Gantt and Yvonne Agazarian introduce the systems-centred concept of the "group mind" that links systems-centred thinking and interpersonal neurobiology via the systems-centred method of functional subgrouping. SCT's functional subgrouping, a group method for conflict resolution that facilitates discriminating and integrating differences in the service of development, is discussed from the interpersonal neurobiological framework as a tool for developing the group mind, considering how it facilitates emotional regulation, creates a secure relational context, and potentiates neural integration.

In Chapter Five, "Introducing couples to group therapy: pursuing passion through the neo-cortex," Don Ferguson describes a practical application of neurobiological research to couples groups, drawing from the work of couples' therapists who have applied the neurobiological research. This couples group model combines psycho-education about how the brain works, links this to the challenge of managing the "reptilian brain" in relationships, and introduces an eight-session couples' group model.

In Chapter Six, Bonnie Mark-Goldstein and Pat Ogden, in "Sensorimotor psychotherapy as a foundation of group therapy with younger clients," offer an overview of applying IPNB in their sensorimotor therapy with children. The examples included here are quite rich and give the flavour of how the group works, including how the leaders' holding capacity provides the foundation on which children can find the safety to change.

Mitchel Adler, in Chapter Seven, presents his group model: "Hunger and longing: a developmental regulation model for exploring core relational needs". He emphasises the regulatory function of the group in managing issues surrounding our core limbic longing for connection. He articulates his eight-stage model for managing the relational issues that arise in group therapy, using an IPNB perspective in attuning to the importance of the regulatory function of the leader and the group.

In Chapter Eight, Gloria Batkin Kahn and Darryl Feldman offer their model for working with couples: "Relationship-focused group therapy (RFGT) to mitigate marital instability and neuropsychophysiological dysregulation". Drawing from the neurobiology of attachment theory, they describe using separate therapy groups as a support and adjunct to couples therapy in order to help both spouses in their neuropsychophysiological regulation as part of increasing intimacy and stability in the marriage.

We end the book with Chapter Nine that moves beyond group therapy to an experiential learning group where Bonnie Badenoch applies her understanding of group process and IPNB in a training context: "A transformational learning group: inviting the implicit". The rich examples included here focus particularly on how the leader shapes the group and the group shapes the leader in an ongoing dance that can potentially support implicit transformation.

References

Badenoch, B. (2008). *Being A Brain-wise Therapist: A Practical Guide to Interpersonal Neurobiology*. New York: Norton.

Burlingame, G. M., MacKenzie, K. R., & Strauss, B. (2004). Small group treatment: evidence for effectiveness and mechanisms of change. In: M. Lambert (Ed), *Bergin and Garfield's Handbook of Psychotherapy and Behavior Change* (5th edn) (pp. 647–696). New York: Wiley.

Bion, W. R. (1959). *Experiences In Groups*. London: Tavistock.

Cozolino, L. (2006). *The Neuroscience of Human Relationships: Attachment and the Developing Social Brain*. New York: Norton.

Cozolino, L. (2010). *The Neuroscience of Psychotherapy: Healing the Social Brain* (2nd edn). New York: Norton.

Iacoboni, M. (2008). *Mirroring People: The New Science of How We Connect With Others*. New York: Farrar, Straus & Giroux.

Porges, S. W. (2009a). The polyvagal theory: new insights into adaptive reactions of the autonomic nervous system. *Cleveland Clinic Journal of Medicine, 76*: 86–90.

Forges, S. W. (2009b). Stress and parasympathetic control. In: L. R. Squire (Ed.), *Encyclopedia of Neuroscience, Vol. 9* (pp. 463–469). Oxford: Academic Press.

Schore, A. N. (1994). *Affect Regulation and the Origin of the Self: The Neurobiology of Emotional Development*. Hillsdale, NJ & England: Lawrence Erlbaum.

Schore, A. N. (2012). *The Science of the Art of Psychotherapy*. New York: Norton.

Siegel, D. J. (1999). *The Developing Mind: Toward a Neurobiology of Interpersonal Experience*. New York: Guilford.

Siegel, D. J. (2007). *The Mindful Brain*. New York: Norton.

Siegel, D. J. (2012). *The Developing Mind: How Relationships and the Brain Interact to Shape Who We Are* (2nd edn). New York: Guilford.

CHAPTER ONE

Integrating interpersonal neurobiology with group psychotherapy*

Bonnie Badenoch and Paul Cox

We human beings are hardwired to connect with one another throughout life, to seek the most attuned attachments available to us. Our initial relationships shape the very structure of our brains, and the constant sea of interpersonal encounters in which we swim continues to modify our brain wiring (Schore, 2003a,b; Siegel, 1999). These experiences create embodied anticipations of how relationships will be for us. They are then tucked away in long-term memory, continuing their influence by guiding our choice of a partner, our style of parenting, our levels of resilience and hope, our capacity to make meaning of our lives, and other psychological and interpersonal capacities.

While all forms of psychotherapy use the power of the therapeutic relationship to help patients increase personal well-being and enhance their relational capacity, the rich interpersonal environment of group therapy offers unique opportunities for patients to touch one another's inner worlds and provide support for each other, all within the rich holding environment provided by the therapist, initially, and one

*This is an adaptation of an article originally published in *International Journal of Group Psychotherapy*, 60(4): 462–482.

another, eventually. The brain's capacity to change (neuroplasticity) is heightened in environments that provide moderate emotional arousal (Cozolino, 2002), attuned and therefore regulating interpersonal relationships (Schore, 2009; Siegel, 2006), support for coming into contact with experiential awareness of memories (Badenoch, 2008), and experiences that disconfirm earlier implicit learnings (Toomey & Ecker, 2009).

In this chapter, we will explore the framework of interpersonal neurobiology (IPNB), a scientifically-grounded theory developed by Allan Schore (2003a,b) and Daniel Siegel (1999), to illuminate how relationships shape the brain throughout the lifespan, and then explore how aspects of IPNB can support the group therapy process. We suggest that both the therapist's holding capacity and the group members' mindful awareness of their own inner worlds, as well as their empathic awareness of one another, can be increased by understanding and practicing some core principles about brain and mind. For those of us leading groups, this knowledge often brings clearer seeing of our own mind, as well as the minds of individuals in the group, subgroups, and the group-as-a-whole. The practice of observing our own mind and the minds of others builds a layer of processing via increased integration between certain aspects of the prefrontal cortex and limbic regions, creating a broader perspective, increased bodily and emotional regulation, and a sense of confidence and stability, often followed by increased compassion (Siegel, 2007). As the limbic region grows calmer through this integration, reactivity (internal and behavioural) decreases, while calm holding capacity increases, providing safety for a larger range of experience to emerge in the group (Badenoch, 2008).

A rich river of communication is always unfolding below the level of conscious awareness as well. Changes in integration influence the quality of these micro-second interactions that reveal themselves through gaze, prosody of the voice, body posture, and movement, along with other visual and auditory messengers arising from the right hemisphere implicit world (Schore, 2009). As these signals emanate from a more integrated right brain, they can also support increases in safety and vulnerability, which we might regard as the initial conditions for deep change (Badenoch, 2011).

As we think about integrating IPNB principles into group therapy, one starting place might be sharing information about the brain and mind, not in the spirit of psycho-education only, but also as support for attunement and regulation. If we therapists have internalised these concepts so that we carry not only a left hemisphere knowledge, but also a right hemisphere felt sense, then group members have an enhanced opportunity to experience these for themselves through resonance with us (Iacoboni, 2009). This kind of whole-brain learning is far more compelling at the level of implicit and behavioural change than concepts by themselves (Badenoch, 2011). As patients learn about their brains and minds, they may be able to experience some of their struggles as neurobiological issues rather than character flaws. This can lead to a felt sense of a decrease in shame and blame while heightening self-compassion, in and of themselves powerful agents of neuroplasticity (Lutz, Greischar, Rawlings, Ricard, & Davidson, 2004). Fostering the group's awareness of the processes of brain change also provides a foundation for hope that even longstanding struggles may be alleviated. When therapists are able to offer these discoveries about the brain in a mode appropriate to the group and at the right empathic moment, this new framework for seeing and understanding may support both a paradigm shift (new explicit awareness) and a new felt sense that arises from the first stirrings of changes in implicit memory. Over time, these subtle shifts can build on each other, leading to increases in the subjective experience of wholeness, stability, spontaneity, and resilience, and the interpersonal qualities of increased empathy, attunement, receptivity, and compassion for others (Badenoch, 2008; Siegel, 2006).

Within the framework of IPNB, we could explore many concepts; however, for greater clarity we will limit ourselves to three that seem appropriate starting points for considering the benefit of IPNB to group therapy: early brain development, including implicit, explicit, and autobiographical memory; group as a source of regulation for the emotions and autonomic nervous system through interpersonal connection mediated by mirror neurons and resonance circuits; and four domains of neural integration—integration of consciousness, interpersonal, vertical, and bilateral integration.

Brain development in the first two years of life: implicit, explicit, and autobiographical memory

While research (Field, Diego, & Hernandez-Reif, 2006) is confirming that our nervous systems, neurochemical patterns, and even attachment behaviours begin to be shaped by our mother's state of mind and body even before birth, we are going to begin with infancy. While a full thirty-eight per cent of our genome is devoted to brain development, attachment theorists and neuroscientists recognise that interactions with our mothering person or people are responsible for establishing the very structure of our limbic and cortical regions (Siegel, 1999). In the process, our brains encode templates, in the form of implicit memories and embodied anticipations (sometimes called mental models) that will remain largely below the level of conscious awareness, guiding our perception of our value, the degree to which we are safe in the world, and what we can expect in relationships. In the group therapy situation, both we, as therapists, and group members bring these unseen implicit patterns into the collective experience where they influence every interaction.

When we are born, our attachment system comes into full flower, seeking proximity and safety with the person who has been carrying us (Siegel & Hartzell, 2003). Mothering person and baby begin a dyadic dance that encodes experiences in the baby's largely undifferentiated brain. Our limbic system, particularly the amygdala in the right hemisphere, begins to form implicit memories of these experiences. They are made up of bodily sensations, behavioural impulses, emotional surges, perceptions of safety or danger, and possibly, fragmentary sensory experiences—the feel of grandfather's beard, the fragrance of mother's powder, the way light glints off the glass vase (Badenoch, 2011; Siegel, 1999). For the first twelve to eighteen months, this is the only kind of memory we make—embodied, wordless, yet rich and foundational to our view of the world. We are forming a perceptual reservoir through which all later experience will pass before encoding in our brains or coming into our awareness. As the same kinds of interpersonal experiences are repeated, they organise into embodied anticipations (also called mental models), engrained expectations of how the relational world works, held below the level of conscious awareness (Schore, 2003a,b; Siegel, 1999). When implicit memories are present later in life, we do not experience the sensation of remembering, but instead have the felt sense of them happening now. Because they have no time stamp, we cannot say "I remember . . .", but instead simply experience them as this moment's truth.

We can do a simple practice to taste implicit memory. Take a moment to close your eyes and call to mind a pleasant experience that happened in the last two weeks. Sit with it for a bit. Then tell yourself the story of the memory—"I played Frisbee with my dog in the park last Sunday". Notice that you are explicitly clear that this joyous romp happened in the past. Then notice how you are feeling in your body. In all likelihood, there will be remnants of the felt experience, perhaps an expansive feeling in the chest that speaks of joy or the behavioural impulse to run and cavort. The latter part is the implicit aspect of the memory, and is present in this moment. We could say that implicit memory is the eternally present past (Badenoch, 2011), and it lies at the heart of the group experience.

In adulthood, these embodied experiences, as modified to some degree by later relational encounters, influence the way we approach relationships of all sorts, including those established in group therapy. Toomey and Ecker (2007) make the important point that these core, unseen, and perceptually-based "knowings" shape our overall view of the world, our assessment of the current situation, and our behaviour within that situation. This leads to a painful circle in which what we implicitly "know" is continually confirmed by how we perceive what is happening and how our behaviour tends to shape situations in the direction of the expected form.

All memories have an implicit layer, but as we move into our second year of life, the pieces of implicit memory begin to be gathered into another form of remembering called explicit memory. In the developing limbic area, the amygdala (central to implicit memory) links with the hippocampus (the cognitive mapper of explicit memory) to assemble the pieces of implicit memory into a whole experience and place a time stamp that marks it as past. Then we can know, "This happened yesterday". However, this does not mean that the implicit memory has become past—only that it is now connected to a new resource, explicit memory. While this capacity begins in the second year, genetically guided neural integration between the amygdala and hippocampus takes a while, so for most of us who grew up in reasonably safe homes, explicit memory becomes more continuous and stable between ages four and six (Siegel, 1999).

At about twenty-four months, we are ready for a new developmental step as these limbic regions begin to link with the mid-line structures of the prefrontal cortex, first in the right hemisphere with the felt sense of our self in our history, and then in the left hemisphere where our story finds words and we can say, "I remember when . . .". This is called autobiographical memory. If we have been reasonably well-nurtured in our earliest days, this stage of integration begins to establish our capacity for empathy, something that develops naturally as long as enough nurturance is present (Warneken & Tomasello, 2006). While genetically-guided, these stages of integration can also be interrupted. Certain events, especially traumatic ones, can interfere with these early stages of linking between implicit and explicit memory and also disrupt established integration at any stage in life (Schore, 2003a). The flood of stress chemicals and the mind's tendency to dissociate under extreme stress can keep the implicit layer of memory disintegrated from explicit and autobiographical recall, leaving the person at the mercy of his or her implicit memories (Badenoch, 2008; Schore, 2009). This loss of freedom to consciously choose one's response is one of the most debilitating and discouraging aspects of dissociated implicit memories.

Understanding these different types of memory may enable a group therapist to see people entering group with greater clarity and to discern the patterns of implicit memory in the movement or sensations of the body, the upwelling of emotion, and perceptions that do not make sense in current reality. Set against the background of each member's history, these implicit struggles do make sense and can lead to more thorough empathy and a broader holding capacity. For example, a group member might be convinced that everyone in the room is against him, even though the group's acceptance and empathy are clear to the therapist. Understanding the implicit origins of this perception might help the group therapist maintain connection rather than move into an attempt to counteract this felt reality by cognitive means, a process that does not yield comfort in the moment or change in the implicit memory (Toomey & Ecker, 2007). As this man feels understood and accepted in the midst of his perception, the implicit memory may become available for transformation precisely because feeling felt and known in that moment provides a disconfirming experience (Ecker & Toomey, 2008).

One of the strengths of group therapy is the high likelihood that the neural networks holding early implicit experience will be triggered as other members bring their struggles into the group. At the same time, group can become an empathy-rich environment for holding the pain and fear that emerges. In our clinical experience, as both therapist and group members understand more about brain development, they become more capable of seeing other members (and themselves) with understanding and compassion. Such attunement helps to repair the circuits of regulation not only for the receiver of care but the giver of care as well (Schore, 2003b; Siegel & Hartzell, 2003).

The implicit memory templates that govern our relationships appear to change in two primary ways: below the level of conscious awareness, attunement can enable rewiring of the limbic region into patterns of secure attachment (Schore, 2003b); and, at a more conscious level, allowing these memories to emerge in their emotional vividness makes them available for transformation (Badenoch, 2008; Ecker & Toomey, 2008). Through such living contact, implicit memories come into explicit awareness and may now meet experiences in the current world that disconfirm the truth of earlier implicit knowledge. When that happens, these earlier implicit memories may then become available for taking in new relational information that changes our felt sense of them, as well as for incorporation in the developing coherent narrative of the person's life (Badenoch, 2008; Ecker & Toomey, 2008). When implicit neural networks are activated in group, the members, supported by the therapist, can amplify the sense of attunement to the specific kind of struggle the member is experiencing, and, consequently, potentiate the possible repair. For example, if the person is experiencing shame, the felt sense of acceptance can initiate implicit change; if danger, then an embodied sense of safety held by the group.

At the same time, a group that includes visceral experience of implicit memories as a conscious part of its mission can use the group's combined compassionate energy to create a safe space for such work. Often, instead of reacting with aggravation or fear when another person is activated, the other group members may be able to come from a more kind, regulated, clear-seeing perspective; a state that is good for everyone in the room. To get a better sense of implicit and explicit memory in the group experience, we consider the example of John, a member of a group engaged in processing post-traumatic stress symptoms. For John, his implicit and explicit memories are split from each other, limiting John's freedom to consciously choose his responses.

> John, a sixty-two-year-old ex-Marine Vietnam veteran, nervously walked into his first trauma therapy group and took a seat facing the door while also keeping his eye on the opposite window. He came to the group at the

suggestion of his individual therapist, who thought it might help him with his war trauma. As other members of the group trickled in, John continued his vigilant watch, not consciously aware of his own anxiety or the developing social interactions of the other members. When the therapist entered the room, the wind caught the door, slamming it loudly. John quickly left the room without thought or explanation.

From John's history, the therapist knew that, at nineteen, he was caught in a fire-fight during which half of his company was killed or wounded. In response to the slamming door, John's nervous system, body, and limbic circuits were immediately activated in the implicit memory of Vietnam. The speed with which these circuits fired in response to perceived threat made it impossible for him to override his behavioural impulse and choose to stay in the room. Sadly, not only had this experience left him vulnerable to sudden, loud noises, but it had also dramatically altered his perception of life's possibilities. Always on guard and fearing loss, he held himself back from forming close relationships. Currently, his third marriage was failing and he was estranged from his three children. While John had some explicit recall of some of his experiences in Vietnam, the implicit underlayer of these terrifying events remained split off, out of conscious awareness, and lodged primarily in his body and nervous system, while always informing his perceptions and behaviours in the relational world.

It seemed best for John to delay entering this trauma-focused group, but his psychiatrist encouraged him to spend some time in what he thought might be a safer setting, a post-traumatic stress disorder (PTSD) psycho-educational group instead. In this more structured, educationally-oriented setting, John began to understand about the brain processes that had protected him in Vietnam, but were now injuring his ability to feel safe or form relationships. He started to develop a picture of how he might be able to approach the implicit memories step by step and allow the group to help him regulate and rework the pain. John was a contractor and the group leader's use of house-building metaphors helped him to connect to John. He was then more open to understanding how gradually approaching the implicit aspect of his traumatic memories, while being held by the therapist and fellow group members in a safe environment, with the potential to offer a different experience in the present, could serve to build a stronger frame for his house. As understanding grew and likely as he felt seen as well, shame receded. John agreed to continue his medication and meet again with the leader of the trauma-focused psychotherapy group. We can imagine that he not only strengthened the circuitry of knowledge in the left hemisphere, but in the caring relationship with the therapist, also sent some soothing regulatory fibres from his middle prefrontal region to his amygdala. This kind of whole-brained care lies at the heart of increasing the capacity for calmness and flexible responses to implicit arisings.

He re-entered the trauma group six months later, and this time could stay and talk with others who also suffered with hypervigilance and anxiety. His understanding of his brain's processes gave him enough of a bird's eye view to observe his body and nervous system as they began to dysregulate when the implicit memories emerged, and this gave him time to ask for help from other group members and the leader. Some of the helplessness he had experienced since Vietnam began to abate, and, with it, a greater sense of safety gradually emerged. Also, with the vivid but sensitively shared recollections of other group members about a spectrum of experiences in Vietnam, additional aspects of his experience came trickling back into explicit view. As he incorporated these into his meaningful life narrative, he even discovered some positive aspects of his experience. He recalled with a sense of pride how his platoon had controlled an important position in a particular battle, and understood that some of that perseverance now showed up in his ability to finish houses in challenging settings with demanding customers. This broader and more balanced view is one sign that implicit memories were no longer dominating him with their constant sense of danger, that he now has time and space within his neural networks to sit with both the positive and negative aspects. This signalled increases in integrative wiring between the body, limbic, and middle prefrontal cortex on the right and bilateral integration across the hemispheres. When John left group after a full year of weekly contact, he carried himself differently, had formed some significant bonds with other members, and reported feeling relatively safe in the world for the first time in memory.

Group as a source of regulation

One way to think about John's initial experience in the trauma group is to consider that on the first day of group, he was easily dysregulated, meaning that his limbic system, particularly the amygdala which encodes fear as well as pain (LeDoux, 2003), was hypersensitive to threat, leaving him vulnerable to even minor disturbances. When the door slammed, his amygdala accessed the implicit memory of battle in Vietnam and, perceiving threat, sent signals to his hypothalamus and pituitary, activating his stress response system. His cortisol levels shot up even higher than their usual elevated state, and his body went into active fight/flight mode. Without conscious decision, he left the room. If we had been with him in the hallway as he left, we might have seen his rapidly beating heart and dilated eyes telling us of a sympathetic nervous system on overload. Even had he been able to hear our words of reassurance, it is unlikely that he would have been able to make use of our presence to help him return to a state of regulation. A brief review of the autonomic nervous system is helpful in understanding his reaction.

When our nervous system perceives threat, our social engagement system shuts off and we lose the ability to use others as a source of soothing and regulation (Porges, 2007). However, when we once again feel safe, or have a *neuroception of safety*, to use Porges' phrase, then we are able to connect with others through facial expression, eye contact, body language, prosody of voice, and other non-verbal means that are part of interpersonal co-regulation.

Porges' research has identified a three-part autonomic system that operates as a hierarchy. When we have a neuroception of safety, the ventral vegal branch of the parasympathetic comes online to dampen the sympathetic nervous system and give us the calmness needed for intimate joining. This myelinated circuit allows us to send and read social signals that invite connection, leading to mutual regulation and generally empathic relationships. When we perceive threat, the sympathetic branch activates, attenuates the social engagement system, and prepares our organism to defend against the threat with a "fight" or "flight" response. Still further, if we perceive a danger as life threatening, the unmyelinated dorsal vagal branch of the parasympathetic activates a "freeze" response, often seen as collapse, a shut-down, or disassociation. When the dorsal vagal system is dominant, all of our systems become diminished, not only cutting us off from social contact with others, but decreasing our level of consciousness and our response to pain.

With a group therapist who understands this hierarchical structure in the autonomic nervous system, the group-as-a-whole can be supported in gradually becoming havens of safety and regulation for all members. Teaching group members about how our nervous systems respond often proves useful in heightening the group's collaboration in keeping the space safer, as well as increasing members' capacity to identify more clearly when an individual, a subgroup, or the group-as-a-whole has entered a sympathetic or dorsal vagal state—without judgment, holding the upset with compassion.

Under traumatic historical circumstances like John's or those with childhood attachment difficulties or overt trauma, it may take only the slightest, sometimes subliminal, stimulus (internal or external) to move a person from regulation (ventral vagal) to dysregulation (sympathetic or dorsal vagal). It is precisely at this juncture that group therapy can become a resource for reworking traumatic memories. Initially, especially in groups whose members have somewhat similar life histories, there is a high probability that when one group member accesses an implicit memory of loss or trauma, for example, one or more others in the group may also have similar neural networks activated. One way implicit memory can be changed is through emotional contact with the encoded experience coupled with a disconfirming experience (Alberini, 2005; Ecker & Toomey, 2008; Nader, 2003; Walker, Brakefield, Hobson, & Stickgold, 2003), so that a group's greater likelihood of activating these neural networks can be an advantage (rather than a threat). When group members have been prepared for the possibility of emerging implicit memories, and also are grounded in awareness of the importance of a safe space for regulating and changing these memories, the group-as-a-whole (with the guidance of a calm, containing therapist) can become a powerful regulating resource for each member.

Research regarding mirror neurons (Carr, Iacoboni, Dubeau, Mazzlotta, & Lenzi, 2003; Iacoboni, 2009) and resonance circuits (Siegel, 2007) can help us understand how this process works. These findings describe how the state of mind of one person is internalised by the body, nervous system, and brain of another, affecting functioning in the moment, and, with repetition, creating a permanent representation of the other (Badenoch, 2008, 2011). In this way, we develop an inner community of all those with whom we have had significant emotional contact, including their intentions and emotions in regard to us. One implication for group therapy is that if the therapist and group-as-a-whole are attending to their own regulation as a way to maintain a safe space, then those who are in the midst of an unfolding implicit memory may be able to use resonance with that calm inner state as a way to both regulate the intensity of the memory and have a different experience that can permanently modify the implicit encoding.

In well-established groups, we have seen such synchrony develop where one person moving into an intense implicit state pulls the rest of the group into a calm, empathic, holding state of mind, very like a dance of neural circuits operating between brains for the betterment of the whole. The group is then able to stay with the person who is in the midst of reworking a memory, providing a rich experience that combines not only containment, but often deep empathic understanding because of similar life histories. After weeks or months, these group members also report that in their daily lives, they experience the group as with them, particularly in stressful or triggering moments, so the regulating capacity of the group becomes a potent ongoing internal resource. Making these ideas overt in the group gives the conscious, attending mind an opportunity to assist in the development of such a rich, regulating environment.

Domains of neural integration: integration of consciousness, interpersonal, vertical, and bilateral integration

In creating a framework to understand how the various regions of neural processing become linked, Siegel (2006, 2007) has identified nine domains of neural integration that correlate with the subjective experiences of mental coherence and well-being, as well as with increased capacity for empathic relationships. Understanding the embodied and relational brain, as well as groups of brains, to be complex systems, not in a metaphorical sense, but according to scientific definition (Prigogine & Stengers, 1984; Robertson & Combs, 1995; Skinner, Molnar, Vybiral, & Mitra, 1992; Taylor, 1994), can help us see how billions of ongoing neural firings become organised into the coherent experience of daily life. As complex systems, our brains are self-organising and seek to continually link differentiated brain circuits into a coherent whole, moving from simplicity to complexity/coherence, and faltering only when there are constraints that block this natural movement (Siegel, 1999; van Pelt, Corner, Uylings, & Lopes Da Silva, 1994).

Building on this view of how brains develop, Siegel suggested that the evidence for increasing brain integration is greater flexibility, adaptability, coherence, energy, and stability of our thoughts, feelings, behaviours, and perceptions, what he called the FACES (Flexible, Adaptive, Coherent, Energised, and Stable) of mental health (Siegel,

2006). Discussing and encouraging a developing felt sense of these domains of neural integration with members of the group, particularly in terms of the FACES indicators, can encourage increased awareness of change in self and others. In one recent group, for example, two members commented appreciatively that they noticed another member being able to pause before making a snappy comeback, giving him time to choose words that reflected empathy rather than defence. Using the language of neural integration, one said, "Your mind is becoming more flexible". As the group paused, the man receiving the feedback said that using brain language helps him gain a deeper understanding of how participation in the group is changing him, and also seems to stop him from reflexively pushing away the compliment. It seems that it is not only the knowledge of integration, but the felt sense of how it is unfolding that gives these ideas their power. Helping members sit with the embodied experience because we have done that work ourselves is perhaps the most efficient way for us to encourage the movement from thought to embodied experience.

We will consider four domains of neural integration with examples of how they might be brought into the group therapy process. Returning to our previous discussion of regulation, we highlighted how the implicit memories that have the most negative affect on functioning reflect a state of neural disintegration, meaning that they are not connected to the larger flow of the developing brain. To review, this usually occurs because the chemicals of high stress and the mind's capacity for protective dissociation have partially or completely blocked linkage between the amygdala (implicit layer of remembering) and the hippocampus (assembly of implicit pieces into explicit memory), or the memory is from the first four or five years of life when explicit memory is either absent or spotty. In either case, as discussed above, these memories operate autonomously when triggered, taking over sensation, behaviour, and perception as though the original experience were happening in the present. The sufferer loses freedom of conscious choice, often accompanied by feelings of extreme helplessness. These experiences almost always dysregulate the nervous system, making them even more difficult to manage.

We begin with the *integration of consciousness*, defining it as the mind's capacity to observe, preferably with kindness, the states of mind that continually flow through awareness (Siegel, 2007). We emphasise kind observation rather than more detached witnessing because recent research has found that meditative practice of loving-kindness (wishing self and others well) and compassion (feeling the suffering of others) builds the circuitry that maps bodily responses to emotion (in the insula) and a right hemisphere region that processes empathy (the temporal parietal junction) (Lutz, Brefczynski-Lewis, Johnstone, & Davidson, 2008). In a recent study of self-compassion *vs.* global self-esteem, Neff and Vonk (2009) found that "self-compassion predicted more stable feelings of self-worth than self-esteem and was less contingent on particular outcomes" (p. 23). In addition, self-compassion predicted "less social comparison, public self-consciousness, self-rumination, anger, and need for cognitive closure" (p. 23). When we build our capacity to consistently reflect on our inner world with kindness, research suggests that we begin to initiate neuroplastic change in the direction of greater self-awareness and empathy for others.

Introducing the idea and practice of mindfully viewing these continual changes in our states of mind can be revolutionary for group members who have felt helplessly caught up in the flow of implicit experience. Adding an element of mindfulness practice and/or compassion meditation to each group session can build this capacity. For group therapists who personally practice some form of mindfulness, mirror neuron resonance with the therapist's state of mind will help facilitate the group's development of this state. Not only is attentional focus useful as a way to regulate one's own internal state, but it can also have great interpersonal power when the group-as-a-whole kindly attends to the emerging experience of one or more members. Energy and information constantly flow not only within brains, but between brains. Whether we are practicing this to help ourselves or others, just the act of observing in this way has an overall integrating effect on the brain (Siegel, 2007).

Integration of consciousness involves what could be called intrapersonal integration when one part of our mind observes and cares for another part of our mind (Badenoch, 2008). In contrast, when we turn our kind attention toward others, we are practicing *interpersonal integration* (Siegel, 2006). As we discussed briefly above, our lives are continually interwoven with each other via resonance circuits, for good or ill. Through these circuits, two people in a relationship may attune with each other, creating an internal experience of each other's actions, intentions, and emotions, coupled with the sensory experience (sight, sound, touch, taste, smell) that accompanies the encounter. Under conditions of sufficient neural integration, this blossoms into attuned connection with one another, fostering development of an internal image of each other's being—what Siegel (2007) called an ISO, the *internal state of the other* in the moment. As the relationship continues, our minds may gradually also develop a NOTO, a *narrative of the other*, offering us a sense of the other's ongoing internal presence (Siegel, 2007). We literally carry each other within our minds. These resonant experiences lie at the root of our capacity for empathy (Iacoboni, 2009).

However, not all encounters leave a legacy of empathy and neural integration. Implicit memories, particularly those that have been created by poor attachment or trauma and remain dissociated, change our perceptual frame of reference so that we may not be able to clearly resonate with another person. The incoming relational information gets caught by the amygdala's previously encoded appraisal, reaching the integrating middle prefrontal region in a state altered by these perceptions, preventing the full experience of empathy (Iacoboni, 2009). Consequently, we see the person primarily through the eyes of our encoded bias. The most difficult part is that we are unaware that we are not seeing what the other person intends to convey.

Both kinds of interpersonal experience find rich expression in therapy groups. Initially, as each member is invited into vulnerability, his or her perceptual biases gradually enter and influence the conversation. For example, James senses that he wants to get away from Melissa, and with empathic support from the group and the therapist, is able to find the internal knowing that her voice quality and rhythm of speech set his body on edge because they are similar to those of his harsh mother. As he draws emotionally close to painful experiences with his mother, the group, supported by the therapist, finds the resources to remain in attunement with his process. Sustained by the safety and regulation they are creating, James' integrating brain brings more of the memory of his mother into embodied consciousness. The implicit memory becoming grounded in explicit memory signals the integration of the amygdala and hippocampus. Resonating with his empathic compatriots, his right hemisphere limbic region is also integrating with the middle prefrontal, laying the groundwork for emotional regulation of this particular patch of memories. In addition, because the embodied implicit memory is alive in the room, it can

receive the quiet gentleness of the group as a disconfirming experience, potentially changing the implicit memory at the root (Ecker &
Toomey, 2008). As his nervous system continues to quieten, he
emerges from the memory, and speaks eloquently of the pain caused
by his mother's constant cruel carping and dissatisfaction. As this new
narrative unfolds, he is also able to gradually look at Melissa with
eyes of gratitude for being the gateway to this experience, rather than
with his former frightened and defensive eyes.

Not every group experience goes this smoothly, particularly in the
beginning when implicit memories may be strongly activated in every
group member's deeper mind. However, as long as the therapist
remains grounded in non-judgment and empathy, the process of
interpersonal integration can begin and then resonate through the
group mind, building the circuits of empathy and expanding the individual and group window of tolerance for strong emotion bit by bit.
Group members also internalise us therapists who then become living
internal examples and resources for the felt experience of interpersonal integration. At the same time, each uncovered and regulated
implicit neural blockage removes another obstacle to integration and
provides a broader foundation for empathy in the group-as-a-whole.

As we can begin to see, no domain of integration stands alone. We
set out to talk about our selected four domains sequentially, but each
draws in others as befits a brain moving as a whole toward more
complexity and coherence. As we talk of James' "awareness of his
body's reaction to Melissa", followed by his "access to memories of
his mother", and his subsequent ability to "regulate the intensity of
his response", we are speaking of the process of *vertical integration*.
The body, limbic region, and neocortex in one hemisphere (in this
case, the right) become linked in a way that allows memory to be
drawn into a regulated whole. When a dissociated implicit memory
(comprised of body and partial limbic connections) comes out of isolation into availability, and may first be embraced by the hippocampus
(where explicit memories are made), and then by the integrative fibres
of the middle prefrontal cortex (insight, empathy, and regulation),
vertical integration occurs. Over time, these repeated experiences of
co-regulation by the group build the capacity for a felt sense of self-
regulation, establishing a calmer baseline for the autonomic nervous
system. In this way, the person becomes more resilient in the face of
stressful conditions.

In this more regulated state, the next natural development is to add our new understanding of the meaning and impact of these experiences to our life narrative. James spontaneously began to piece together how his mother's verbal cruelty had altered his relationship not only with Melissa, but with several other women in his life. This kind of emotionally-grounded storytelling is the hallmark of *bilateral integration* between the right hemisphere, where the visceral and emotional parts of our developing coherent narrative lives, and the left hemisphere, where these felt sense experiences find words and can be explicitly shared. Not all changes in implicit narrative become explicit, but all will nonetheless affect our perceptions and behaviours in ways that alter our lived narrative. As we uncover and then assemble the diverse pieces of our narrative, our lives take on their unique and meaningful shape and we grow closer to a subjective sense of well-being and connection with others.

Group therapy can provide the safe and accepting environment that allows dissociated implicit memories to be held in kindness long enough to receive the disconfirming experience that is offered by the group's growing capacity to resonate with and meet individual members with the very experience their systems need in this moment of their distress. In this way, support for vertical integration is an ongoing core process of groups. At the same time, the commonality of wounding in groups may often bring many more opportunities to naturally access the implicit world than individual therapy typically provides. The flow between implicit intensity, regulating kind attention, and accurate disconfirming experience may become a beautifully executed ongoing dance as groups mature.

However, group therapy probably makes one of its greatest contributions as an ample container for collaborative storytelling. Siegel and Hartzell (2003) describe this process as one of the cornerstones of secure attachment. By their second birthdays, children begin to make sense of their world through telling and retelling their experience of joyous and hurtful moments, while their parents support the ever-deepening story. When the process is complete, these elements have completed the journey of vertical and bilateral integration to become part of the meaningful narrative of their lives, with few implicit hooks left to disrupt them later.

Because therapy group members often share some common implicit experiences—abandonment, shame, terror, grief—they can easily collaborate with one another in making meaning of the experiences that led to these painful states. In almost every group, as processing gives way to narrative, both verbal and non-verbal support flows easily between the brains, minds, and bodies of members. As James began to talk about his mother's influence on his later relationships, Nancy leaned forward, Andy slowly nodded his understanding, Mark looked down in sadness but with a deep sigh of assent, and Melissa, whose own mother's verbal cruelty had significantly impacted her relational abilities, listened intently, empathised verbally, and, as James finished, began her own story. During these frequent moments of profound interpersonal integration, the group is doing a great deal of neural repair work, deepening vertical integration and supporting the movement of energy and information across the corpus callosum from the right hemisphere to the left. One by one, the implicit hooks are undone.

In summary, this chapter highlights aspects of IPNB that can be useful to the group therapist and to group members in moving toward the goal of integrating the experience of IPNB into group practice. Adding the IPNB lens may enable us as group therapists to sharpen the ways in which this collaborative effort contributes to greater neural integration, emotional regulation, and interpersonal richness.

Reflections on mind, brain, and relationships in group psychotherapy

A discussion of Bonnie Badenoch and Paul Cox's chapter "Integrating interpersonal neurobiology with group psychotherapy"*

Daniel J. Siegel

Bonnie Badenoch and Paul Cox have created an exciting summary of the application of principles derived from the interdisciplinary view of interpersonal neurobiology (IPNB). My deepest hope is that these ideas are helpful in supporting the journey toward healing. Harnessing the "consilient" lens of IPNB with which we draw from a wide array of sciences and reflective practices to construct a view of being human, we can dive deeply into the notion of a "triangle of well-being" that frames an approach to the process of change: mind, brain, and relationships are the three irreducible anchor points of our human experience. Mind can be seen as having a core process that regulates the flow of energy and information; brain is the mechanism by which energy and information flow throughout the whole body, and relationships are the ways we share energy and information flow with one another through patterns of communication. With a mind that is resilient and coherent, the brain is integrated, and relationships empathic. This is the triangle of well-being (Siegel, 2007; 2010b).

A group psychotherapist's knowledge of IPNB can help frame the process of change as this triangle is envisioned to represent how

---

*First published in *International Journal of Group Psychotherapy*, 60(4): 483–485.

integration—the linkage of differentiated parts into a coherent and adaptive whole—promotes health. Impediments to integration lead to states of chaos, rigidity, or both. From a group perspective, honouring other members' inner worlds and supporting their expression enables differentiation to flourish. Actively engaging with others to seek and respect their communication of the inner world of the mind links members to one another through these reflective connections. As Badenoch and Cox beautifully reveal, group dynamics can help or hinder this integration process. A therapist can keep a "pulse" on integration by observing closely for the emergence of chaos or rigidity and then exploring where in the members' interactions—or in a given individual member's inner experience as projected out onto the group—differentiation and/or linkage might be impaired.

With this chapter's open invitation to consider how IPNB principles might be of benefit to the group therapy experience, we are invited to reframe the goal of therapy and the process of transformation itself. Integration is seen to be the heart of health. Transformative experiences recruit the sharing of information and energy flow within relationships to actively move the synaptically stuck brain to fire off in new ways—ones that are now shaped toward integration. What this means in practical terms is that we can first detect chaos and/or rigidity and then look for impediments to differentiation and/or linkage. Next, we identify which of several broad domains of integration might be blocked. And finally, we stimulate neuronal activation and growth or "SNAG" the brain (Siegel, 2007)—we help the group focus attention in a way that will "push" the brains in the room toward more integrative states. The adage in neuroscience that "neurons which fire together, wire together" is the powerful principle we can harness as psychotherapists to be sure that moment-to-moment experience of creating states of compassion and empathy, realisation and break-through, are transformed from temporary states of discovery and relief into long-term enduring traits of health and resilience. This change we seek to cultivate through the group's process is integration. The key to moving there is the focus of attention: our attention stimulates new patterns of neural activity beyond the old, non-integrated ways of being.

In group therapy, as in psychotherapy in general, we discover that the "system" has an innate drive toward integration, toward healing. As open systems capable of chaotic behaviour, we are complex, non-linear, dynamical systems that have an innate drive to maximise complexity (Siegel, 1999; 2010a). The mathematics of complexity reveals that the linkage of differentiated elements of the system achieves this "self-organisational flow" that is the most flexible and adaptive. The subjective feeling of this integrative state is harmony. In Badenoch and Cox's clinical examples, one can feel the emergence of such integrative complexity through the group process that emerges within therapy. The great news of this view is that it illuminates the process by which we are the facilitators of change, not its creators. Ours is a role of collaboration to liberate the innate drive to heal, an inner potential present in each group member that has become buried, often beneath layers of pain and defence, rigid thought, and chaotic feeling. Finding a way to free the group members' natural drive to move toward integration is the central goal of therapy from an IPNB perspective. A group therapist can feel that state of integration emerge as members respect one another and with the profoundly integrative act of kindness and compassion—toward the self and other—reach out to lend a hand in the miraculous movement of healing and trans-formation that we are so privileged to experience.

References

Alberini, C. M. (2005). Mechanisms of memory stabilization: are consoli-dation and reconsolidation similar or distinct processes? *Trends in Neuroscience, 28*(1): 51–56.

Badenoch, B. (2008). *Being a Brain-wise Therapist: A Practical Guide to Interpersonal Neurobiology*. New York: Norton.

Badenoch, B. (2011). *The Brain-savvy Therapist's Workbook*. New York: Norton.

Carr, L., Iacoboni, M., Dubeau, M., Mazzlotta, J., & Lenzi, G. (2003). Neural mechanisms of empathy in humans: a relay from neural systems for imitation to limbic areas. *Proceedings of the National Academy of Sciences of the United States of America, 100*(9): 5497–5502.

Cozolino, L. (2002). *The Neuroscience of Psychotherapy: Building and Rebuilding the Human Brain*. New York: Norton.

Ecker, B., & Toomey, B. (2008). Depotentiation of symptom-producing implicit memory in coherence therapy. *Journal of Constructivist Psychology, 21*(2): 87–150.

Field, T., Diego, M., & Hernandez-Reif, M. (2006). Prenatal depression effects on the fetus and newborn: a review. *Infant Behavior and Development, 29*(3): 445–455.

Iacoboni, M. (2009). Imitation, empathy, and mirror neurons. *Annual Review of Psychology, 60*: 653–670.

LeDoux, J. (2003). *Synaptic Self: How Our Brains Become Who We Are.* New York: Penguin Putnam.

Lutz, A., Brefczynski-Lewis, J., Johnstone, T., & Davidson, R. J. (2008). Regulation of the neural circuitry of emotion by compassion meditation: effects of meditative expertise. *PLoS ONE, 3*(3): e1897.

Lutz, A., Greischar, L. L., Rawlings, N. B., Ricard, M., & Davidson, R. J. (2004). Long-term meditators self-induce high-amplitude gamma synchrony during mental practice. *Proceedings of National Academy of Sciences, 101*(46): 16369–16343.

Nader, K. (2003). Memory traces unbound. *Trends in Neuroscience, 26*(2): 65–72.

Neff, K. D., & Vonk, R. (2009). Self-compassion versus global self-esteem: two different ways of relating to oneself. *Journal of Personality, 77*(1): 23–50.

Porges, S. W. (2007). The polyvagal perspective. *Biological Psychology, 74*(2): 116–143.

Prigogine, I., & Stengers, I. (1984). *Order Out of Chaos.* New York: Bantam.

Robertson, R., & Combs, A. (Eds.) (1995). *Chaos Theory in Psychology and the Life Sciences.* Hillsdale, NJ: Lawrence Erlbaum.

Schore, A. N. (2003a). *Affect Dysregulation and Disorders of the Self.* New York: Norton.

Schore, A. N. (2003b). *Affect Regulation and the Repair of the Self.* New York: Norton.

Schore, A. N. (2009). Right brain affect regulation: an essential mechanism of development, trauma, dissociation, and psychotherapy. In: D. Fosha, D. J. Siegel, & M. Solomon (Eds.), *The Healing Power of Emotion: Affective Neuroscience, Development, and Clinical Practice* (pp. 112–144). New York: Norton.

Siegel, D. J. (1999). *The Developing Mind: How Relationship and the Brain Interact to Shape Who We Are.* New York: Guilford.

Siegel, D. J. (2006). An interpersonal neurobiology approach to psychotherapy: awareness, mirror neurons, and neural plasticity in the development of well-being. *Psychiatric Annals, 36*(4): 247–258.

Siegel, D. J. (2007). *The Mindful Brain: Reflection and Attunement in the Cultivation of Well-being.* New York: Norton.

Siegel, D. J. (2010a). *Mindsight.* New York: Random House.

Siegel, D. J. (2010b). *The Mindful Therapist*. New York: Norton.

Siegel, D. J., & Hartzell, M. (2003). *Parenting From the Inside Out: How a Deeper Self-understanding Can Help You Raise Children Who Thrive*. New York: Jeremy P. Tarcher/Penguin Putnam.

Skinner, J. E., Molnar, M., Vybiral, T., & Mitra, M. (1992). Application of chaos theory to biology and medicine. *Integrative Physiological and Behavioral Science, 27*(1): 43–57.

Taylor, J. G. (1994). Non-linear dynamics in neural networks. *Progress in Brain Research, 102*: 317–382.

Toomey, B., & Ecker, B. (2007). Of neurons and knowings: constructivism, coherence psychology, and their neurodynamic substrates. *Journal of Constructivist Psychology, 20*(3): 201–245.

Toomey, B., & Ecker, B. (2009). Competing visions of the implications of neuroscience for psychotherapy. *Journal of Constructivist Psychology, 22*(2): 95–140.

Van Pelt, J., Corner, M. A., Uylings, H. B. M., & Lopes DaSilva, F. H. (Eds.) (1994). The self-organizing brain: from growth cones to functional networks. *Progress in Brain Research, 102*: 1–446.

Walker, M. P., Brakefield, T., Hobson, J. A., & Stickgold, R. (2003). Dissociable stages of human memory consolidation and reconsolidation. *Nature, 425*(6958): 616–620.

Warneken, F., & Tomasello, M. (2006). Altruistic helping in human infants and young chimpanzees. *Science, 311*: 1301–1302.

CHAPTER TWO

Mirror neurons: their implications for group psychotherapy*

Victor L. Schermer

G roup psychotherapy, in its ongoing search for understanding the patient and the group, often borrows from other disciplines to formulate its theoretical framework and practical methodology. One excellent source to draw from is neuroscience, since it seeks correlations between the brain, emotion, and behaviour, and especially now, because it has begun to investigate matters pertaining to social interactions.

Among the recent intriguing findings of neuroscience has been the discovery of mirror neurons, brain cells that fire in response to perceiving another's action in ways similar to when one is rehearsing or performing the action oneself (Iacoboni, 2008, pp. 8–21). Much as other neurons are specialised for cognition, memory, emotion, and so on, these brain cells, by virtue of their location within complex neural networks, connect individuals to each other by *registering perceived behaviours, emotions, and intentions of others "as if" one were enacting or experiencing them oneself*. Mirror neurons appear to account for the immediate intuitive recognition of others as similar to oneself, so well stated by the philosopher Maurice Merleau-Ponty when he wrote,

* First published in *International Journal of Group Psychotherapy*, 60(4): 486–513.

". . . now it is precisely my body which perceives the body of another person, and discovers in that other body a miraculous prolongation of my own intention, a familiar way of dealing with the world" (Merleau-Ponty, 1976, p. 354).

For clarification purposes, in what follows, three concepts will be used that are related but distinct from one another. "Mirror neurons" are the nerve cells described above. "Mirror systems" refers to neural networks that include mirror neurons but also may involve other parts of the brain that play a role in mirroring, imitation, empathy, and identification. "Mirroring" as such consists of psychological and interpersonal processes in which individuals model, reflect upon, and learn from each other (Foulkes & Anthony, 1965; Pines, 1998). Mirror neurons very likely play a significant role in complex human mirroring, but their precise role is still under investigation. Moreover, the discovery of mirror neurons in monkeys using electrode implants that can measure the activity of a single cell preceded the evolving research on humans, in which the locus of activity of specific neurons can only be inferred using less sharply focused functional magnetic resonance imaging (fMRI). However, the mirroring properties of regions of the human brain in which these neurons reside are being verified by emerging research. Thus, when the phrase "mirror neurons" is used in connection with humans and groups, it may more precisely refer to mirror systems and/or regions of the brain that contain mirror neurons, since human research in which individual nerve cells are invasively stimulated is rare for ethical reasons.

It can be said that in the world of mirror neurons and mirror systems, individuals attune to one another and represent themselves in and through each other, challenging the premise that minds function in relative isolation. Contrary to the traditional Cartesian dualism separating mind from the body and the material world, mirror systems are distinctly *relational*, forming a possible linkage among embodied selves, suggesting that, by extension, the mind/brain may be inherently social and intimately linked to its environmental and group context (Cozolino, 2006). Individuals are not social "atoms". Rather, they are in many respects "reflecting mirrors" of the interpersonal world that surrounds them.

Because they form a possible "hardwired" basis for social relations and identification, mirror neurons should be of great interest to group psychotherapists. Even as other elucidations of neural functions, from conditioned reflexes (Pavlov, 1927) to the pleasure centre (Olds & Milner, 1954) to neural networks (Edelman, 1987; Hebb, 1949) to the relationships between emotions, cognition, and attachment (Damasio, 1999; Schore, 1994; Siegel, 1999) have gained our attention, so too the study of mirror neurons and related neural networks may help us integrate our understanding of the brain with that of psychotherapy and the group. Emerging knowledge about mirror systems can enrich and modify the way therapists understand individuals, groups, and the treatment process as well as elucidate the nature of some mental disorders. Although the understanding of mirror neurons as such is in the investigative "cutting edge" and cannot always be definitively interpreted and applied, it nevertheless can stimulate thinking about groups, generate hypotheses, and encourage the exploration of new possibilities for theory and practice. In what follows, the implications of mirror neurons and systems for group psychotherapy are explored in that spirit of creative understanding rather than offering hard and fast conclusions.

A suitable beginning can be made by reviewing some of the relevant neuroscience research. With that database, some potential implications for the theoretical understanding of groups and group therapy can be taken up. Finally, the application of such understanding to clinical practice can be explored. Proceeding in such a step-wise manner, one can first state the assumptions that lead from neuroscience to psychology and then consider the implications for group dynamics and treatment, pointing to possibilities for clinical intervention.

Research findings on mirror neurons and systems

Mirror neurons were discovered in a primate laboratory in Italy in the late 1980s (Iacoboni, 2008, pp. 10–11). The research subjects were macaque monkeys. A sophisticated electrode that registered the impulses in a single neuron in the motor cortex (in a segment concerned with planning, selecting, and executing actions) repeatedly indicated that a particular neuron fired whenever the monkey made a grasping hand movement. The purpose of the ongoing research was not psychological, but biomedical, to study the neurological substrate of the initiation of physical movements. On one occasion, the researcher noticed, from the clicking sound of the computer loudspeakers, that the same neuron fired when he himself made a similar motion. This was totally unexpected and may have been one of those rare and paradigm-changing moments when a scientist makes a serendipitous observation that ultimately alters the prevailing understanding of an aspect of nature.

The fact that the neuron was located in the motor cortex meant surprisingly that the neuron was not cognitively processing self–other relationships but registering, and in a sense "rehearsing", an identity between its own movements and those of another organism. Since no one had ever observed nerve cells to respond in this way, a flurry of interest was then set off in the same laboratory, whose staff replicated the finding and tried a number of variations to assure that it was a reliable phenomenon. Guided by the leader of their team, Giacomo Rizzolatti, their published reports (e.g., Gallese, Fadigia, Fogassi, & Rizzolatti, 1996; Rizzolatti & Craighero, 2004; Rizzolatti, Riggio, Dascola, & Umilta, 1987) set off research activity worldwide. Still later, studies involving humans utilising functional magnetic resonance imaging (fMRI) and other non-invasive brain imaging techniques that, though with less precision than single-neuron electrodes, show the activity of neural networks and regions of the brain. As a result, what is very probably mirror neuron activity has been shown to occur in humans in approximately the same parts of the brain as in the monkeys (Iacoboni, 2008, pp. 59–62).

Since then, a host of studies have been undertaken to study the nature of mirror neuron systems in a variety of stimulus conditions with regard to intersubjectivity (Gallese & Goldman, 1998), emotions (Carr, Iacoboni, Dubeau, Mazziotta, & Lenzi, 2003), psychiatric disorders (Gallese, 2006), and political choices (Iacoboni, 2008, pp. 244–258). It appears that mirror neurons fire not only in response to specific movements, but in more sophisticated ways that embody complex psychological qualities of empathy, intentionality, and goal-directedness, responding to a variety of stimuli, including facial expressions, gestures, vocal inflections, other social cues, and body language (Iacoboni, 2008, pp. 79–105).

Importantly, the responses of mirror neurons are associated with other brain centres that monitor and regulate affects, cognition, and memory. They do not operate in isolation, but may form a neurological component of social and emotional intelligence. While caution must be exercised in drawing specific conclusions from these early investigations, mirror neurons may play a role in interpersonal processes such as the attunement of a mother to her infant's emotional states (Iacoboni, 2008, pp. 126–129), the ways in which individuals recognise each other's subjective states (intersubjectivity) and establish rapport (LaFrance, 1982), and complex choice behaviour such as selecting a political candidate (Iacoboni, 2008, pp. 244–258). In addition, hypotheses have been proposed about potential mirror neuron deficiencies in severe developmental disorders such as autism, which involve difficulty with social behaviours and information processing (Gallese, 2006; Williams, Whitten, Suddendorf, & Ferrett, 2001).

As noted above, mirror neurons fire when an individual engages in a goal directed activity or observes someone else doing so. This capacity of mirror neurons to respond to the behaviours of self and other in a similar way, thereby forming a link and equation between the two, is bound to be intriguing to the group therapist, who uses social interaction as a treatment modality. What does this discovery imply for the understanding of groups and group treatment? How can it be applied practically in group work? Although these questions are far from being fully answered, it is possible to state some broad premises about the neurological basis of social behaviour from the data that has already accumulated and will help to set the stage for a discussion of more specific implications and applications for group therapy.

Implications of mirror neurons for understanding human interaction, communication, and groups

In general and very importantly, mirror neurons link organisms of the same or similar species to one another at a precognitive level that antecedes language and logical reasoning. Evolution apparently connected members of a given primate group to one another before the advent of language and reflective cognition as such (De Waal, 2001). It appears now that mutual recognition and identification are the progenitors of reason, self-consciousness, and culture rather than vice versa. This understanding overturns the cherished assumption that social behaviour results mainly from a learning process mediated by a formal language. Instead, humans seem to come equipped with the ability to interact with one another through a primitive recognition of similarities and differences between self and other, and that is likely also activated in early mother–infant interactions. Mirror neurons support the notion of an innate pre-linguistic responsiveness to others that also may prefigure social interaction in dyadic and group situations.

Thus, mirror neurons provide an avenue of "hardwired" evidence supporting the group therapists' belief that human beings are inherently relational. Furthermore, mirror neurons transcend basic attachment behaviour (Bowlby, 1968) because while attachment implies following, staying in close proximity to, and receiving safety, nurturing, and soothing from the maternal figure, recognition and mirroring imply the potential to compare responses, imitate, and learn from one another. Importantly for group work, attachment and mirroring are thus related but different neuropsychological phenomena. Furthermore, the pre-cognitive "instant recognition" inherent in mirror neuron activity may explain why some group formations can occur in short order, pointing to "grouping" as being, like primary attachment, a "wired-in" tendency of our species. Children not only bond to survive the "dependency" stage of development by having their safety needs met, they may also be "hardwired" to form "primary groups of belonging" (Rouchy, 1995) where group cooperation and culture becomes possible. Social learning and social norms appear to be partly based upon the inherent capacity for recognition of similarity and identification that resides in mirror neuron activity.

A variety of observations from primate behaviour in nature as well as infant research thus suggests that social and cooperative behaviour is not simply, as Freud believed, an outcropping of rational minds (egos) overcoming instinctual tendencies (the id), but an inborn component of our nature that itself has evolutionary survival value. Group therapists and relational psychologists can increasingly point to evidence from neuroscience that supports their relational bias, hitherto considered "soft" and speculative by biologists, as well as by many psychoanalysts, behaviourists, and cognitive psychologists. Research studies on mirror neurons and other aspects of the "social brain" (Cozolino, 2006) are converging to provide a stronger "natural sciences" foundation for systems-based group psychotherapy than ever before.

Mirror neurons and group-as-a-whole theories

This expansion of the linkage between brain and social behaviour can also support and illuminate group-theoretical perspectives. For example, mirror neurons offer a potential neurological grounding for group-as-a-whole concepts and a partial explanation for them. If individuals are autonomous creatures driven by primary needs for security and survival, then, as Stacey (2005) has argued, it is quite a stretch to think of group fields (Lewin, 1951), matrices (Foulkes, 1948), basic assumptions (Bion, 1959), and "living human systems" (Agazarian, 1997) that transcend the individuals who comprise them. But if humans are neurologically prepared to respond to similarities in one another, then it is understandable that individuals could organise into holistic social networks. Attuned to link to one another by recognition and action (the two poles of mirror neurons' functioning), individuals are poised to form the larger social units of which they are a part, whether the dyad, the family, or the group. Thus, it can be proposed that mirror systems and related neural networks serve as a biological substrate for systemic group-as-a-whole relations.

Each important group-as-a-whole perspective has a particular tie-in to mirror neurons and related neural structures. For example, Lewin's (1951) "field" theory articulates the tendency to organise and respond according to group intentions (Agazarian & Peters, 1981) through behaviours, attitudes, roles, and purposes that mirror one another. The group "field" could thus be understood as a "final common path" emerging from the resonance of intentions mediated by mirror neurons. The archaic and abstract model of the "electromagnetic" field that Lewin used in his early formulations could be reconceptualised in terms of neural "electrochemical" fields forming complex "maps" in the brain (Damasio, 1999). That is, Lewin's "field" could be understood as a coordinated neuropsychological map of the group-as-group that is mediated partially by mirror neurons and their potential for self–other resonance.

Similarly, Foulkes' (1948) "group matrix" speaks to communications networks that occur among the group members, emphasising the social nature of the self. Mirror neurons provide a possible link that connects individuals as "nodal points" to one another. Mirror neurons also help account for the fact, emphasised by Foulkes, that the self which defines our individuality, autonomy, and agency, is paradoxically social in nature. For it is through the identification of one's own behaviour and self-image with those of another that an organised sense of self is established. Mirror neurons register these similarities and provide a basis for socially-defined selfhood.

Finally, Bion's "basic assumptions" represent unconscious group formations that result from pre-cognitive mutual adaptations, that is, what Bion called the "protomental" level (Symington & Symington, 1996, pp. 138–140). "Protomental" is a useful term to characterise how a variety of social phenomena, not only those related to mirror neurons, are configured in the brain. Basic assumptions are "proto"- mental insofar as the processing is non-conscious (the person not aware of thinking thoughts), rather informing and conditioning our embodied relations with one another. As the philosopher Merleau-Ponty wrote,

> When my gaze meets another gaze, I re-enact the alien existence in a sort of reflection. There is nothing here resembling "reasoning by analogy" . . . Between my consciousness and my body as I experience it, between this phenomenal body of mine and that of another as I see it from outside there exists an internal relation which causes the other to appear as the completion of the system. (Merleau-Ponty, 1976, p. 332)

As group therapists well know, and as Bion stated, as soon as individuals make contact with one another, a group begins to form. It is almost as if the group is waiting for the members to "embody" it. That is, "grouping" occurs beneath the radar of reflective cognition, in the same manner in which mirror neurons operate. For example, Turquet's (1975) distinction between "IM" (individual member) and "MI" (membership individual) suggests that a member comes into the group as a "singleton" (his term), and encounters a group in which she comes to reflect its collective identity, but Turquet implies a degree of conformity pressure beyond the direct causation of, say, mirror neurons. Similarly, Karterud and Stone's (2003) supraordinate "group self" could be considered the result of collective mirror neuron activity creating an emergent group entity that manifests the individual selves of the members. This group "self" is not a conscious agent, though. It is rather an ever shifting functional entity that has a collective identity and intentionality. In this sense, the group is a "house of mirrors" in which we are it and it is us.

A philosophical "turn"

To probe still more deeply, mirror neurons, by responding to both self-initiated and others' behaviours also make a direct neural connection between perception and action. That is, the perception of others is structured by the neuron's own tendency towards innervating action. Furthermore, research has shown that mirror neurons respond not simply to behaviours, but more subtly as a function of the intentions and goals of those actions as well. Thus a mirror neuron that fires when the subject sees someone lifting an ice cream cone may not fire when the identical movement is used to lift a hammer (Iacoboni, 2008, pp. 29–34). The fact that perceptions, intentions, and actions are related to one another in this way contradicts the traditional sharp distinctions between stimulus and response, perception and behaviour, stressed by the behaviourists Pavlov and Skinner. Their notion of a distinct stimulus evoking a particular response, and the two becoming linked by "conditioning" was first articulated in the eighteenth century by the philosophers Locke (1996) and Hume (1993). Freud (1953) adopted a similar perspective in formulating his concepts of mental associations and representations. Mirror neurons suggest that perception and action are unified and not, as stimulus-response psychology supposes, separate functions.

On the other hand, the oneness of perception and action is consistent with late nineteenth and early twentieth century philosophical and psychological trends that formed a basis for modern group psychology. Gestalt psychology (King & Wertheimer, 2005) emphasises the self-organised, patterned nature of perception. Pragmatist philosophy (Dewey, 2004; James, 1909) highlights the functions, agency, and intentions that inform a person's nexus with the world. "Symbolic interactionism", a sociological approach based on the work of George Herbert Meade (1934), holds that social relations are organised into mutually recognisable meanings and actions. Phenomenology (Husserl, 1999; Merleau-Ponty, 1976) asserts that much of our experience is inherently relational: "No man is an island". Pioneering group systems theorists such as Lewin, Foulkes, Helen Durkin (1964), James Durkin (1981), and Agazarian (1997) have all made use of such understandings. Mirror neurons suggest that our brains are organised along meaning-laden, relational, and systems lines rather than the "reflex-arc" notion of discrete stimulus-response packages as such.

The study of mirror neurons has re-kindled many of the discussions of the role of language (Iacoboni, 2008) in the development of the self and social life that occurred among the early pragmatist thinkers. Mirror neuronal activity occurs somewhere between impulsive or instinctual actions and reflective linguistic reason, between the group as an unthinking "mass" responding in a "blind", automatised way and the group as a community of reflective, thinking selves. Mirror neurons point to the importance of an intermediate zone, in some ways similar to, but not precisely the same as, Winnicott's (1971) "transitional space", in which there is an overlap between self and other. Much of the following discussion about the implications of mirror neurons for group therapy emphasises the hitherto neglected importance of such an intermediate zone of human activity in the work of group therapy.

Implications for group psychotherapy

The development of new understanding of psychotherapy groups based on mirror neurons and related developments in neuroscience requires a "leap of faith" in which one becomes willing to reconsider some assumptions about how to run groups. For example, dynamic group therapists are taught that they should maintain an "objective" distance from the group and interpret to the group from an independent, detached perspective. (It should be said that some therapy approaches—interpersonal and gestalt in particular—have long recognised that the abstinent, interpretive stance is sometimes less effective than a relationally based and mutually responsive dialogue. The skill of a leader in fact involves moving adeptly between the two positions.) Mirror neurons suggest that, like it or not, the therapist is non-consciously resonating with the group, cannot avoid doing that, and might better work from the "inside", utilising his or her "natural" responses to influence the group, much like the monkey who made the same motion as the experimenter. (Remember that, by inadvertently evoking the curiosity of the researcher, the monkey made scientific history in the process! Unfortunately, unlike the experimenter, the monkey will never "know" about the ripple effect of his response. The group therapist is in the enviable position of representing both the monkey *and* the knowing researcher.)

For example, therapists who work with substance abusers, borderlines, and other difficult populations discover rather quickly that an objective, detached stance often results in greater resistances and "acting out" rather than the hoped for insight and adaptive change.

Such patients seem to induce the therapist to come down to their level. Once, as a novice working in a drug and alcohol facility, the author discovered this quite by chance. In one of the groups he conducted, he almost desperately, through a process of counter-identification, found himself mirroring their highly charged, angry responses. His face turned red, the veins and muscles in his neck tensed, his back arched, and he told the clients they were hopeless cases unworthy of treatment. He immediately recoiled, fearing that he had "acted out" in an unconscionable manner and that the group would retaliate or disintegrate. To his surprise, the members relaxed, smiled, and said that not only was he right in confronting them, but that they also liked the way he reacted because it made him emotionally "real" to them. His reputation in the facility rose, as the members told other patients and staff that he was the best therapist on the unit!

Thankfully, the author was savvy enough to know that their favourable response to his loss of control was a transference resistance and rebellion that he had unwittingly joined, and that it would eventually be necessary to "work it through" with them. But from a "mirror neuron" standpoint, their wounded selves were temporarily mirrored and "understood" because the therapist manifested an unreflective aspect of their self-systems. When it is used as an active intervention, modern psychoanalysts (Spotnitz, 1976) call this process "joining", and Lichtenberg (2008) has coined the felicitous phrase "wearing the attribution". Lichtenberg, in particular, advocates the more introspective process, and in retrospect, the author's simply considering with the group the possible accuracy of their attribution might have had a still more beneficial impact than his "over-reaction", but the point here is that sometimes the group members need to find a mirror in the therapist in order to feel understood and connected. Mirror neurons and systems suggest that therapists should sometimes seek constructive ways to use "self in role" to mirror the group's emotions and reactions. Such periodic interventions could facilitate both the feeling of being understood and the strength of the therapeutic alliance. It also provides therapeutic leverage to the group-as-system.

The importance of such direct mirroring as a gateway to the therapeutic process was further brought home recently while the author was reviewing the literature on mirror neurons. At the time, he was individually treating a severely paranoid schizophrenic patient who was having ongoing experiences in which his "heart is being broken—I mean it—my physical heart—is being damaged by telepathic communications from the people around me". Both because of his disorder and the medication that was being used to control it, his body and face were stiff and inhibited. Subjectively, the author noticed that he felt emotionally cut off from the patient. Thinking about this experience, he wondered whether the patient's inhibition was insufficiently triggering his mirror neurons. So he took the chance of pointing out to him that he seemed very shy and could try to "play-act" being more animated. Therapist and patient then engaged in a "game" in which both exaggerated their facial and body movements. The patient genuinely enjoyed the process and relaxed quite a bit. Since that time, his therapy has been more productive and the rapport significantly improved.

It is impossible to say whether the "mirroring game" helped the therapist or patient more. It may be that it simply helped both feel more relaxed. In a certain sense, with respect to mirror neurons, it does not matter who is who. Nevertheless, one might hypothesise in this respect that activating the mirroring responses played a role in stimulating a mutually empathic linkage between the patient and therapist.

As an example of mirroring (and the lack thereof) in the group, consider the phenomenon of scapegoating, which can severely disrupt the group and cause patients to be extruded. A particular patient, Joe, joined an outpatient group, and engaged in "refusal", that is, he participated passively, but "refused" to acknowledge it. He maintained his apartness by responding mechanically rather than empathically to the other members. Eventually, they confronted him about it. He acknowledged the validity of their feedback. But he drew a symbolic circle around himself by folding his arms and speaking in a monotone. The group expressed compassion towards him, but they mirrored his "refusal" by in turn speaking to him without any emotion. The non-verbal mirroring of his isolation eventually led to his dropping out of the group, despite the therapist's valiant efforts to include him. This is a case where the therapist might have wished there were no mirror neurons! It was as if those nerve cells equated action and perception, self and other, in such a way as to create distance rather than closeness. A helpful intervention in this case might have been to enhance the "social intelligence" (Goleman, 2006) of the scapegoated patient by inculcating empathic skills. The group could have been enlisted as "trainers", thus further increasing their investment in him.

Using mirror neurons as a starting point, several specific components of group therapy can be targeted as areas for creative intervention: 1) mirroring and identification among group members; 2) therapist attunement and interpretation; and 3) leadership styles and therapist training.

Mirroring and identification

Mirror neurons, by virtue of their non-conscious recognition of enacted similarities, suggest that the therapist especially attend to non-verbal, gestural expressions of bonding and mutuality that emerge in the group. Research suggests that, as noted earlier, mirror neurons can register shared intentions, goals, and emotions. This may impact the ongoing cohesion, norms, and goals of a particular group or session. Everyone knows that a really good party host can influence the success of an event by the way (s)he introduces people to each other, creates mini-interactions, and offers a drink or hors d'oeuvre that sets things in motion. In terms of mirror neurons, (s)he is evoking behaviours that the party-goers spontaneously mimic for each other, in this way bringing people together mirroring each others' expectations and wishes for a good time. While group therapy clearly has different objectives from a party, the pre-verbal mirroring among the members is just as important. Mirror neurons suggest that the affective tone of each session will begin to emerge early in the process well before focal themes are articulated, and the group therapist should be alert to expressions of how the mirroring process is going and what it may lead to later. One group, for example, began with a lengthy discussion of whether the lighting and temperature of the room needed adjusting. It soon became apparent that a new group member, whose self-preoccupied "coldness" was disrupting the "warmth" of the mirroring process, needed some "light" shed on her monopolising the group time by a lengthy sharing of her recent dreams without being fully "included" in the group. When this interactive problem was clarified, the members stopped adjusting the Venetian blinds and the thermostat! They were able to help the new patient adjust her mirror neuron "thermostat" to that of the group.

Scheidlinger (1955) pointed out the importance of identification in group formation. Foulkes and Anthony (1965) held that mirroring (which they defined as perceiving aspects of oneself in others) is the means by which members "reflect" each others' "insides" and acquire self-understanding. Cohen (2000) offered evidence suggesting that, among group members, "intersubjective" feedback or what some have called "I statements" (sharing about one's own experience in response to another) is more effective therapeutically than what he called "cybernetic" feedback (members providing observations, information, and inferences about each other, i.e., "you" or "they" statements). The type of processing done by mirror neurons lends support to the value of intersubjective feedback. It is as if the mirror neurons automatically grasp "I" input from others in terms of the self and its potential for action (hence change), while "objective" information about oneself does not register so easily, especially as, from another perspective (Kohut, 1977), it challenges the individual's narcissism. For group therapists, this implies that interventions geared to strengthen and shape healthy mirroring and identification in the group should be offered prior to interpretations "about" the group and its members.

Therapist attunement and interpretation

The same principle can be applied to the role of the therapist. Mirror neuron research is consistent with Kohut's (1977) self-psychological emphasis on empathic understanding prior to the explanation or interpretation of patients' dynamics (Stone, 2005). It is also consistent with mother–infant research suggesting the importance of mother's attunement to the infant's needs (Stern, 1985, p. 142). Such attunement emerges in the budding relationship between them and entails recognition of self in other, of other in self. It is possible that mirror neurons represent what is probably one among several underlying "neuro-substrates" of attunement that allow for mother's awareness of her baby's inner states of mind and emotion prior to or along with deliberate reflection about them. Often, unlike the attuned mother, who is profoundly preoccupied with and centred in the infant, some group therapists tend to share abstract observations "about" the group or its members. This can be a helpful way of relating, but not if done prematurely, before the members have achieved a sense of mutual attunement and rapport with the therapist regarding whatever issue is at hand.

Typically, such premature interpretations are either ignored by the group or "reacted to" in a defensive manner which in turn induces countertransference reactions in the therapist. (Paradoxically, therapists often see this malformation as a validation of the interpretation!) For example, in a therapy group consisting of men and women in troubled relationships, the women became inhibited and silent whenever the male members shared and vice versa. The therapist interpreted this defensive withdrawal in terms of their relationships with their non-group partners, pointing to parallels and similarities between the intra- and extra-group interactions. Such interpretation led to a fight/flight climate in which the men and women divided sharply into warring subgroups. The therapist then introspected that he himself tended to "take sides" with the men. He changed his tactic from one of seemingly detached observation to a more "mutually attuned" stance, "trying to get inside" what the members were feeling in the present moment. Then, he formulated his subsequent interventions as mirroring statements such as: "I find that I feel a bit hurt and angry when there is fighting in the group, and I wonder if you might too". And when a female member spoke of her husband's detachment from her as he sat in his recliner watching sports events, the therapist interjected, "I feel almost as if I'm watching such an event in the group right now. I feel outside of things, both like your husband in the recliner watching TV and you feeling left out of his world. I wonder if the women in the group feel that way about the men here". The therapist's resonance with the group climate seemed to allow the men and women in the group to respond more empathically to one another. The male and female subgroups acknowledged similarities in their feelings and for the first time formed "surrogate couples" (Feldman & Kahn, 2009) which enabled them to rehearse new insights and behaviours before trying them out with their real life partners.

When a group is going well, the members sometimes feel as if they can read each others' minds, as if they can anticipate what someone is going to do or say next. Instead of being considered magical thinking, such intuitions could be understood as a mirror systems effect taken to a level where the members create in their own selves transient mirror neuron "models" of what is co-occurring amongst them. This type of cohesion is therapeutic in that it helps the members feel less alone with their problems and "in tune" with each other, very similar to the kind of synchrony that occurs within some jazz groups when their improvisations dovetail and build on each other. Well functioning support groups, such as those of Alcoholics Anonymous, are especially known for that "we" feeling, where members readily recognise something of themselves in one another and no longer feel so alone and isolated. Mirror neurons may be a part of what brings people together in consort with each other.

Recently, considerable attention has been given to Lawrence's (2005) work on "social dreaming". Mirror neurons offer a clue as to how dreams, usually private experiences that occur when the dreamer sleeps, can become a group "not-me possession" (Winnicott, 1971) that is social and public. It has been shown (Iacoboni, 2008, pp. 115–121; 196–200) that mirror neurons connect to "deeper" centres of brain activity, for example via the insula to the limbic system, the "feeling centre" of the brain. Thus, collective dreams perhaps can be understood partly in terms of mirror neurons facilitating resonances among members' emotions and memories. So the notion of a "group dream" thereby may have a neurological basis.

Leadership styles and therapist training

As previously discussed, mirror neurons suggest that group leaders should add "mirroring" to the already well-established "neutral observer" and "consultant" roles. Cohen, Ettin, and Fidler (1998) proposed a dual model of group leadership in which the leader is sometimes "transcendent" and sometimes "immanent". These terms, borrowed from religious writings regarding a God who is "above" and a God who is "with" his people, refer secularly to leaders who detach from the group in order to observe, intervene, and interpret *vs.* those, perhaps more "charismatic" or "transformational", who identify with their groups and "suffer" (meaning "to experience and to endure") along with them. Cohen and colleagues contend that both are legitimate modes of group leadership. They point out how the "immanent" style can help transform the characteristics of primitive "basic assumption" groups into "work groups". For example, by experiencing and becoming "part of" the dependency group rather than challenging it, the childlike dependency can be transformed into productive inter-dependence among the members. Leaders like

Mahatma Gandhi, Martin Luther King, and Nelson Mandela served *both* transcendent *and* immanent roles. They stood "above the crowd" to gain a broader, more humanistic perspective on the human condition, and then they "walked with" their followers as role models who were also willing to suffer with them. Similarly, group therapists may need to maintain sufficient objectivity to see a bigger and perhaps more rational picture, and yet to convey this to the group, they may at times need to "walk along" with them. Mirror neurons suggest that the "immanent" style serves a very important function not only for the group, but for the brain itself, which in some sense equates the actions of self and other for the crucial purpose of social learning. Mirror neuron responses facilitate acquisition of new behaviours and link the activities of individuals into a coordinated whole, both of which are essential functions of therapy and training groups. Therapists need to take this into account in their role as group facilitators.

The implications for educating and training group leaders, therapists, and consultants are perhaps more nuanced, because training must inculcate a conscious knowledge base for conducting groups, including the neuroscience perspective discussed here. Training includes developing a professional, responsible, and ethical stance towards the group at a high level of consciousness beyond the capability of mirror neurons. Training is indeed a "whole brain" process that includes left and right brain (verbal–cognitive *vs.* intuitive–imagistic) functioning as well as the overriding decision-making capabilities of the frontal areas of the cortex, and so on. Learning of concepts and theories as well as "hands on" experiences with groups is equally important.

The existence of mirror neurons reinforces two maxims of excellent training: a) that trainers use "role modelling" of leadership behaviour in their teaching; and b) that students are trained subjectively as well as objectively in group work. That is, students should acquire the intuitive ability to experience the group "phenomenologically", in "raw" form, without imposing theoretical assumptions prematurely, and to understand how they are inevitably responding as a participant in the group as well as conducting it. Parts of the leader's brain, such as the mirror neuron system, are automatically connecting to the group outside of immediate consciousness. This is not simply "countertransference" but an inevitable aspect of group formation. Leaders need to be educated in the ways they co-participate in the group development.

One vivid and potentially harmful example of co-participation is vicarious traumatisation (Pearlman & Saakvitne, 1995). In one post-9/11 group which the author supervised, the therapist frequently suffered brief traumatic reactions to the collective trauma the group brought for healing. Fortunately, and thanks to the talent and good emotional adjustment of the therapist, his vicarious "mini-traumatisations" resolved well in a relatively short time through self-insight, and he was able to use these reactions in ways that allowed the group and him to "mirror" one another's "wounds" in productive ways. When, at the termination of the group, the members were asked for feedback about what helped them most, they emphasised their deep and consistent feeling that the therapist was "one of us, and part of our family".

Finally, a parenthetical point can be made regarding training through the use of videotaped therapy sessions. There is evidence (Iacoboni, 2008, pp. 160–161) that mirror neurons are more activated when directly watching a live activity than on a TV monitor. This supports the notion once expressed to the author by an experienced videotape technician who noted that watching videos of therapy sessions "misses something" and that use of videos should not be used in place of direct "in the room with the patient" experience. It is as if the trainee's nervous system can process information in face-to-face contact that cannot be gained from books, transcriptions, or videotaped illustrative material. This is not to say that the latter do not have an important place, but that group training is incomplete without a liberal amount of "hands on" experience. In addition, supervisors sometimes must paradoxically trust the intuitions of their less experienced supervisees above their own, because the latter are present in the room when the group sessions occur, while the supervisor typically must rely on their reports as "secondary sources".

Mirror neurons and psychiatric disorders

Some years ago, the author treated a patient who presented a puzzling difficulty. He impressed the therapist as a polite and gentle person, bright and articulate despite his awkwardness and insecure "Woody

Allen" persona. Yet by his own report, and quite unusually, he had been extruded from several therapy groups as if there were something objectionable about him. The clinic receptionist, ordinarily a tolerant individual, remarked how she found him "obnoxious and unbearable". The therapist did not. He did notice, however, the rare peculiarity that the patient never arose to leave his sessions until the therapist stood right beside him and physically ushered him out the door! The normal gestures and saying "Our time is up, we need to stop for today" had no effect whatever. Something was amiss. Thinking about the situation, the therapist wondered if the patient could have organic brain damage. When he asked the patient if he ever injured his head, he said that several years earlier he was in a serious auto accident in which he suffered a concussion and wound to his skull. Suspecting possible brain trauma, the author referred him for neuropsychological evaluation. The report indicated a probable lesion which, according to the report was located in "the part of the brain that regulates social behaviour". Here was an object lesson in how brain changes can be the source of apparent personality disorders. It will never be known whether the patient's mirror neuron system was damaged, but that is certainly a possibility. In any case, he could not properly respond to social cues on account of the neurological impairment, hence his offensiveness to those around him.

Thus, it is possible, although the evidence is as yet sparse, that mirror neuron deficits may be implicated in some psychiatric disorders. One strong candidate for investigation is infantile autism. Autistic children experience deficits in social learning, emotional responsiveness, and comprehension of facial expressions. It is conceivable that a malfunction of mirror neurons may be involved in such difficulties, since these nerve cells "read" others' intentions. Gallese (2006) has offered a theory and research paradigm for investigating such a possible relationship between autism, intentionality, and mirror neurons.

Although significant research has yet to be done, it is interesting to consider that similar malfunctions may be implicated in a number of major mental illnesses. For example, does severe psychological trauma impinge on mirror neuron firing, thereby contributing to mistrust and other relational symptoms of post-traumatic stress? Do antisocial personalities have a deficit in mirror neurons that limits conformity to social norms? Does severe depression cause a malfunction of the mirroring process, leading to apathy and lack of responsiveness? At this time such hypotheses are untested, but they may be studied in the future using the fMRI technology.

For now, though, it is certainly possible for group therapists to note and address difficulties in mirroring in particular patients who appear to lack appropriate responses to others, and to use the group for reme-dial purposes by developing their social learning capacities. There are opportunities to capitalise on the supportive and educational aspects of the therapy group to encourage skill development, thus helping both the member and the group-as-a-whole. Furthermore, recent knowledge of "neural plasticity", the capacity of the brain to develop new receptors and connections, as well as evidence that brain chem-istry can be enhanced via psychotherapy (Cozolino, 2002, pp. 300–302), should encourage therapists to inquire whether social difficulties that seem biologically based, and therefore resistive to change, might nevertheless benefit from the group experience.

Summary and conclusions

Mirror neurons represent concrete evidence that some brain cells and neural networks respond equally to particular behaviours and inten-tions in self and other. They suggest that many social processes are rooted in non-reflective registering of similarities that link individuals together and facilitate interpersonal and group relations. They provide "hardwired" evidence that the brain may be configured to form groups by virtue of cells that respond similarly to behaviour of self and other. Each person's inner narratives and meaningful under-standing of his or her "life world" (Dilthey, 1972) begin with non-reflective experiences embedded in the group and culture. Self, world, and group are united from birth. Since persons and their living contexts are inseparable, they can form networks that have self-organ-ising characteristics. Mirror neurons constitute a potential neuropsy-chological link between the individual and the group-as-a-whole.

On the level of technique and practice, mirror neurons suggest that therapists make greater use of mirroring techniques. In effect, some degree of mirroring and identification needs to occur in the group and in its relation to the therapist, before cognitive interpreta-tions can be metabolised by the group and used in the interests of insight and self-development. Mutual empathy precedes understanding. Involvement in the co-created "life world" of the group fosters individuated self-experience and self-awareness. Group therapists are inevitably co-participants in the group. Ample use of the therapist's group involvement (immanent leadership) may sometimes offer a better working strategy than a potentially rigid, detached "surgical" stance. It is perhaps timely to re-think therapist style, technique, and training in light of what is being learned about the social brain.

Deficits in mirror neuron functioning may help explain some of the social-interpersonal aspects of psychiatric disorders. While research on this subject is too new to draw hard and fast conclusions, when treating patients who have difficulty with social understanding and empathy, it might be useful to think about how groups facilitate neural plasticity and how mirroring processes can be activated in the group in ways that are productive and healing for such patients, rather than leaving them, as so often happens, to be scapegoated, extruded, de-selected, or relegated to "lower level of functioning" treatment approaches.

The newness of mirror neuron research reminds therapists, however, to proceed carefully in their inferences regarding groups. The human brain is perhaps the most complex unit in the universe and has levels of functioning that have barely begun to be understood. From the beginnings of psychiatry, applications of neurology to psychiatry have had mixed results. Reading the bumps on skulls (phrenology) was a scientifically accepted methodology at one time (Sabbatini, 1996). In nineteenth century Vienna, hysteria was attributed to "railway spine", (Sulloway, 1979, pp. 37–39), an injury to the nervous system from the vibrations of trains! Deciphering the extent to which mirror neurons influence social behaviour remains a new and uncertain science. At the same time, there is sufficient evidence to warrant the consideration of how mirror neurons form a neural substrate of social behaviour. Moreover, that evidence converges with the findings of other disciplines such as ethology, anthropology, and infant research to suggest a picture of social experience as a central component of human nature that operates at non-conscious levels. Most communication (sixty-five per cent, according to one estimate) is non-verbal (Andersen, 2007; Birdwhistell, 1970). Mirror neurons may help account for this fact, since they appear to rapidly "read" gestures and facial expressions.

Finally, mirroring is but one among many ways that people connect with one another to form groups. Brain regions at both higher (cognitive) and lower (instinctual; appetitive) levels than mirror neurons play important roles in processing emotions and relationships. Furthermore, the left and right hemispheres operate in differing, complementary ways in social relations. Mirror neurons are but one among many neural networks, and group relations are a "final common path" that incorporates several of these complex mechanisms operating in tandem. However small their place in neural circuitry, it is likely that mirror neurons have a large impact on some aspects of group development and treatment. Archimedes said, "Give me a lever long enough and a fulcrum on which to place it, and I shall move the world". There are times when these few nerve cells located in a segment of the motor cortex may make all the difference when running groups.

Acknowledgements

The author would like to thank Dr Yvonne Agazarian, Marianne Bentzen, and Dr Malcolm Pines for their helpful comments regarding a preliminary draft of this article.

References

Agazarian, Y. M. (1997). *Systems-centered Therapy for Groups*. New York: Guilford.

Agazarian, Y. M., & Peters, R. (1981). *The Visible and Invisible Group*. London: Routledge and Kegan Paul.

Andersen, P. (2007). *Nonverbal Communication: Forms and Functions* (2nd edn). Long Grove, IL: Waveland.

Bion, W. R. (1959). *Experiences in Groups*. London: Tavistock.

Birdwhistell, L. (1970). *Kinesics and Context*. Philadelphia, PA: University of Pennsylvania Press.

Bowlby, J. (1968). *Attachment and Loss. Vol. 1: Attachment*. New York: Basic Books.

Carr, L. M., Iacoboni, M., Dubeau, M. C., Mazziotta, J. C., & Lenzi, G. L. (2003). Neural mechanisms of empathy in humans: a relay from neural systems for imitation to limbic areas. *Proceedings of the National Academy of Sciences, 100*(9): 5497–5502.

Cohen, B. D. (2000). Intersubjectivity and narcissism in group psycho-therapy: how feedback works. *International Journal of Group Psychotherapy*, 50(2): 163–179.

Cohen, B. D., Ettin, M. F. & Fidler, J. W. (1998). Conceptions of leadership: the "analytic stance" of the group psychotherapist. *Group Dynamics: Theory, Research and Practice*, 2(2): 118–131.

Cozolino, L. (2002). *The Neuroscience of Psychotherapy: Building and Rebuilding the Human Brain*. New York: Norton.

Cozolino, L. (2006). *The Neuroscience of Human Relationships: Attachment and the Developing Social Brain*. New York: Norton.

Damasio, A. (1999). *The Feeling of What Happens: Body and Emotion in the Making of Consciousness*. New York: Harcourt Brace.

De Waal, F. (Ed.) (2001). *Tree of Origin: What Primate Behavior Can Tell Us About Human Social Evolution*. Cambridge, MA: Harvard University Press.

Dewey, J. (2004). *How We Think*. Whitefish, MT: Kessenger.

Dilthey, W. (1972). The rise of hermeneutics, F. Jameson (Trans.). *New Literary History*, 3(2): 229–244.

Durkin, H. (1964). *The Group in Depth*. New York: International Universities Press.

Durkin, J. E. (Ed.) (1981). *Living Groups: Group Psychotherapy and General Systems Theory*. New York: Brunner/Mazel.

Edelman, G. (1987). *Neural Darwinism: The Theory of Neuronal Group Selection*. New York: Basic Books.

Feldman, D. B., & Kahn, G. B. (2009). The integration of relationship-focused group therapy with couples treatment. *International Journal of Group Psychotherapy*, 59(1): 109–126.

Foulkes, S. H. (1948). *Introduction to Group Analytic Psychotherapy*. London: Heinemann.

Foulkes, S. H., & Anthony, E. J. (1965). *Group Psychotherapy. The Psychoanalytic Approach*. London: Penguin.

Freud, S. (1953). *On Aphasia: A Critical Study*, E. Stengel (Trans.). New York: International Universities Press.

Gallese, V. (2006). Intentional attunement: a neurophysiological perspective on social cognition and its disruption in autism. *Brain Research*, 1079(1): 15–24.

Gallese, V., Fadigia, L., Fogassi, L., & Rizzolatti, G. (1996). Action recognition in the premotor cortex. *Brain*, 119(2): 592–609.

Gallese, V., & Goldman, A. (1998). Mirror neurons and the simulation theory of mind-reading. *Trends in Cognitive Science*, 2(12): 493–501.

Goleman, D. (2006). *Social Intelligence: The New Science of Human Relationships*. New York: Random House.

Hebb, D. O. (1949). *The Organization of Behavior*. New York: Wiley.

Hume, D. (1993). *An Enquiry Concerning Human Understanding*. Indianapolis, IN: Hackett.

Husserl, E. (1999). *The Essential Husserl*, D. Welton, (Ed.). Bloomington, IN: Indiana University Press.

Iacoboni, M. (2008). *Mirroring People: The New Science of How We Connect With Others*. New York: Farrar, Strauss, and Giroux.

James, W. (1909). *The Meaning of Truth*. New York: Longmans, Green.

Karterud S., & Stone W. N. (2003).The group self: a neglected aspect of group psychotherapy. *Group Analysis, 36*(1): 7–22.

King, D. B., & Wertheimer, M. (2005). *Max Wertheimer & Gestalt Theory*. New Brunswick, NJ: Transaction.

Kohut, H. (1977). *Restoration of the Self*. New York: International Universities Press.

LaFrance, M. (1982). Posture mirroring and rapport. In: M. Davis (Ed.), *Interaction Rhythms: Periodicity in Communicative Behavior* (pp. 279–298). New York: Human Sciences.

Lawrence, W. G. (2005). *Introduction to Social Dreaming*. London: Karnac.

Lewin, K. (1951). *Field Theory in Social Science*. New York: Harper & Row.

Lichtenberg, J. (2008). The (and this) analyst's intentions. *Psychoanalytic Review, 95*: 711–727.

Locke, J. (1996). *An Essay Concerning Human Understanding*. Indianapolis, IN: Hackett.

Meade, G. H. (1934). *Mind, Self, and Society*, C. W. Morris (Ed.). Chicago, IL: University of Chicago Press.

Merleau-Ponty, M. (1976). *The Phenomenology of Perception*, C. Smith (Trans.). London: Routledge and Kegan Paul.

Olds, J., & Milner, P. (1954). Positive reinforcement produced by electrical stimulation of the septal area and other regions of the rat brain. *Journal of Comparative Physiological Psychology, 47*(6): 419–427.

Pavlov, I. P. (1927). *Conditional Reflexes*, A. V. Anrep (Trans.). London: Oxford University Press.

Pearlman, L. A., & Saakvitne, K. W. (1995). *Trauma and the Therapist: Countertransference and Vicarious Traumatization in Psychotherapy With Incest Survivors*. New York: Norton.

Pines, M. (1998). Reflections on mirroring. In: *Circular Reflections: Selected Papers of Malcolm Pines* (pp. 17–40). London: Jessica Kingsley.

Rizzolatti, G., & Craighero, L. (2004). The mirror neuron system. *Annual Review of Neuroscience, 27*: 169–192.

Rizzolatti, G., Riggio, L., Dascola, I., & Umilta, C. (1987). Reorienting attention across the horizontal and vertical meridens: evidence in favor of a premotor theory of attention. *Neuropsychologica, 25*(1A): 31–40.

Rouchy, J. C. (1995). Identification and groups of belonging. *Group Analysis, 28*(2): 129–141.

Sabbatini, R. (1996). Phrenology: the history of brain localization. *Brain and Mind: Electronic Magazine on Neuroscience* (www.cerebromente.org.br/n01/frenolog/frenologia.htm).

Scheidlinger, S. (1955). The concept of identification in group psychotherapy. *American Journal of Group Psychotherapy, 9*(4): 661–672.

Schore, A. N. (1994). *Affect Regulation and the Origin of the Self: The Neurobiology of Emotional Development*. Mahwah, NJ: Lawrence Erlbaum.

Siegel, D. J. (1999). *The Developing Mind: Toward a Neurobiology of Interpersonal Experience*. New York: Guilford.

Spotnitz, H. (1976). *Psychotherapy of Preoedipal Conditions: Schizophrenia and Severe Character Disorders*. New York: Jason Aronson.

Stacey, R. (2005). Social selves and the notion of the "group-as-a-whole". *Group: The Journal of the Eastern Group Psychotherapy Society, 29*(1): 187–209.

Stern, D. (1985). *The Interpersonal World of the Infant*. New York: Basic Books.

Stone, W. N. (2005). The group-as-a-whole: self-psychological perspective. *Group: The Journal of the Eastern Group Psychotherapy Society, 29*(2): 239–256.

Sulloway, F. G. (1979). *Freud: Biologist of the Mind: Beyond the Psychoanalytic Legend*. New York: Basic Books.

Symington, J., & Symington, N. (1996). *The Clinical Thinking of Wilfred Bion*. London: Routledge.

Turquet, P. M. (1975). Threats to identity in the large group. In: L. Kreeger (Ed.), *The Large Group* (pp. 87–144). London: Constable.

Williams, J. H., Whitten, A., Suddendorf, T., & Ferrett, D. I. (2001). Imitation, mirror neurons, and autism. *Neuroscience and Biobehavioral Review, 25*(4): 287–295.

Winnicott, D. W. (1971). Transitional objects and transitional phenomena. In: *Playing and Reality* (pp. 1–25). New York: Basic Books.

CHAPTER THREE

Group psychotherapy and neuro-plasticity: an attachment theory perspective*

Philip J. Flores

Introduction

B rain mapping studies (Braun, Schweizer, Elbert, Birbaumer, & Taub, 2000), electrostimulation studies (Rizzolatti & Sinigaglia, 2006), and studies of brain receptors (Insel & Quirion, 2005) have provided researchers with neuroimaging techniques that have made it actually possible to record and visualise changes in brain function, neurochemistry, synaptic strengthening, neuronal connectivity, and synaptogenesis. As a result, there is mounting evidence of the brain's plasticity throughout the lifespan which dislodges the pre-1980s notion that the brain is hardwired at birth and not subject to alteration in adulthood (Morris, et al. 2001; Taub & Uswatte, 2000; Weis, et al., 2000). Terms like cortical re-routing, neurogenesis, intensive operant shaping, and brain neuronal reorganisation are reflective of these findings suggesting that the brain, like the rest of the body, can be altered intentionally. In fact, it may be a useful metaphor to consider that just as aerobics sculpt the muscles, so psychotherapy may sculpt the gray matter by reorganising associative neural networks in ways group psychotherapists are only beginning to fathom.

---

* First published in *International Journal of Group Psychotherapy* 60(4): 546–570.

These advancing techniques have provided attachment theory with concrete evidence that helps explain not only how the brain operates, but also how it responds to psychological interventions. For instance, a number of comparative studies have demonstrated regional metabolic changes in the brain (Saxena, et al., 2003), normalisation of ventricle and dorsal brain structures in basal ganglia, amygdala, and hippocampus (Furmark, et al., 2002; Goldapple et al., 2004), and increased regional blood flow in limbic system as a result of psychological interventions. Kay's (2008) review of numerous functional magnetic resonance (fMRI) studies, comparing subjects with similar diagnosis and age, have found that those subjects receiving psychotherapy for a year showed marked changes in structural and neurobiological markers while control subjects receiving no treatment did not. Lehto and colleagues' (2008) study, utilising pre-treatment neuroimaging on depressed subjects revealed reduced serotonin uptake in the medial forebrain bundle compared with healthy non-depressed individuals. After a year of therapy, the treated individual's single photon emission tomography (SPET) patterns had returned to normal. Untreated patients stayed the same.

Neurobiology and attachment theory

Attachment theory (Bowlby, 1988), as part of the development of the newer relational models within psychodynamic theory, represents a conceptual revolution that has emerged over the last few years which has attempted to synthesise the best ideas of psychoanalysis, the cognitive sciences, and neurobiology. Attachment is an instinctual, primary behavioural system that evolved to enhance infant survival, but "continues from the cradle to the grave" (Bowlby, 1979a, p. 129). The attachment system has three primary functions: 1) regulation of proximity to a care-giver in time of stress; 2) provision of comfort and security (safe haven); and 3) development of a secure base which makes exploration possible. More recent evidence reveals a fourth function in that secure attachment primes the brain for the capacity for mentalisation, an absolutely necessary process that equips the individual for collaborative and cooperative existence with others, a task for which the brain was evolutionarily designed (Fonagy, Gergely, Jurist, & Target, 2002). Research (Mikulincer & Shaver, 2007a) has identified four individual differences in attachment styles: 1) secure; 2) insecure–avoidant; 3) insecure–ambivalent; and 4) insecure–disorganised. These styles predict a range of psychological and interpersonal variables across the lifespan (Ainsworth, 1991; Main & Hesse, 1990). As Ainsworth (1989) and Bowlby (1979b) emphasise, insecure attachments are primarily defensive strategies designed to maintain contact with abusive, rejecting, unavailable, or inconsistent caregivers. These patterns of relating are reciprocally influenced and, once established, are difficult to extinguish, becoming self-perpetuating across a person's life span (Mikulincer & Shaver, 2007a).

The contributions that attachment theory has to offer in informing the application of group treatment have only rarely been addressed in the literature (Flores, 2004; Mikulincer & Shaver, 2007b). Prior to the accumulated evidence from developmental neurobiology (Siegel, 1999), the neurosciences (Schore, 2003a; Sroufe, 1996), and developmental psychoanalysis (Stern, 1985) that support Bowlby's work, attachment theory had been exiled to the fringes of psychoanalytical theory and judged to only have relevance for social psychology and child development. One reason why attachment theory may have gone unnoticed is because Bowlby's theories were not just a matter of offering a slight revision of psychoanalysis, but in actuality, "attachment theory proposes a completely new framework from which to understand clinical and developmental phenomena" (Cortina & Marrone, 2003, p. 14).

While classical developmental theory has always recognised the importance of early childhood experiences on adult psychopathology, attachment theory has placed the significance of these early attachments in a broader perspective. Intimate long-lasting relationships are seen as an integral part of human nature and the inability to establish long-lasting gratifying relationships is directly related to the quality of early attachment experiences (Schore, 2003a; Siegel, 1999). The mechanisms by which we become and stay attached to others have a biological basis and are increasingly discernible in the basic structure of the brain (Cozolino, 2006; Siegel, 1999), and these attachments have far reaching implications for optimal health, social functioning, and even survival (Lewis, Amini, & Lannon, 2000; Mikulincer & Shaver, 2007a; Ratey, 2002). Lannon (1996) captured these sentiments perfectly when he says, "Attachment is not just a good idea; it is the law".

The mandate for attachment

Clinical experience and research findings from treatment outcome studies, child development, animal studies, and evidence gathered from the neurosciences with both adults and children have confirmed the importance of attachments (Lewis, Amini, & Lannon, 2000; Norcross, 2002; Schore, 2003b; Stern, 2004). An integrative analysis of these findings has important implications for a group therapy format that emphasises a relational or interpersonal approach to group treatment. A review of these recent discoveries suggests four basic tenets:

1. Attachment cannot be reduced to a secondary drive (Diamond & Marrone, 2003).
2. The central nervous system (CNS) of all social mammals is an open feedback loop requiring stabilisation (Lewis, Amini, & Lannon, 2000) and ongoing external regulation by attachment relationships (Schore, 2003a).
2. This requirement for external regulation and stabilisation is a biological necessity and is not age or phase specific (Bowlby, 1980; Siegel, 1999).
3. The establishment of attachment and secure base in therapy predicts successful treatment outcome (Norcross, 2002; Safran & Muran, 2000).

Attachment is a fundamental motivation in its own right and cannot be reduced to a secondary drive

Attachment theory, like self psychology (Kohut, 1984), can be considered an offspring of object relations theory. While these three theories share important similarities, they hold different allegiances to classical drive theory. The most decisive factor that differentiates attachment theory from the other two theories is the degree to which it differs from classical drive theory on the importance of attachment. Attachment theory holds firmly to the position that the pains, joys, and meaning of attachment cannot be reduced to a secondary drive. Attachment is recognised as a primary motivational force with its own dynamics, and these dynamics have far-reaching and complex consequences (Bowlby, 1973).

The CNS of human beings is an open feedback loop requiring
stabilisation and ongoing external regulation by attachment
relationships

Attachment theory holds the position that our CNS is an open feedback loop, which requires input and external regulation from "attachment figures". Secure attachment creates stable neurophysiological
homeostasis and the lack of it produces disruptions in neurophysiological systems. Furthermore, strong attachment bonds relentlessly
shape developmental phenomena including the physiological and
neurobiological maturation of the brain (Cozolino, 2002; Siegel, 1999),
the capacity for affect regulation (Fonagy, Gergely, Jurist, & Target,
2002), and the internalised self-object representations (internal working model) that organises and influences a person's behaviour in relation to others (Diamond & Marrone, 2003), as well as self-esteem,
cognitive appraisal capacities (Milkulincer & Shaver, 2007a), and self-
image (Lewis, 2000). Human beings regulate each other's physiology
and modify the internal structure of each other's nervous system
through the synchronous exchange of emotions. The nature and
impact of this interactive regulatory relationship is the basis for attachment and the memory of it is recorded in the change that takes place.

This requirement for external regulation and stabilisation is a
biological necessity and is not age or phase specific

Bowlby criticised the position of classic psychoanalytic theory of oral-
ity—that viewed adult attachment needs as indicative either of
pathology or regression to immature behaviour—because these
conceptualisations were derived from outdated theories unsupported
by subsequent research evidence. Attachment theorists see both one-
to-one and group or network attachments as necessary because originally they served a biological function to insure survival. During early
development, attachment helps secure assistance for the infant during
times of threat or danger. However, as the individual grows older,
"affiliative relationships" with peers and groups become more important because they involve greater reciprocity and a semantic order
(Lichtenberg, Lachmann, & Fosshage, 1992). Affiliative relationships
are not based purely on physical proximity, but are mediated by a
complex set of meanings and representations.

The establishment of attachment and secure base in therapy predicts
successful treatment outcome

Because the strength and quality of the therapeutic alliance accounts for the greatest variance in successful treatment outcome (Norcross, 2002; Safran & Muran, 2000), it is crucial that group therapists recognise the power of attachment bonds and use this information wisely. One of the primary advantages and benefits of group psychotherapy is the shared opinion that a properly constructed group environment not only provides a neurobiological organising function, it also extends opportunities for understanding and correcting dysfunctional interpersonal patterns (Buchele, 1995; Gans & Alonso, 1998; Ormont, 2001; Rutan & Stone, 2001; Yalom & Leszcz, 2005). It may be useful to view interactions in group as not just overt behaviours or even primarily psychological functions, but as neurobiological in nature. Schore (2003a) and Siegel (1999) have proposed that alterations in external interpersonal interactions are registered as concurrent changes in the person's neurophysiology and emotional states, and have assembled related research that supports this possibility. These neurobiological changes may be reflective of alterations or modifications of what is commonly referred to as self and object representations. Such an approach takes on added significance when one considers that all psychopathology manifests itself interpersonally and, as Tronick and Gianino (1986) propose, all psychopathology may be the outcome of repeated unsuccessful efforts to repair misattunements and empathic failures. From this viewpoint, new attachment experiences that challenge the validity of early working models are what make personal development and successful psychotherapy possible.

Mentalisation, narratives, and self-reflective function

Talking intimately with another about oneself is a developmental function that not all adults achieve; securely attached individuals are at an advantage to develop this ability (Fonagy, Gergely, Jurist, & Target, 2002). Mentalisation captures the essence of this developmental achievement. It involves both a self-reflective and an interpersonal component, that ideally provides a capacity to have an experiential understanding of feelings or mental states in self and others. Mentalisation is not just a cognitive process because it extends beyond an intellectual understanding and represents the ability to *link thinking to feeling*, thus helping the person ". . . to connect to the meaning of one's emotions" (Fonagy, Gergely, Jurist, & Target, 2002, p. 15).

Knowing oneself and sharing that knowledge with another requires the capacity of putting one's feelings into words, a developmental task that requires the acquisition of inner speech or what Meares (1993) refers to as self-narrative. Attachment theory, especially because of the work of Mary Main (1995) and her development of the Adult Attachment Interview (AAI), has shown a connection between attachment status in childhood and narrative styles in adulthood. Fonagy, Steele, Steele, Higgitt, and Target (1994) describes this reflexive self function (RSF) as the ability to think about oneself in relation to another which is a necessity for empathy and reciprocal altruism.

A clinical example will help illustrate these ideas.

Andrew was referred to group by his individual therapist because of his difficulties maintaining relationships. After a number of weeks into the group, Andrew's style of relating became painfully obvious to the group leader and the other group members. He had great difficulty connecting to others interpersonally about the emotional material stirred up in the here and now of the present relationships in the group. Andrew could be supportive and compassionate of others' painful experiences or stories, but he could not stay engaged with others once the interpersonal exchange required that people relate beyond the historic content of their experience. When Andrew spoke about himself, he could not keep others engaged. Group members would become distracted or drift off because his exchanges became bogged down in the minute details of his painful past history. People in group could feel sorry for Andrew, but they could not feel drawn in by him. It was not that it was unusual for new group members to feel compelled to tell their story when they first joined the group; that was not the problem. Andrew's problem was that he remained trapped in his narratives. His stories became rote and stereotyped. It took a concerted effort by the group leader to steer the group away from their eventual indifference or boredom and their stereotyped responses to Andrew (i.e., "Oh, that's horrible, you had a terrible childhood, I can't believe they did that to you", etc.), and guide them to deal directly with the feelings that Andrew evoked in them. Using his knowledge of Mary Main's work on narrative styles and attachment, the therapist was able to cut across the dichotomy between historical truth and narrative truth. By focusing on the form of Andrew's narratives, rather than their content, the group leader was able to help the group and Andrew see that Andrew's preoccupation with his history was a way for him to stay attached to his past pain and hurt in the hope of evoking protective attachment behaviour in potential care-givers. The group leader's actions in this example are an important reminder that therapists are more helpful when they attend as much to the way their patients talk as to what they talk about.

The confluence of attachment theory and the neurosciences: implications for informing the application of group psychotherapy

Secure base and exploration

If group psychotherapy is to become more grounded in scientific theory, group therapists must pay closer attention to the vast amount of research evidence and information that the neurosciences are generating about the human brain. Our task, as group theorists, is to integrate this information and translate these discoveries into meaningful and practical clinical applications to help inform more effective group treatment. One of the important contributions generated by neuroscience research is the recognition that neurogenesis and brain plasticity are amplified by certain experiences and optimally enriched environments (Doidge, 2007; Ratey, 2002). Not all environments provide the types of activities and experiences that enhance brain plasticity, learning and change. First and foremost, the proper interpersonal environment must be established to ensure that the brain will be primed for exploration and discovery, without which positive brain change, learning, and retention of that learning is impeded (Berns, 2005; Kempermann, Gast, & Gage, 2002). Research evidence like this suggests that group therapists should take seriously the tasks of developing the types of group environment that best delivers these crucial elements.

The strength of a secure base captures one of the important paradoxes of attachment theory: secure attachment liberates (Lewis, Amini, & Lannon, 2000). Just as a securely attached child will take more risks exploring a strange room, while in the presence of a secure attachment to its mother, a securely attached group member will take more risks in exploring his/her internal world and the relationships with other members in the group if the group environment serves as a secure base. However, secure base does not mean a rigidly controlled environment that sacrifices spontaneity, complexity, diversity, and the messiness of real relationships. Attachment oriented group therapy with its emphasis on cohesion or secure base does not mean an unrealistically supportive, safe environment. Rather, it pertains to creating an environment where personal agency and differences can be safely explored, which allows the inevitable conflict that arises in any authentic relationship to be addressed. The group is secure when members can protest, disagree, and challenge each other and the group leader without fear of abandonment or violence. As Cozolino (2006) and Siegel (2006) emphasise, the human mind emerges from patterns embedded within the flow of energy and information contained inside the brain as well as between and among brains. The group leader's task from this perspective is to promote and integrate the diverse pieces of energy and information within the group into a coherent whole that allows the group to move between the shores of rigidity and chaos. The group leader's aim is to foster a process of shared reflection that generates multiple perspectives on experience, helping group members from getting trapped in the "reality" of one view.

Five factors to consider for promoting brain plasticity and change in group

1. Enriched environments, emotional arousal, and optimal levels of stress are required for brain change (Ratey, 2002; Sapolsky, 2005).
2. Experience over explanation: procedural memory and the importance of working in the implicit domain (Stern et al., 1998).
3. Strong attachment bonds prime the brain for change (Lewis, Amini, & Lannon, 2000, Norcross, 2002).
4. The brain is social and hardwired for cooperation, caring, and fairness (Denninger & Witte, 2007; Ratey, 2002; Sapolsky, 2005).
5. Initial changes in the brain are just temporary: the advantages of long term therapy (Medina, 2008; Sapolsky, 2005).

Enriched environments, emotional arousal, and optimal levels of stress are required for brain change

The brain is driven to pursue novelty and challenge (Berns, 2008), and some of the greatest sources of novelty, challenge, and satisfaction come from the necessity of negotiating the demands of ongoing intimate relationships. The brain's drive for the novelty experienced in relationships is as strong as any other primary drive because the pleasure experienced as the result of the dopamine release when a relationship is successfully managed is highly rewarding (Young, 2009). Because relationships are also challenging and emotionally arousing, they are highly effective in inducing high enough levels of optimal stress to stimulate cortisol, which primes the brain and body for action (Sapolsky, 2005). All authentic relationships are unpredictable and require constant ongoing cooperation and attention. Becoming locked into rigid styles of relating not only dooms a relationship, it also does little for priming the brain for novelty and exploration, two crucial components for brain plasticity (Berns, 2008; Ratey, 2002).

Rutan (2003) suggested that "just belonging to a group" can have a therapeutic effect. Lewis, Amini, and Lannon (2000) provide evidence of why and how secure attachment helps create central nervous system homeostasis and stabilisation which reduces cortisol to more manageable levels, thus combating the debilitating effects of chronic stress that interferes with learning and memory (Sapolsky, 2005). There are few things as stressful as isolation. This is a fact so well recognised that when researchers are conducting animal studies on stress, isolation is the primary method for inducing stress in their subjects (Ratey, 2002). While optimal levels of stress enhance learning and memory, chronic stress and too much anxiety interfere. Stress engraves memories important to survival, but too much of it cannibalises the very structure (i.e., hippocampus, which is crucial for learning and memory) that does the engraving (Ratey, 2002). This is why it is crucial that group therapists put great effort in creating the optimal therapeutic environment that balances security with emotional arousal.

Experience over explanation: procedural memory and the importance of working in the implicit domain

There has been a growing recognition (Stern et al., 1998) that new conceptual tools are required to explain how change occurs as the result of psychotherapy, both in individual and group psychotherapy. It has long been recognised that "something more" other than interpretation, explanation, or insight is required in successful treatment. Attachment theory has helped provide a different theoretical perspective that has resulted in a shift from an emphasis on the symbolic, verbal declarative realm to a greater emphasis on the procedural, implicit relational realm. Learning and change are recognised as occurring through the relationship and intersubjective moments ("moments of meeting") between or among the participants that create new neurological organisations, thus altering procedural knowledge and the implicit unspoken rules of being with others.

Writing about the advantages of an attachment perspective, Fonagy and colleagues (2002) recommended that an alteration of treatment technique needs to be carefully considered since many psychoanalytic propositions about development have turned out to be naïve and inadequate. For instance, the focus on memory and the retrieval of forgotten or repressed experience is now generally discarded in favour of an approach that examines the interpersonal and interactional aspects of relationships that have been retained as implicit procedures or patterns of actions that come to organise later behaviours (Fonagy, Gegely, Jurist, & Target, 2002). Memory is no longer conceived of as a caldron of recorded, stored formative experiences, waiting to be retrieved by uncovering analytic work (Diamond & Marrone, 2003). Rather, formative experiences emerge as analogous procedures representing an intricately interlinked sequence of events that become organised as mental models (Cortina & Marrone, 2003). These internal working models (Bowlby, 1980) exist, encoded at the limbic level and are readily observable through an individual's style or manner of relating. Once a rule is learned and becomes a basic part of implicit memory, the rules are difficult to unlearn because this information is not readily available for conscious recall. The goal of group therapy, from this perspective, is the observation of implicit rules of behaviour or patterns of interaction, the identification of maladaptive models, and the subsequent strengthening, and establishment of more adaptive rules of engagement.

The world Grand Master chess player Gary Kasparov (2007), in his book aptly titled: *How Life Imitates Chess*, captures these sentiments perfectly when he writes,

Rote memory is far less important than the ability to recognize meaningful patterns. When we tackle a problem, we never start from scratch, we instinctively look for a past parallel. We work out the authenticity of the parallels to see if we can work out a similar receipt from these slightly different ingredients . . . .. We depend on these patterns the way we depend on our autonomic nervous systems to keep us breathing. A champion chess player can spot a simple checkmate in three moves without hesitation even if he has never seen that exact position before in his life. (pp. 54 & 120)

When group members become emotionally attached in group therapy, not only is their implicit memory engaged, the biological mechanisms that permit implicit memory to be modified are also engaged. The link between memory and emotions is crucial for learning and plasticity to be maximised. Since all emotional learning takes place at the limbic level (Lewis, Amini, & Lannon, 2000; Ratey, 2002) and the limbic system is anatomically interconnected with memory, emotionally charged information is stored and encoded here, functioning as a motivational map. The amgydala, as a central arousing component of the limbic system, flags significant events, as if to say, "Remember this. This is important". From a psychobiological standpoint, group psychotherapy can be thought of as a delicate establishment of regulatory attachment relationships aimed at stabilising physiology and emotions, and revising the emotional memory of attachment patterns. If relationships are powerfully established, group members will eventually began to extract the new rules that govern their relationships with others and the modification of their nervous system has begun. The attachment model emphasises experience over insight, implicit learning over explicit learning. This is the reason why explanations and self-help books rarely change anything. Experience over time is what produces change in therapy. Insight has little effect as an agent of change. Insight is often the result of change.

Our emotional brain, as often as not, resonates with others, frequently without words or cognition. A wordless communication that we often ignore or take for granted reflects a process that Lewis, Amini, and Lannon (2000) call *limbic resonance*, which involves "a symphony of mutual exchange and internal adaptation whereby two mammals become attuned to each other's inner states".

A clinical example will help illustrate the power of limbic resonance and wordless emotional communication.

Mark, an extremely bright, thirty-five year old MBA had been in an outpatient therapy group for about six months when he began describing a series of difficulties in what had been, until recently, a promising career. He had been on a fast track for a VP position at a Fortune 500 company when two job changes were made necessary because of his recurrent difficulties with both of his bosses at two different blue-chip companies.

After describing a particularly troublesome encounter with his new CEO at work, Mark gave the group a troubled look and stated, "I wish I knew what the hell was bugging my boss".

"Think it has anything to do with your authority conflicts?" one group member asked.

"Authority conflicts?" Mark asked. "What are you talking about?"

Another group member promptly offered, "Maybe you do the same thing with your boss that you do with our group leader".

"What?" Mark looked befuddled.

"Yeah", another member nodded in agreement. "It isn't so much what you say, but what you do. You're always rolling your eyes and smirking at the group leader whenever he speaks".

A fourth group member chimed in. "You have this weird grin on your face whenever you respond to Dr A. Because I've gotten to know you in the group over the last few months, I now understand that you get that silly smile whenever you're nervous. But, I could see how someone could interpret it the wrong way, like you were mocking them or making fun of them".

Mark was shocked to learn that his behaviour was so transparent. He had no idea that he was communicating a message he did not even consciously know he was sending. With the group's continual monitoring and challenging of him, Mark's "acting out" with the group leader diminished dramatically over the next few weeks. As his awareness of his implicit communication increased within the group, he was able to translate this change outside of the group with his boss as he attempted to salvage his once promising career.

One night he entered the group gushing with excitement as he described how he had taken the group's feedback and applied it successfully in response to an especially challenging encounter with his new boss. Because Mark's struggle was a universal theme that the entire group could identify with and because he delivered his experience with such heart felt sincerity, his story galvanised the entire group with the richness of its authenticity and raw emotional honesty. Mark's struggle and his reported success was no longer just Mark's success: it had morphed into a shared group triumph. Mark had changed. Gone was his usual bravado or self-righteous indignation. Instead, Mark spoke with humility and honesty about his fears as he struggled to overcome his sense of crippling entitlement and destructive indifference.

The group, as well as the group leader, felt impacted by the enormity of Mark's achievement. An emotional contagion hung rich and heavy in the room as the entire group bathed in the shared elation of his victory. It was a tender and moving moment for everyone.

Tears welled up in the group leader's eyes. As he beamed at Mark, a single tear trickled down the corner of his eye.

Mark caught a glimpse of the group leader out of the corner of his eye. He turned and gawked at him.

"Is that a tear?" Mark asked; astonished at what he saw.

The group leader nodded yes.

Mark burst into tears. "You really get it, don't you? It matters to you that I was able to accomplish this, doesn't it?"

The group leader smiled warmly and nodded again, choosing not to hide or disown what was obvious to everyone in the group. It was also a feeling that the entire group shared with him at this second.

Mark put his head in his hands and sobbed for a few moments. Gasping for breath, he looked around at the group and shook his head. "My father never noticed my successes".

He clenched his fist. "He would usually just stare at me with such indifference. If he even bothered to speak, it was usually something critical. How I could have done it better. Don't get a big head".

Mark looked up at the group leader. "The only way I could get any kind of reaction from my father was when I screwed up. Then he would notice".

Even though the group leader had not uttered a single word, his communication was unmistakably obvious and had a profound emotional impact on Mark as well as the rest of the group. The discourse at that moment in group did not call for emotional neutrality, contrivance, or even interpretation. Instead, it required transparency and authenticity equal to the demands of the genuine human encounter that had just unfolded in the group. The remainder of the session was spent with the rest of the group joining in a rich and poignant exploration around the simple power inherent in a person's non-verbal emotional response to another. It was an important reminder to the entire group of the potency of authentic engagement in the reparative process and the basic human need to be noticed and truly seen by another. Words, in such authentic encounters, are usually incidental.

Strong attachment bonds prime the brain for change

Attachment theory suggests that therapy works because of one basic principle: exposure to people changes people—or more accurately, a powerful attachment experience can alter a person's central nervous system (Siegel, 2006). When group members become attached in group, not only are their central nervous systems engaged, but they also engage the biological mechanisms that permit their brains to be modified (Lewis, Amini, & Lannon, 2000; Ratey, 2002). If the therapeutic relationship is powerfully established, group members will eventually begin to extract the new rules that govern the relationship with the group leader and other group members and the modification of their nervous system has begun. From a neurobiological standpoint, group psychotherapy is a delicate establishment of regulatory attachment relationships aimed at stabilising physiology and revising implicit emotional memory of attachment patterns (Lewis, Amini, & Lannon, 2000).

Attachment is not just an abstract concept; it is a complex physiological process. The brain is profoundly social and highly plastic, malleable, and pliable throughout one's lifespan (Doidge, 2007; Ratey, 2002). The evidence about the way our brains function and are wired explains why we are biologically determined to form strong attachment bonds with others and how these relationships relentlessly shape and sculpt our neurophysiology and neurobiology (Siegel, 2006). However, our experience-dependent brain is not a passive recipient to either internal or external environmental influences. It is not an inanimate vessel that we fill. Rather, the brain is more like a complex, dynamic eco-system constantly adapting to its ongoing experiences. We cannot expose our brain to toxic relationships any more than we can selectively introduce drugs into the system and not expect the entire brain to be profoundly impacted.

Mirror neurons: learning by observation and imitation

The brain is a dynamic and adaptive system with a built in capacity for fairness, cooperation, and care-giving (Denninger & Witte, 2007;

Eisler & Levine, 2002; Quartz & Sejnowski, 2002) and it is the mirror neuron system that allows for this capacity for empathy, imitation, and learning through observation and understanding the intention of others because these inherent social, interpersonal features enhance survival of the species. The instantaneous understanding of the emotions of others, rendered possible by the emotional mirror neuron system, is a necessary condition for empathy that lies at the root of most of our more complex interpersonal relationships (Rizzolatti & Sinigaglia, 2006).

Constructing environments that ignore or fail to promote the need for care-giving, care-seeking, mutuality, and reciprocity interferes with the genetically programmed brain's need for attachment. When care-seeking behaviour is met by effective care-giving behaviour (attunement, empathy) or the opportunity to repair ruptures, all parties feel regulated and satisfied. This satisfaction reflects a need that all developmentally mature adults have in their drive to give and receive in relationships. In contrast, if care-giving is ineffective (poor attunement, the care-giver distracts the care-seeker from fully exploring his/her experience), no secure base is established and exploration is inhibited. Unmet care-seeking and all the behaviour associated with it (acting out, clinging, manipulation) remains active, and old defensive rules for survival in a hostile, un-empathic environment get activated (McCluskey, 2002).

Attachment is tied to biological motivations other than mere survival or reproduction. Caring does good things to the brain, whether the person is receiving it or providing it. Research evidence (Eisler & Levine, 2002) points to the importance of intrinsic motivations in most mammals for pleasure and positive affect (i.e., caring, cooperation, love, and bonding). Cooperation with others activates the pleasure centres of the brain, the same parts that are stimulated by rewards like food and money (Berns, 2008). This satisfaction reflects the need that all developmentally mature adults have: the need to give and receive in relationships. Evidence accrued from studies (Quartz & Sejnowski, 2002; Sapolsky, 2005) with both animal and human subjects confirms that social mammals' brains are hardwired for cooperation and trust; at least until they gather evidence that it either costs them too much or that they are being taken advantage of by another. In short, the brain is hardwired to recognise when it is giving more than it receives (King-Casas et al., 2005). It is essential, therefore, that the group leader constructs an environment that not only promotes cooperation and caring, but also allows for the repair of the inevitable ruptures and betrayals that occur in any authentic ongoing relationship.

Initial changes in the brain are just temporary

Attachment and practice over an extended period of time are required to produce long lasting changes in the brain (Sapolsky, 2005). Repetitive attachment potentiates the synapses and they work better through increased experience that strengthens the neural connections. In a process called long-term potentiation (LTP), excitation is prolonged allowing synapses to become synchronised in their firing patterns and organised into neural networks ("Neurons that fire together, wire together", Hebb, 1949). Information is not contained in single neurons or single synapses. Rather, information is contained in patterns of excitation, in networks of excitation, where the same neurons can overlap in different networks and be used in different settings (Sapolsky, 2005). The more a neural pathway is utilised, the more it is etched into the brain (Doidge, 2007). The neuronal circuits that do not get activated or are under-utilised experience loss of synaptic strength or pruning. Familiarity, intensity, and extended duration in time are all required for an attachment relationship to be able to provide the kind of stabilisation and modification of the central nervous system that translates into long-lasting brain change (Lewis, Amini, & Lannon, 2000). Short term treatment does not allow for enough practice for extinguishing negative plasticity and "rewiring" the new implicit rules of relatedness.

Conclusion

The neuroscience of group psychotherapy

A model of group treatment that integrates the new discoveries of the neurosciences is needed in order to offer a better translation of the implications that these research findings have for informing the clinical application of group therapy. Bowlby (1979a) and Kohut (1984) suggested years ago that the origins of the specific pathogenesis in an individual's early development is not so much related to the particular rearing practices of the parents as it is to the emotional climate of the home. In a similar fashion, it is not so much the specific techniques or approach of the group leader that influence successful treatment outcome, as it is the creation of the proper therapeutic climate that allows for the conditions that optimise brain plasticity and neurogenesis. While any attempt to translate the complexities of neurobiological and neurophysiological functions of the brain as it relates to overt behaviour will always teeter on the edge of reductionism and over-simplification, this paper represents a beginning effort at interpreting how research findings in the neurosciences may guide group therapists in creating the type of group climate that fosters neuroplasticity.

Equally important, the contributions from the neurosciences do not lead to the need for the development of another new model of group treatment, but actually may help validate many current methods already being utilised. Just as attachment theory offers a trans-theoretical formula that identifies and substantiates what all effective therapeutic models and treatments already do, the field of "interpersonal neurobiology" helps validate the venerable notion that talking with someone will alter neural pathways and synaptic strength— especially if the encounter is meaningful and occurs within the context of emotional arousal, attunement, and a strong emotional bond. All forms of group psychotherapy, from psychodynamic, interpersonal, and systems-centred theory (SCT) to cognitive behavioural therapy (CBT), are successful to the degree to which they accomplish this task and enhance growth in relevant neuron-circuitry.

References

Ainsworth, M. D. S. (1989). Attachment beyond infancy. *American Psychologist*, 44(4): 709–716.

Ainsworth, M. D. S. (1991). Attachments and other affectional bonds across the life cycle. In: C. Parkes, J. Stevenson-Hinde, & P. Marris (Eds.), *Attachment Across the Life Cycle* (pp. 33–51). London: Routledge.

Berns, G. (2005). *Satisfaction: Sensation Seeking, Novelty, and the Science of Finding True Fulfillment*. New York: Henry Holt.

Berns, G. (2008). *Iconoclast: A Neuroscientist Reveals How to Think Differently*. Boston: Harvard Business Press.

Bowlby, J. (1958). The nature of the child's tie to the mother. *International Journal of Psychoanalysis, 39*: 350–373.

Bowlby, J. (1973). *Attachment and Loss: Vol. II. Separation: Anxiety and Anger.* New York: Basic Books

Bowlby, J. (1979a). *The Making and Breaking of Affectional Bonds.* London & New York: Routledge.

Bowlby, J. (1979b). On knowing what you are not supposed to know and feeling what you are not supposed to feel. *Canadian Journal of Psychiatry, 24*(5): 403–408.

Bowlby, J. (1980). *Attachment and Loss: Vol. III. Loss.* New York: Basic Books.

Bowlby, J. (1988). *A Secure Base. Clinical Applications of Attachment Theory.* London: Routledge.

Braun, C., Schweizer, R., Elbert, T., Birbaumer, N., & Taub, E. (2000). Differential reorganization in somatosensory cortex for different discrimination tasks. *Journal of Neuroscience, 20*(1): 446–450.

Buchele, B. J. (1995). Etiology and management of anger in groups: a psychodynamic view. *International Journal of Group Psychotherapy, 45*(3): 275–286.

Cortina, M., & Marrone, M. (2003). *Attachment Theory and the Psychoanalytic Process.* London: Whurr.

Cozolino, L. (2002). *The Neuroscience of Psychotherapy.* NewYork: Norton.

Cozolino, L. (2006). *The Neuroscience of Human Relationships: Attachment and the Developing Brain.* New York: Norton.

Denninger, J. W., & Witte, J. M. (2007). The neurobiology of group psycho-therapy. *Presentation at the Annual Meeting of the American Group Psychotherapy Association,* Austin, TX, February 2007.

Diamond, N., & Marrone, M. (2003). *Attachment and Intersubjectivity.* London: Whurr.

Doidge, M. (2007). *The Brain That Changes Itself.* New York: Penguin.

Eisler, R. & Levine, D. S. (2002). Nurture, nature, and caring: we are not prisoners of our genes. *Brain and Mind: Special Issue on Brain Development & Caring Behavior, 3*: 9–52.

Flores, P. J. (2004). *Addiction as an Attachment Disorder.* Northvale, NJ: Jason Aronson.

Fonagy, P., Gergely, G., Jurist, E. L., & Target, M. (2002). *Affect Regulation, Mentalization and the Development of the Self.* New York: Other Press.

Fonagy, P., Steele, M., Steele, H., Higgitt, A., & Target, M. (1994). The theory and practice of resilience. *Journal of Child Psychology and Psychiatry, 35*(2): 231–257.

Furmark, T., Tillfors, M., Marteinsdottir, I., Fischer, H., Oossiota, A., Langstrom, B., & Fredrikson, M. (2002). Common changes in cerebral blood flow in patients with social phobia treated with citalopram or cognitive-behavioral therapy. *Archives of General Psychiatry, 59*(5): 425–433.

Gans, J. S., & Alonso, A. (1998). Difficult patients: their construction in group therapy. *International Journal of Group Psychotherapy, 48*(3): 311–326.

Goldapple, K., Zindel, S., Garson, C., Lau, M., Bieling, P., Kennedy, S., & Mayberg, H. (2004). Modulation of cortical-limbic pathways in major depression. *Archives of General Psychiatry, 61*(1): 34–41.

Hebb, D. O. (1949). *The Organization of Behavior: A Neuropsychological Theory.* New York: Wiley.

Insel, T. R., & Quirion, R. (2005). Psychiatry as a clinical neuroscience discipline. *Journal of the American Medical Association, 294*(17): 2221–2224.

Kasparov, G. (2007). *How Life Imitates Chess.* New York: Bloomsbury.

Kay, J. (2008). Neurobiology of psychotherapy. *Grand Rounds, Department of Psychiatry & Behavioral Sciences, Emory University School of Medicine,* Atlanta, GA, June 2008.

Kempermann, G., Gast, D., & Gage, F. H. (2002). Neuroplasticity in old age: Sustained fivefold induction of hippocampal neurogenesis by long-term environmental enrichment. *Annals of Neurology, 52*(2): 135–143.

King-Casas, B., Tomlin, D., Anen, C., Camerer, C. F., Quartz, S. R., & Montague, P. R. (2005). Getting to know you: reputation and trust in a two-person economic exchange. *Science, 308*: 78–83.

Kohut, H. (1984). *How Does Analysis Cure?* Chicago: University of Chicago Press.

Lannon, R. (1996). Attachment theory and group psychotherapy. *Presentation at the Annual Meeting of the American Group Psychotherapy Association,* San Francisco, CA, February 1996.

Lehto, S. M., Hintikka, J., Niskanen, L., Valkonen-Korhonen, M., Joensuu, M., Saarinen, P. I., Vanninen, R., Ahola, P., Tihonen, J., & Letonen, J. (2008). Midbrain serotonin and striatum transporter binding in double depression: a one-year follow up study. *Neuroscience Letters, 441*(3): 291–295.

Lewis, J. M. (2000). Repairing the bond in important relationships: a dynamic for personality maturation. *American Journal of Psychiatry, 157*(9): 1375–1378.

Lewis, T., Amini, F., & Lannon, R. (2000). *A General Theory of Love.* New York: Random House.

Lichtenberg, J. D., Lachmann, F. M., & Fosshage, J. L. (1992) *Self and Motivational Systems.* Hillsdale, NJ: Analytic Press.

Main, M. (1995). Clinical aspects of attachment: the work of Mary Main. *Lecture given at Conference, University College, London.*

Main, M., & Hesse, E. (1990). Parents unresolved traumatic experiences are related to infant disorganized attachment status: is frightened and/or frightening parental behavior the lining mechanism? In: M. Greenberg, D. Cicchetti, & E. M. Cummings (Eds.), *Attachment in the Preschool Years* (pp. 161–182). Chicago: University of Chicago Press.

McCluskey, U. (2002). The dynamics of attachment and systems-centered group psychotherapy. *Group Dynamics: Theory, Research, & Practice, 6*(2): 131–142.

Meares, R. (1993). *The Metaphor of Play.* Northvale, NJ: Jason Aronson.

Medina, J. (2008). *Brain Rules.* Seattle, WA: Pear.

Mikulincer, M., & Shaver, P. R. (2007a). *Attachment in Adulthood: Structure, Dynamics, and Change.* New York: Guilford Press.

Mikulincer, M., & Shaver, P. R. (2007b). Attachment, group-related process, and psychotherapy. *International Journal of Group Psychotherapy, 57*(2): 233–245.

Morris, D., Crago, J., Uswatte, G., Wolf, S., Cook, E. W. III, & Taub, E. (2001). The reliability of the Wolf Motor Function test for assessing upper extremity function following stroke. *Archives of Physical Medicine & Rehabilitation, 82*(6): 750–755.

Norcross, J. C. (2002). *Psychotherapy Relationships That Work: Therapist Contributions and Responsiveness to Patients.* Oxford, NY: Oxford University Press.

Ormont, L. (2001). Meeting maturational needs in the group setting. *International Journal of Group Psychotherapy, 51*(3): 343–360.

Quartz, S. R., & Sejnowski, T. J. (2002). *Liars, Lovers, and Heroes: What the New Brain Science Reveals About How We Become Who We Are.* New York: HarperCollins.

Ratey, J. J. (2002). *A User's Guide to the Brain.* New York: Random House.

Rizzolatti, G., & Sinigaglia, C. (2006). *Mirrors in the Brain — How Our Minds Share Actions and Emotions.* Oxford, NY: Oxford University Press.

Rutan, J. S. (2003). *Belonging to a Group,* unpublished manuscript. Harvard University, Boston, MA.

Rutan, J. S., & Stone, W. N. (2001). *Psychodynamic Group Psychotherapy* (3rd edn). New York: Guilford Press.

Safran, J. D., & Muran, J. C. (2000). *Negotiating the Therapeutic Alliance: A Relational Treatment Guide.* New York: Guilford Press.

Sapolsky, R. M. (2005). *Biology and Human Behavior: The Neurological Origins of Individuality.* Chantilly, VA: The Teaching Co.

Saxena, S., Brody, A. L., Ho, B. S., Zohrabi, B. S., Maidment, R. N., & Baxter, L. R. (2003). Differential brain metabolic predictors of response to Paroxetine in obsessive-compulsive disorder versus major depression. *American Journal of Psychiatry, 160*(3): 522–532.

Schore, A. N. (2003a). *Affect Dysregulation and Disorders of the Self.* New York: Norton.

Schore, A. N. (2003b). *Affect Regulation and the Repair of the Self.* New York: Norton.

Siegel, D. J. (1999). *The Developing Mind: Toward a Neurobiology of Interpersonal Experience.* New York: Guilford.

Siegel, D. J. (2006). The social brain in human relationships: insights from interpersonal neurobiology. *Presentation at the Annual Meeting of the American Group Psychotherapy Association,* San Francisco, CA, March 2006.

Stern, D. N. (1985). *The Interpersonal World of the Infant.* New York: Basic Books.

Stern, D. N. (2004). *The Present Moment: In Psychotherapy and Everyday Life.* New York: Norton.

Stern, D. N., Sander, L. W., Nuhum, J. P., Harrison, A. M. Lyons-Ruth, K., Morgan, A. C., Bruschweilerstern, N., & Tronick, E. Z. (1998). Non-interpretive mechanisms in psychoanalytic therapy: the "something more" than interpretation. *International Journal of Psycho-Analysis, 79*(5): 903–921.

Sroufe, L. A. (1996). *Emotional Development. The Organization of Emotional Development in the Early Years.* New York: Cambridge University Press.

Taub, E., & Uswatte, G. (2000). Constraint-induced movement therapy based on behavioral neuroscience. In: R. G. Frank & T. R. Elliott (Eds.), *Handbook of Rehabilitation Psychology* (pp. 475–496). Washington, DC: American Psychological Association.

Tronick, E. Z., & Gianino, A. (1986). Zero to three. *Bulletin of the National Center for Clinical Infant Programs, 6*(3): 1–6.

Weis, T., Miltner, W. H. R., Huonker, R., Friedel, R., Schmidt, L., & Taub, E. (2000). Rapid functional plasticity of the somatosensory cortex after finger amputation. *Experimental Brain Research, 134*(2): 100–203.

Yalom, I. D., & Leszcz, M. (2005). *The Theory and Practice of Group Psychotherapy* (5th edn). New York: Basic Books.

Young, L. J. (2009). Molecular neurobiology of social attachment. *Grand Rounds, Emory University,* Atlanta, GA, April 2009.

CHAPTER FOUR

Developing the group mind through functional subgrouping: linking systems-centred training (SCT) and interpersonal neurobiology*

Susan P. Gantt and Yvonne M. Agazarian

I n this chapter, we build a link between the emerging insights of interpersonal neurobiology and the systems-centred group method of functional subgrouping as a tool for developing the "group mind". We propose a definition of group mind that differs from the ones formulated by Le Bon (1896) who emphasised crowd psychology, McDougall (1920) who focused on individuals thinking together, and Durkheim (1966) who emphasised the *collective* of the society as an organism. Instead we propose a definition of "group mind" that integrates interpersonal neurobiology (IPNB) and systems-centred theory (SCT) and practice.

Interpersonal neurobiology

The last fifteen years have brought a new understanding of the brain and especially of its neuroplasticity (Badenoch, 2008). Certain genetic potentials in the brain are now recognised as experience-dependent for activation (Kandel, 2006). A growing body of research has now

* This is an adaptation of an article originally published in *International Journal of Group Psychotherapy*, 60(4): 514–544.

demonstrated that repeated neuron firings at synapses can increase the density of neural circuits and form new ones, validating Hebb's (1949) idea that repeated firings of one neuron followed by the firing of another strengthen this neuronal connection. For example: individuals who meditate have increased neural thickening in the middle prefrontal cortex and right insula areas of the brain, areas associated with attention, interoception, and sensory processing (Lazar et al., 2005); London cab drivers have larger hippocampal volume, an area of the brain related to spatial mapping (Terrazas & McNaughton, 2000); musicians have thickening in auditory areas of the cortex (Menning, Roberts, & Pantev, 2000); and both novel experience and exercise stimulate the formation of new stem cells (neurogenesis) in the hippocampus (Song, Stevens, & Gage, 2002).

The extraordinary proliferation in research on neuroplasticity has accelerated the focus on the relationship between the brain, the mind, and interpersonal relationships. Notably, Badenoch (2008, 2011), Cozolino (2006, 2012), Ogden, Pain, and Minton (2006), Panksepp (2001, 2008), Porges (2007), Schore (2003a,b, 2012), Siegel (1999, 2006, 2007, 2012), and Tronick (2006, 2007) have linked brain functioning and interpersonal experience, an area of focus now called interpersonal neurobiology (IPNB).

Siegel (1999) proposed a definition of mind as an embodied and relational process that regulates the flow of energy and information "at the interface of neurophysiological processes and interpersonal relationships" (Siegel, 1999, p. 21). Further, mind ". . . develops across the lifespan, as the genetically programmed maturation of the nervous system is shaped by ongoing experience" (Siegel, 2006, p. 249). This definition emphasises the role of experience and interpersonal relationships in brain development and the ongoing plasticity of the brain. Further, Siegel (1999, 2007) highlighted the role of the middle prefrontal region (consisting of the anterior cingulate, orbitofrontal, medial, and ventral regions of the prefrontal cortex) in integrating information from the body, limbic region, and cortex. He emphasised this integrative processing as crucial in interpersonal relationships and attachment patterns. In addition, focusing attention activates neuronal firing which, with repetition, can lead to the development of new and sustained patterns of neuronal activation. For example, using sensory awareness exercises to activate the right-brain can be useful with avoidantly-attached patients to stimulate not only the right-brain but also the neural connection between the right and left hemispheres (Siegel & Hartzell, 2003). Lastly, Siegel (2007) conceptualised the existing research in terms of domains of neural integration, for example, cortical to subcortical (vertical integration) and right to left (horizontal integration), proposing that effective psychotherapy enhances processes of neural integration.

Schore (2003a,b) focused on how the therapeutic relationship alters neurobiological processes related to affect regulation, building on his seminal work in understanding how affective regulation patterns originally developed in the context of early attachment relationships. Schore (2010) stressed the importance of the right-brain or "right mind" as a non-conscious, implicit core system. With its strong links to the limbic and brainstem, the right is uniquely important in implicit emotional functioning with its rapid processing of information related to safety and self-regulation. Importantly, he has emphasised that right-brain implicit processing links not only to "right-brain unconscious processing of exteroceptive information from the outer world and interoceptive information from the inner world", but also to "implicit affect, implicit communication, and implicit self-regulation" (Schore, 2010, p. 181). Drawing from his understanding of the neurobiology of early development of affect regulation structures in the right-brain, Schore linked neurobiological research to the remediation of affect regulation structures in psychotherapy. He emphasised the importance of implicit micro-second right-brain to right-brain communications between therapist and patient for developing increased right-brain complexity and capacity for regulating affective experience. This kind of implicit experiential learning (Greenberg, 2007) "certainly include(s) a dysregulating affective experience that is communicated to an empathic other . . . with an opportunity for interactive affect regulation, the core of the attachment process" (Schore, 2010, p. 194). Thus Schore stressed that the heart of change in psychotherapy is in the interpersonal regulation of "affective-autonomic arousal that allows for repair and re-organization" (Schore, 2010, p. 194) of right implicit functioning.

Cozolino (2006, 2012) also reviewed the brain research literature extensively and identified aspects of psychotherapy that maximise neural integration: a) the therapeutic relationship makes the attachment circuits in the brain more modifiable; b) moderate emotional arousal creates the kind of new experience that promotes neural plasticity; and, c) neural activation enables a re-regulation between cognitive and emotional processing, including developing narratives that guide new behaviour.

In short, IPNB has utilised research on the brain to understand how the interpersonal processes of psychotherapy help change the brain function and structure in the direction of greater neural integration and more secure attachment, and influence the implicit process of emotional regulation and right brain functioning. IPNB applies neuroscience research in considering how to deliberately enhance the impact of psychotherapeutic processes on neuroplasticity, neural integration, and emotional regulation.

Models of the brain

Although summarising the research bases of interpersonal neurobiology is beyond the scope of this chapter, it is useful to describe basic models of brain function that are relevant for our discussion. One long-standing model divides the brain into three areas: brainstem, limbic, and cortex. The oldest region in terms of phylogeny is the *brainstem*, which manages the physiological state of the body, for example, heart rate, breathing, arousal. Next is the *limbic* area, the emotional/motivational centre in the brain, which includes the *amygdala*, *hippocampus*, and *hypothalamus*, among other structures. In new situations, the *amygdala* makes a rapid judgment about safety. This judgment motivates action—to stay present and engage if there is safety, or to defend or flee if there is danger. The amygdala encodes these experiences as implicit memories. For the first twelve to eighteen months of life, implicit memory is the only kind of memory available. Implicit memories are encoded as behavioural impulses, bodily sensations, emotions, perceptions, and sometimes, fragmentary images. When activated, we experience these implicit memories in the present as "the way it is" (B. Badenoch, personal communication, 2009), rather than recalling it as a past experience. These implicit encodings form the basis of our "taken for granted" assumptions, perceptions, and beliefs about our selves, our relationships, and our sense of how trustworthy the world is. Understanding this is especially important in group therapy as implicit relational assumptions always influence members' relating without explicit awareness of that influence. For example, a group member reports his belief that the leader is unresponsive to him even though other group members experience the group leader as very responsive to him. For this member, whose parent was consistently unavailable, this belief was an important implicit assumption for him to discover and explore.

At about twelve to eighteen months, the *hippocampus* matures and explicit memory gradually develops. The hippocampus integrates implicit memories into a coherent memory with a timeframe. I can then know, "There was a dog here yesterday who was scary" instead of feeling fearful without a context. Responding to the perception of safety or lack of safety, the *hypothalamus* and the pituitary control the neuroendocrine system, which prepares our body through a release of neurohormones that facilitate remaining in connection if safe, or fight, flee, or freeze if not safe. The limbic region adjoins the middle prefrontal region of the cortex, that, when integrated with the limbic, provides for emotional and relational regulation, as well as a sense of ourselves in the meaningful flow of our history. As the ventromedial prefrontal circuitry comes into play, we can say "I", for example, "I was scared by the dog yesterday". The *cortex*, the outer layer of the brain, receives our sensory information (occipital, parietal, and temporal lobes) and integrates it with information from the body and limbic areas into a fully formed experience.

Another perspective highlights the differential functioning of the right and left hemispheres. Each lobe is a specialised processing system, with the left biased toward linguistic processing and the right toward emotional and bodily experiences (Cozolino, 2006). The right brain dominates early development (the first two years), and is strongly involved in stimuli appraisal, holistic and emotional under-standings, implicit emotional regulation, establishing attachment patterns, and mapping body awareness (Schore, 2010; Siegel, 1999). The right brain has stronger limbic connectivity, is more inward-look-ing, and more oriented to withdrawal and reflection. Paradoxically, the attention of the right brain is more to the whole than the parts, to the context, the relational, and to novelty (McGilchrist, 2009), all of which guide us to look outward. So perhaps we might say that from an inward focus on our relationship to the other, we look out at the world of connections. The left brain is more linear, logical, literal, and language-dominated (Siegel & Hartzell, 2003), and more outward toward the world, with an approach orientation that focuses on how to create systems that will facilitate getting what we need and want (McGilchrist, 2009).

Other research has generated models that describe integrated neural networks. IPNB has focused on the "social brain" (Cozolino, 2006) that includes both the limbic (amygdala, hippocampus, hypothalamus) and the middle prefrontal regions of the cortex, mostly in the right hemisphere (Badenoch, 2008) that work together in processing and integrating inner emotional and bodily experience and social information. The IPNB paradigm has also emphasised the importance of integrating the linguistic left hemisphere that creates meaningful narrative with the input of felt experience from the holistic right hemisphere.

Another focus has been on resonance circuitry that includes the mirror neuron system (Iacoboni, 2007, 2009), the insula, superior temporal cortex, amygdala, and the middle prefrontal areas. This circuitry works so that we feel others' experience in ourselves as our brain fires in response to what we are seeing in another. Central to this process are our mirror neurons which when we see a goal-directed grasping action in another fire in a similar pattern as if we were doing the action ourselves. Of even greater significance is the research showing that mirror neurons code facial actions, especially those related to the mouth (Ferrari, Gallese, Rizzolatti, & Fogassi, 2003) leading to credible hypotheses that mirror neurons may facilitate our emotional understandings of others. Mirror neurons include neurons that are strictly congruent, like grasping for a banana, which accounts for about one third of our mirror neurons, as well as those that are broadly congruent, and fire for actions that are logically related and may be essential for cooperation. Mirror neurons develop early through the act of imitating. Imitating is automatic for humans and leads to increased liking and empathy for others (Chartrand & Bargh, 1999). In applying these models, Siegel (2007) has emphasised fostering integration between the middle prefrontal cortex and the limbic regions in working with attachment issues in psychotherapy. Schore (2003a,b) has emphasised the importance of implicit right-brain functioning and the role of psychotherapy in repairing and re-organising emotional processing and regulation in the direction of greater complexity and adaptation in right-brain functioning, something that occurs when the orbitofrontal cortex and amygdala in the right hemisphere become integrated.

A theory of living human systems and systems-centred therapy

The idea of a "group mind" builds from a theory of living human systems (TLHS) and its systems-centred therapy (SCT) (Agazarian, 1997). As a systems theory, a theory of living human systems can be applied to any living human system, whether a group, a single person, a couple, a family, a team, an organisation, or even a nation. TLHS defines a hierarchy of isomorphic systems that are energy-organising, goal-directed, and system-correcting.

For a living human system, *hierarchy* defines a set of three systems, where each exists in the context of the system above it and simultaneously is the context for the system below it in the hierarchy. Living human systems always exist in context, never in isolation. This hierarchy of interdependent systems organises the flow of energy and information toward the goals of survival, development, and transformation. For example, a psychotherapy group can be conceptualised as a set of three systems, schematised as three concentric circles. The innermost circle is the person system, the source of energy for the system hierarchy. In the middle circle, member systems link to the context and are fuelled by the person systems. Member systems also organise to form transient subgroup systems whenever there are differences. In turn, the group-as-a-whole, the outermost circle of the three, integrates the subgroup organisations of energy and information. Organisation of energy and information in each system impacts the other systems in the hierarchy: each system both influences the development of the system above it and below it, and is simultaneously influenced by them. In the first meeting of a new therapy group, everyone will be in a "stranger" situation, managing all the inevitable human feelings in a new context. This is the context of the whole group, represented by the largest of our three concentric circles. People (represented by the smallest circle in our three) bring in their feelings as members as they speak of them: the feelings early in a new group are likely to cluster into two subgroups (represented by the centre circle in our concentric drawing), a subgroup of people who are anxious and the subgroup who is excited. The subgroup system(s) exist in the context of the whole group (in this case, the context is a new group) and the subgroups are the context for the person system as people explore their feelings in this new group.

Continuing with the definition, the systems in a defined hierarchy are isomorphic (defined as similar in structure and function), for example, the person, member or subgroup, and group-as-a-whole will be similar in structure and function.

Structure is defined as boundaries that open or close to the flow of energy/information. Boundaries are relevant for a group, its subgroups, and the person system: for example, as people, when our mind is open, we take in information and when our mind is closed, we do not. Group boundaries will be open to information sometimes, and closed to information at other times. For example, in the fight phase, groups are typically more open to exploring frustration and in most new groups in the flight phase, they avoid frustration.

Living human systems *function* to discriminate and integrate information (finding differences in the apparently similar and similarities in the apparently different) in the service of survival, development, and transformation. Thus, whatever one understands about the development in one system in the defined hierarchy of three (person, member or subgroup, and group-as-a-whole) will be similar for the other system levels and therefore useful in understanding the whole of the hierarchy.

For example, with a psychotherapy group, isomorphy defines a similarity between systems in the group: how the subgroups in a group are discriminating and integrating information and opening and closing their boundaries provides information about both the people and the group-as-a-whole. In our example with the anxious and excited subgroups, as the subgroups work, we understand more how the people in the group are managing the newness and the unknown of the beginning group, and also begin to see how the whole group is integrating its two responses to this new situation.

The group mind

Linking Siegel's (1999) definition of mind as a process that regulates the flow of energy and information to the TLHS enables us to operationally define mind in terms of system variables. First, the process of mind would be identifiable in every living human system and building on isomorphy, mind can be operationally defined at each system level in the hierarchy. Thus, we can conceptualise the group mind as the interdependent processes within and between the systems of person, member, subgroup, and group-as-a-whole that regulate the flow of energy and information within the system of the psycho-therapy group. These processes regulate by discriminating and inte-grating information/energy, and titrating the flow of information/energy across the system boundaries.

Our version of group mind provides a schema for linking inter-personal neurobiology and group therapy. In this schema, a central function of group psychotherapy is developing a group mind that regulates the flow of energy and information in which the minds and brains of its group members can develop and transform. As members develop their minds (by regulating the flow of energy and informa-tion and discriminating and integrating information in the direction of increasing neural integration and greater implicit emotional function-ing), more and more potential energy/information can flow through the members into the group. As people contribute more energy/infor-mation, adding still more resources for developing the group mind, and as the group mind develops and transforms, it again changes the brains and minds of the members of the group. This recursive process supports the primary goal of every psychotherapy group. For exam-ple, in a new group, as Betsy joins with others who are anxious, Betsy becomes less anxious; joining with others is regulating. Betsy is then more open to contribute her experience which increases the flow of energy and information into the group so that the group has more resources from its members for developing and transforming. This results in greater complexity in the group, which in turn has greater development and thereby resources to develop its members. In making this proposition, we are not excluding the potential for groups to become mind-numbing and closed-minded instead of mind-devel-oping. For example, the work on "group think" (Janis, 1972), social conformity (Asch, 1951), and obedience (Burger, 2009; Haney, Banks, & Zimbardo, 1973; Milgram, 1963) all point to how group norms can dominate the individual. Berns (Berns et al., 2005) has replicated Asch's study using functional magnetic resonance imaging of the brain, and identified the "distortion" from social pressure as activat-ing the parietal and occipital regions, which suggests that the social context actually impacts the neurophysiology of perceptions.

Clearly, group therapists must work explicitly to develop a group mind that not only potentiates problem-solving, but also creates expe-riences that regulate and develop the minds and brains of the group members. From an IPNB view, this means considering how our groups do or do not create emotional regulation and neural integration. Maximising neuroplasticity requires that we create an experiential group environment that provides a secure relational context, with neural and emotional regulation within and between brains, where moderate levels of emotion can be experienced with the right-brain resonance and responsiveness that enables modulation, development, and greater implicit integration. This facilitates the integration and reintegration of cognitive and implicit emotional elements of human experience that, in turn, increase access to the range of human experience and capacity for implicit and explicit regulation of one's experience with one's self and with others.

Functional subgrouping

Using this framework of "group mind", we posit that functional subgrouping, a core method in systems-centred groups, contributes to developing a group mind with the kinds of experiences that enhance right-brain emotional regulation and neural integration. Functional subgrouping contains emotional arousal and facilitates emotional modulation in the flow of energy/information; creates a secure relational context of right-to-right brain communications; and fosters a group mind that potentiates implicit emotional processing toward greater integration and function.

Functional subgrouping was developed as a conflict resolution method implementing the theoretical idea that living human systems survive, develop, and transform from simpler to more complex through the process of discriminating and integrating differences, both the differences in the apparently similar and the similarities in the apparently different (Agazarian, 1997). Information is the energy of living human systems. However, as human beings, we all react to information that is too different from what we know as though we are endangered (sympathetic nervous system arousal or dorsal vagal activation), and we often close our minds to these differences. By organising communications so that we can contain and modulate our reactions to differences in energy/information, functional subgrouping enables the differences to be used as resources in the service of the group's development.

For example, functional subgrouping interrupts typical group phase communication patterns that fixate group development by avoiding differences (flight phase) or attacking them (fight phase) (Agazarian & Gantt, 2003). In the flight phase, members often try to advise or help others, frequently creating the roles of "identified patient" and "helpers", as when a member talks about being anxious while other group members speak up to reassure, sympathise, or ask about the member's anxiety. In this communication pattern, the flow of energy/information is from "helpers" to "identified patient". Neither the information contained in the "helpers" nor the "identified patient" subsystems is explored. Functional subgrouping interrupts these typical group phase patterns by changing the communication patterns themselves. In this example, all "helpers" explore together in one subgroup their impulse of "wanting to help", and all those "wanting to be helped" explore their impulse in a separate subgroup. The more secure subgroup context of similarity and understanding allows for more regulation of the right-to-right brain communications between members. In the fight phase, group members typically refute differences with "yes, but's" and elect a scapegoat to contain the differences the group has not yet explored (Agazarian, 1997; Horwitz, 1983). Moreno (2007) provided an example of a group starting to scapegoat a member who was angry. Using functional subgrouping enabled the group to explore their different relationships to anger, with one subgroup joining the angry member to explore being angry and another subgroup exploring the pull to withdraw and avoid the anger.

Functional subgrouping interrupts these stereotyped group patterns by introducing an alternative communication pattern: training group members to ask, "Anyone else?" when they are finished with what they are saying. For example, Doris begins by saying, "I'm anxious. Anyone else?". The phrase "Anyone else?" lets others know Doris is finished *and* wants to be joined. Members are then trained to join and build with their similarity and resonance. Donna joins by saying she is anxious, too, and then builds by adding, "I am all fluttery, not knowing how this is going to go. Anyone else?". In this way, functional subgrouping builds resonant subsystems as members join together. In these subsystems of relative similarity, boundaries are more open and small differences more easily tolerated. Thus, without the sympathetic reactivity to differences that triggers survival roles at the expense of development, energy/information can be more easily discriminated and integrated.

As each subgroup works in turn, within the subgroup environ-ment of comfortable similarity, members begin to notice and accept "just tolerable differences" in what was apparently similar. When a member of a subgroup notices a difference that is "too" different, the leader validates the importance of this difference, and asks the member to start a new subgroup when the working subgroup has finished its exploration. This enables groups to explore in the context of subgroups of similarity and resonance. At the level of the group mind, functional subgrouping regulates the flow of energy/informa-tion. For example, as mentioned earlier, a therapy group working in the flight phase would often have one subgroup exploring the impulse to help and "make things right", and the other exploring the wish to be helped and "taken care of". These subgroups contain and explore the human experiences of anxiety and dependency that are inevitable in early group life. This same process is applicable to the exploration of any human experience.

When a subgroup pauses and is ready for a difference, a member starts a "different" subgroup and members who resonate with this difference join together and build this subgroup. In this example, once the anxious subgroup paused, the "excited" subgroup explored. And again, in the new subgroup, members begin to discover those differ-ences with each other that are barely tolerable to them. In the members' shared resonance, mirror neurons and resonance circuits are activated and the subgroup climate supports neural integration. Over time, group members discover the similarities between what were initially two different subgroups, as both discover some relief, and integration takes place in the group-as-a-whole.

Containing emotional arousal and facilitating emotional modulation in the flow of energy and information

Porges (1995, 1998, 2007) has identified three levels of autonomic nervous system circuits that operate hierarchically. These circuits acti-vate differentially depending on "neuroception" of the level of safety or danger in a situation. Neuroception is a process that takes place largely below the level of conscious awareness, yet influences how we relate and interact. The myelinated ventral vagal branch of the parasympathetic nervous system activates to neuroception of safety and is the highest and the only uniquely mammalian level of the three. This circuitry links the heart to the striated muscles in the face, and inhibits sympathetic activation of the heart. Porges calls this ventral vagal circuit the social engagement system in that its activation orients to the unique facial expressions and vocalisations of safety, tuning our ears to also listen for the tones and prosody of safety. This allows for interpersonal regulation and experiences of calm, relaxation, and openness. The middle level of autonomic activation involves the sympathetic branch and activates with a neuroception of threat, accompanied by the possibility of doing something about it. Sympathetic activation prepares us for fight or flight and diminishes social engagement and our ability to take in new information. The lowest level system, the unmyelinated dorsal vagal parasympathetic, takes over when our neuroception of threat leaves us feeling helpless, and initiates a death-feigning, dissociating freeze response.

Creating groups that foster interpersonal neural integration then requires developing group contexts that are experienced as "safe-enough" to activate the social engagement circuits that support "brain to brain" neural modulation. Complexity theory introduced the idea of near-to- or far-from-equilibrium as descriptors of "systems function". To the extent that a system functions near-to-equilibrium, it approximates a closed system and approaches entropy. To the extent a system is functioning far-from-equilibrium, it approaches chaos (Kossmann & Bullrich, 1997).

Functional subgrouping creates a "mid-from-equilibrium" condition (Gantt & Agazarian, 2004), activating the brain's social engagement system. "Mid-from-equilibrium" creates a stable-enough context for system containment while simultaneously introducing the conditions for system change through discriminating and integrating differences and its ongoing process of system correction.

Revisiting the example of the "anxious subgroup"

The experience of an "anxiety subgroup" is more typical of right-brain processing with sympathetic activation in response to neuroception of danger (often referred to as flight/fight). (Canli, Desmond, Zhao, Glover, & Gabrieli (1998) documents a right-brain bias in anxiety disorders.) The left hemisphere orients to making meaning of the right-brain input. The anxiety is then "explained" by left-brain analysis ("this group will not work out for me and is not the right context for me"). The explanation itself creates additional anxiety.

SCT discriminates "explaining" from "exploring". "Explaining" is similar to what Siegel (2007) calls "top-down" thinking that maintains a "usual" view. This generates feelings that pre-empt attention to new or current experiences. In contrast, functional subgrouping supports exploration that is more likely to access the implicit unknown. Joining on resonance and similarities activates the social engagement system, increasing security. Moreover, functional subgrouping emphasises looking at, talking to, and making eye contact with the members of one's subgroup, which heightens the right-brain interchange. As each person in the subgroup speaks, the next speaker reflects him or her until the contributor feels understood, before adding his or her own contribution, increasing attunement. In the example above, as the anxious subgroup worked together, members felt relieved as they discovered others who felt anxious, too. Thus, the social engagement system was activated in the subgrouping process, lowering the sympathetic mobilisation to the "threat" of the new, or the "unknown" as SCT terms it, that is inevitable in every new group. Implicit right-brain communications in the subgrouping process lay the foundation for new right-brain integrations and increased capacity for emotional regulation. As Porges demonstrated, neuroception of safety activates the social engagement system. Functional subgrouping elicits social engagement and deactivates the sympathetic mobilisation to threat.

Fear system

The considerable research on anxiety and the brain's "fear system" is also relevant (cf. LeDoux, 1996). Those brain subsystems that are most relevant for anxiety and fear are the amygdala, the orbitofrontal cortex, and the sensory thalamus, particularly in the right hemisphere. The amygdala is located in the limbic system, the middle part of the brain involved in emotional processing. The amygdala is closely connected by neuronal pathways to both the vagal and sympathetic nervous systems, and potentially has strong connections to the prefrontal cortices. In many ways, our brains are primed to be alert for threat (Cozolino, 2006). A sensory "alarm" is relayed through the sensory thalamus that sends signals to both the amygdala and the cortex. The amygdala processes the sensory input and serves as the fast-track alarm system

(Goleman, 1995). The cortex receives signals from the thalamus as well, but is a slower and more precise response system that discriminates details of the stimulus, makes a more accurate here-and-now assessment of danger, and can then modulate the amygdala response (LeDoux, 1996). LeDoux describes an example of seeing a coiled object in the woods. The amygdala reaction is to run from the "snake", the cortex "collects" more data, recognises a coiled vine, and then sends signals to the amygdala to relax. Depending on the integration in that moment between the prefrontal cortex and limbic regions, the amygdala's activation of an immediate fear response may or may not be inhibited by the slower cortical assessments. Research with post-traumatic stress disorder (PTSD) patients (Shin et al., 2004, 2005) pointed to the interplay in the fear circuitry between an under-functioning orbital medial prefrontal cortex and an overactive firing in the amygdala. When the fast-track amygdala is highly sensitised by previous fearful experiences without enough cortical modulation, the result is the kind of chronic anxiety and fear seen in PTSD and generalised anxiety disorder (GAD) patients. In addition, the amygdala with its fearful associations (including out-of-awareness implicit memories) can send ascendant alarm signals, which the left hemisphere organises into fearful narratives at the expense of the cortex collecting data and modulating amygdala arousal.

Functional subgrouping and modulating fear responses

In groups, differences that are "too" different are often experienced as threats. By teaching group members to join deliberately on similarities, members learn to shift their attention away from their "fast-track" responses to differences. The relief in being joined is usually palpable, an embodied right-to-right experience of security. Thus, functional subgrouping not only activates the social engagement system in the brain, but also directly provides emotional co-regulation, while also supporting cortical assessment and modulation as another means of calming the amygdala.

Once functional subgrouping is established, and the anxious subgroup has joined each other well enough that members start to feel less anxious and more secure, the "anxious" subgroup's task is to check the reality of their fears in the here-and-now. This next step is implemented by asking the subgroup members to talk together to identify the source of their anxiety: "Find out if your anxiety is coming from a thought, a feeling, or the edge of the unknown" (Agazarian, 1997). This kind of question stimulates cortical activity in the brain, fostering cortical and limbic integration. Group members learn to shift their attention away from the limbic/amygdala firing (middle brain), which further modulates their anxieties. Learning to shift one's attention also de-escalates habitual fear priming.

Early in a group's development, members tend to identify their anxiety as coming from a thought, often a negative prediction about the future. As Sally put it: "This group might not be a good place for me to be", a common negative prediction in new groups. Having identified the specific thoughts that are making them each anxious, subgroup members are asked to "turn on their researcher" to find out if they believe they can tell the future. This further engages cortical processes and continues restoration of the neural balance in the fear system. Doing this work in the context of the subgroup maintains the social engagement system activation, fostering the possibility of ongoing mutual regulation of implicit emotional processing, experiences that over time can build permanent connections between the amygdala and middle prefrontal regions. Typically, subgroup members answer "no", and feel calmer still. SCT thinks of this as restoring reality-testing. The next step is asking how each person feels for themselves about having been caught up in thoughts that created anxiety. This is often answered with "I feel compassion" or "sad for me", linking an emotional experience to anchor the cognitive work, an important neural integration, and activating the highly integrative middle prefrontal region. Thus, the security in the subgroup, with its activation of the social engagement system, lowers the mobilisation to threat. The subgrouping also creates enough right-brain to right-brain communication to regulate the emotional arousal and to foster increased right-brain adaptive complexity. This enables settling the fast track amygdala responses to difference, activating the prefrontal cortex to check reality and modulate the amygdala, and thus facilitates integration.

Functional subgrouping creates a secure relational context

Building on similarities to create a resonant communication system

The heart of functional subgrouping is building on similarities and resonance with each other before introducing differences. The earlier example illustrated a beginning group in the flight phase, learning to explore instead of explain. Below we summarise a subgroup in a group in transition from flight to fight:

> John started a subgroup reporting his anger, and saying he felt full of hot energy. Doreen joined, saying she was angry, too, and felt big and energised. Sam joined with his experience of feeling like an angry bull and wanting to ram into things. Jeri joined next, building on Sam's feeling of being a ram: "I can actually feel wanting to paw and charge, as you were saying it. I feel more like a ram actually, and I want to snort, too! I've never felt like a ram before". As Doreen and then others joined, John reported feeling relieved and freer with his experience of anger. Jeri chimed in saying she had never felt so strong, that usually she feels like hiding when others are angry. As the subgroup members continued to join and build on each other, the subgroup discovered an increasing sense of power, solidity, and freedom.

Building on similarities and resonance creates a context of attuned communication *within* the subgroup, right-to-right brain resonance, while simultaneously building a group mind that organises its emerging differences in resonant subsystems. Members increase their attunement to others and develop the ability to accommodate a wider range of different experiences in themselves. This resonant attunement is what Siegel (1999) calls "contingent communication", in which there is an initial alignment of "states of mind". Each person's experience shapes and is shaped by the experience of others within the subgroup as they feel "felt" by one another. The subgrouping experience also matches Schore's (2010) description of right-brain to right-brain communication, where the discriminating and integrating in the subgrouping process provides "repair and re-organization of the right lateralized implicit self, the biological substrate of the human unconscious" (p. 194). The subgroup is emergent, and in this emergent system, new experiences unfold as members build on right-brain resonance, which amplifies the subgroup's capacity to hold their emotions. In fact, group members discover that each person will explore places in the process of subgrouping that they are unlikely to explore alone.

Joining on resonant similarities is an implicit, emotional communication: an exchange of emotional energy/information. The subgroup provides a secure emotional and relational context. Members learn to hold their differences and direct them to another subgroup.

This helps to develop the environment *within* the subgroup of cohesive alignment in similarities, and the environment *within* the group-as-a-whole of making room for all differences. Tronick (Cohn & Tronick, 1989; Tronick, 2006) demonstrated that in interactions between adults and infants, moving from matching to mismatching affective states with infants generated stress in the infant that was "resolved by the reparation back to matching states" (Tronick, 2007, p. 389). In effect, the emphasis in functional subgrouping on joining on similarities ameliorates distressful mismatching that comes from differences that are too different. There is little reason to suppose the distress is any less for adult–adult interactions since responses to differences in groups often precipitate "fight" communication patterns replete with blame and attack.

Functional subgrouping develops a secure context in which the typical human reaction to difference is regulated both by the sense of feeling understood and the sense of security and implicit emotional regulation that develops in the subgroup system. McCluskey (2002) has suggested that functional subgrouping increases the potential for attunement and creates an environment in which early attachment failures can be explored and remediated as internal models are modified at the intuitive, non-verbal, and sensory level. Building on McCluskey's work, SCT suggests that the secure-enough environment of the subgroup system provides the context for activation of the exploratory drive, so essential to human development (Heard & Lake, 1986, 1997). It is the exploratory drive, or "curiosity" as SCT names it, that enables the essential process of discriminating and integrating differences in the service of development, thereby strengthening the implicit right-brain regulation. In effect, a functional subgroup approximates a secure-enough attachment system in the here-and-now experience.

The act of joining in functional subgrouping and finding that someone else understands generates a positive emotional state. As the subgrouping continues, members discover small differences in their experience (which may lead to mild sympathetic activation). In the subgroup environment of similarity and resonance, small differences are more easily accepted without distress or fear. Thus, the subgroup development creates a secure system that contains the aligned *and* slightly different communications, the matches, and the increasingly tolerable mismatches. In this way, functional subgrouping increases the "window of affective tolerance" in implicit right-brain functioning at all system levels, the person, the subgroup, and the group-as-a-whole.

Eye contact is emphasised in functional subgrouping as part of making the emotional connection to the other. Observing others' emotions, especially the facial expressions of those emotions, activates mirror neuron firing just the same as if we were making the facial expression ourselves. Iacoboni (2008) detailed this automatic process of mirror neuron firing in response to others' facial expressions: as the mirror neurons fire, they send signals via the insula to the limbic system, particularly the amygdala, and on to the prefrontal cortex. This process allows us to "feel" the feelings and experience the intentions of others. As the group develops, the subgroups that emerge reflect the conflicts in each phase of group development and the members' challenges related to these human conflicts (Agazarian & Gantt, 2003). In the early phases of flight and fight in a group, the main challenges are commonly related either to anxiety, fear activation, or emotional arousal.

Attachment issues are also reflected early in a group in the tendencies to join subgroups quickly or slowly. For example, someone with an avoidant-attachment style will tend to see every subgroup as "too different" to join, while someone with an ambivalent-attachment may lose his or her own experience by "subgroup hopping". The in-depth exploration of attachment issues is not sustainable until, and unless, the group develops to the intimacy phase. In the intimacy phase, functional subgrouping centres on the exploration of the attachment roles that influence how members subgroup and join in resonant communications with others, often linked to implicit memories. The early attachment issues are then explored in the security of functional subgrouping, with its "good-enough" attachments. In fact, once members have learned the basics of functional subgrouping, they then learn a more nuanced process of subgrouping. The first step is to attune to the last person who has spoken, and then either join in emotional resonance or paraphrase in attunement. This is reminiscent of the imitation that Iacoboni (2008) sees as essential to the development of mirror neuron functioning. The second step is to separate, re-join one's self, and then individuate by adding one's own "build" to the group that will introduce some difference. The third step is to look around the group-as-a-whole and ask "Anyone else?" furthering the individuation and fostering attunement with the larger group. Schore's (2003a,b) work suggests that the micro-attunements that occur in such a secure environment directly rewire early implicit attachment patterns in the direction of greater security. Since implicit memories are not easily accessible through the usual process of remembering, but instead show themselves in automatic, out-of-conscious-awareness relational patterns, the possibility of rewiring through the experiences of connecting and being understood represents an important aspect of the group process.

Developing the group-as-a-whole and neural integration

Previously, SCT has emphasised using functional subgrouping to integrate the conflicts inherent in each phase to facilitate the group through its phases of development (Agazarian, 1997). An IPNB perspective enables the additional view of functional subgrouping in the service of developing the group mind. From a group mind perspective, functional subgroups are differentiated emergent subsystems that influence group functioning and maturation by regulating the flow of energy and information within and between members, subgroups, and the group-as-a-whole. Within the group, functional subgroups contain differentiated functions for the group-as-a-whole in its development as a complex adaptive system. As the subgroups develop functionally by discriminating and integrating information, integration occurs in the group-as-a-whole, and the dynamic subgroups then dissolve. Functional subgrouping can then adaptively contain any number of splits in human experience that reflect current neural integration at the level of person/member, and foster integration in the mind of the group-as-a-whole.

The integration of cortical and sub-cortical structures is easily illustrated by looking at the fear-activation system. As discussed, the right-brain role in fear-activation via the amygdala is moderated by the orbitofrontal cortex. In the earlier example, as the "fight" subgroup worked, the "anxious" subgroup emerged in the group. From the group dynamics perspective, the two subgroups contained the two polarities characteristic of the group's phase of development: fight and flight. From an IPNB view, both subgroups reflect sympathetic mobilisation. Functional subgrouping contains each experience, by activating the ventral vagal circuitry that modulates the sympathetic mobilisation. This then enables cortical involvement with the potential for greater integration within each subgroup in the right-brain implicit communications and restoration of neural balance between the cortical and limbic responses.

In addition, within each subgroup, the exploration of novelty increases, enriching the subgrouping context (importantly, enrichment increases neurogenesis (Gage, 2002)). Subgrouping is particularly important for "memories" or emotional responses that originally occurred under conditions of stress or trauma that were encoded in the amygdala (implicit memories), but not organised by the hippocampus into explicit memories. These implicit "stress" responses are often triggered by a here-and-now group event. In fact, it is common for fear-related implicit memories to be triggered in response to anger, and for group members to be frightened without knowing why. Functional subgrouping provides the containment and contingent communication in which these implicit responses can be explored in the right-brain to right-brain communication leading to greater implicit adaptation and building integration with higher level cortical processing.

"Right-brain subgrouping" promotes vertical integration across modalities of experience. Functional subgrouping, with its emphasis on exploring rather than explaining, mirroring, prosody, and eye contact, creates a "right-brain rich" environment that develops the capacity of members for images, right-brain to right-brain communications, polysemantic understandings, analogic communications, and an increased awareness of sensation and bodily experience. The "fight" subgroup, with its experience of "feeling like a bull", exemplifies how functional subgrouping supports exploration of bodily experience and analogic knowing. In the security of a subgroup, members are more open to exploring human experience. In the earlier phases of a group, the work is to access and develop more of the implicit right brain experience in the subgrouping context that enables greater complexity and adaptation. In later group phases, the emphasis shifts to how to use this right-brain knowing as one relates to one's self and others.

Directing attention to the "fork-in-the-road" between "exploring" one's experience instead of "explaining" it (Agazarian, 1997) develops the capacity for subgrouping by focusing attention through intention.

Recent research (Lazar et al., 2005) has demonstrated that consciously focusing the mind (as in meditation) increases cortical thickness, supporting development of neural connections between the middle prefrontal and limbic regions. Deliberately attending to the energy and information coming from the body strengthens vertical integration—drawing body, limbic, and cortex together. Identifying and describing the experience in one's limbs and facial muscles changes/fires the somatosensory cortex, while attending to visceral shifts in the body fires the orbitofrontal cortex and anterior cingulate, predominantly on the right side (Siegel, 1999). Exploring these body experiences in attunement with subgroup members who are observing similar experiences builds neural capacity for a coherent experience of body knowledge. The attuned resonance in the subgrouping allows members to feel "felt" (Siegel, 1999, 2007) and to feel others in the process of exploring bodily experience.

Functional subgrouping to support left-brain functioning

"Left-brain subgrouping" provides a context for exploring left-hemisphere constructions and verbal communications that may be misattuned or out of date with right-brain input. This process supports members detecting and assessing previously invisible and habitual "top-down" influences, like negative predictions, that are sometimes rooted in implicit memory. Functional subgrouping can be used to explore the ambiguities, contradictions, and redundancies in communications (Shannon & Weaver, 1964; Simon & Agazarian, 2000) that represent a left-brain adaptation to right-hemisphere dysregulation. For example, Sally joins the "worrying" subgroup, saying, "Something bad may happen". This negative prediction is high on ambiguity, which makes it impossible for Sally's subgroup to test it in the here-and-now reality of the group. It is also not the kind of communication that will help the subgroup use its left-brain function to analyse relevant information from their right brains to discriminate whether the right-brain "felt" sense is in response to a current sensory input or an activation of an implicit past neural network.

Subgroup exploration here follows this pattern: first, identify the thoughts that are generating the worry; second, say aloud to each other the specifics of the thought; and third, test and compare the thoughts to the actual observable external reality (Agazarian, 1997).

All of this happens in the resonant attunement with others in the subgroup who are having similar thoughts, thus bringing an element of right-brain repair in as well.

It is not unusual for one subgroup to work with the left-brain exploration and a second with the right-brain experience. Going back to the earlier example with the angry subgroup, as it finished exploring and paused, another subgroup formed.

Dawn reports being frightened and anxious. The therapist encourages her to ask, "Anyone else?". Three other members join and begin exploring the source of their fear. The therapist then leads this subgroup through the systems-centred protocol for undoing anxiety (Agazarian, 1997), and members identify that the anxiety and fright is coming from their negative predictions that the angry subgroup will lose control. The therapist asks the subgroup to find out if they actually believe they can tell the future. The subgroup members respond, "No", and report an immediate relief and decrease in anxiety. As the anxiety is reduced, the subgroup is in effect assuming a reality-testing function for the group-as-a-whole, checking to see if there is any danger in the here-and-now reality.

Functionally, the first subgroup voicing the anger has spoken more for the right-brain experience for the group-as-a-whole (e.g., the somatosensory experience, images, and metaphors). This subgroup's work strengthened access to the right-brain processing. The second subgroup, activated by the anger of the other subgroup, voiced and explored the left-brain worries related to fears generated by the past or speculations about the future. These thoughts translate the anxieties of the right-brain fear arousal in response to the anger into thoughts or explanations that generate and maintain fear arousal. The group's challenge is to contain both human propensities, providing sufficient safety to regulate the response to the differences. When there is good-enough containment, the exploration of both the anger and the source of the anxiety can occur with left- and right-brain processing that is sufficient for an integration of the two in addition to re-organising the implicit right-brain emotional processing. A new neural integration can then be established both within the right-brain systems and between the left- and right-brain processing systems.

As the work continued, each subgroup recognised their similarities with the other subgroup and group insights emerged. For example, after listening to the work of the "anxiety" subgroup, John, who was initially in the "fight" subgroup, acknowledged that he too had often been stopped from exploring his angry feelings by his fears. Further, as he listened to the "anxiety" subgroup work, he felt more confident that his typical fears were not founded in current realities. Others joined in recognising how their thoughts interfere with getting to know their feelings. They also realised how useful it was to separate their thinking from their feelings, and redirect their thinking to clarify reality. In effect, functional subgrouping can develop the group mind through stimulating vertical integration (the middle prefrontal better regulating the limbic circuits especially within the right-brain) and horizontal integration (the left hemisphere providing a new narrative based on here-and-now reality). Describing one's experience to each of the members of a subgroup also promotes horizontal integration of left and right hemisphere functioning. Verbalising and describing one's emotions enhances emotional regulation by creating more of a balance between left and right hemisphere activation (Badenoch, 2008).

Functional subgrouping contains unintegrated splits that reflect a lack of neural integration within and between neural systems. Exploring each side in the containing context of similarity enables each component of brain processing to do the work necessary for the group mind to develop, and to integrate differentiated systems and modes of processing. As each subgroup develops by discriminating differences in what was initially a similar experience, each begins to notice the similarities in what was initially different (Agazarian, 1997). This fosters integration in the group mind of the splits in the group-as-a-whole and isomorphically in its members. Splitting is evidence of lack of integration in a system at all system levels; functional subgrouping organises splits in a way that promotes neural integration.

Summary and conclusions

We have discussed how functional subgrouping can lead to "feeling felt" as members resonate with experiences shared by other members. This creates a secure context and strengthens our social engagement circuitry, allowing for deepening self-awareness and for the repair and reorganisation of right-brain implicit emotional processing.

Functional subgrouping is typically introduced in a group whenever there is a conflict or difference that is too different to be easily integrated. Conflict almost always results in some kind of neurophysiological arousal or de-activation or dissociation that is then contained in the subgrouping process, lowering the reactivity or adaptation that, when unmodulated or unintegrated, leads to personal and interpersonal distress at the expense of neural integration. Thus, using functional subgrouping to resolve group conflicts and integrate differences constitutes the very combination of moderate arousal and the experience of closeness and understanding with one's subgroup that is similar to the conditions that promote neural plasticity and re-organisation of implicit right-brain emotional processing (Badenoch, 2008; Cozolino, 2006; Schore, 2010; Siegel, 1999).

In systems-centred groups, functional subgrouping is often focused on here-and-now experience. Paying attention to the present moment stimulates neural firing of here-and-now sensory input, enabling a shift away from the "known explanations" or "invariant cortical representations" that have been encoded by repeated experience (Hawkins & Blakeslee, 2004). This increases the capacity for exploring the "unknown" in one's experience that both activates and potentiates right-brain processing. Building with others in exploring experience creates a heightened sense in the present moment with the containment and attunement of the subgroup. Within the experiential process of functional subgrouping, each person's mind is shaped by, and shapes others, in the direction of bodily and emotional regulation. This has a strong potential to create new neural activation patterns that support exploring "novelty" (the unknown) without disabling fear while increasing the adaptive capacities of the implicit right-brain emotional processing. Novelty, that is, differences, is essential to the development and transformation of living human systems.

This chapter offers hypotheses that link functional subgrouping to neurobiological research. We have hypothesised first, that functional subgrouping develops the group mind, and second, that it is the group mind that regulates the flow of information and energy. In effect, functional subgrouping regulates affect at all levels of the group system: within the subgroup through attuned right-brain to right-brain communications, within members who are contained within subgroups, and within the group-as-a-whole. This process of regulation meets Siegel's definition for mind: an embodied and relational process that regulates the flow of energy and information. Further, it may be that linking to the IPNB models will enable us as group therapists to more fully implement de Maré's (de Maré, Piper, & Thompson, 1991) idea that "group mind is culture and a living system of dialogue is required . . ." to link the individual with the group mind. Linking the theory of living human systems and especially its method of functional subgrouping to IPNB enables tools for modifying the system variables that impact neurobiological processing.

Acknowledgement

Much appreciation to Marianne Bentzen, Paul Cox, and Rich Armington for their careful reading and helpful suggestions, to Bonnie Badenoch for her most excellent editing and suggestions, and to Roll Fellows for his reading and support of this paper. Some of the ideas here were first presented at the annual meeting of the American Group Psychotherapy Association in 2007 in Austin, TX.

References

Agazarian, Y. M. (1997). *Systems-centered Therapy for Groups*. New York: Guilford Press [reprinted London: Karnac, 2004].

Agazarian, Y. M., & Gantt, S. P. (2003). Phases of group development: systems-centered hypotheses and their implications for research and practice. *Group Dynamics: Theory, Research and Practice, 7*(3): 238–252.

Asch, S. E. (1951). Effects of group pressure upon the modification and distortion of judgments. In: H. S. Guetzkow (Ed.), *Groups, Leadership and Men: Research in Human Relations* (pp. 177–190). Pittsburgh, PA: Carnegie Press.

Badenoch, B. (2008). *Being a Brain-wise Therapist: A Practical Guide to Interpersonal Neurobiology*. New York: Norton.

Badenoch, B. (2011). *The Brain-savvy Therapist's workbook*. New York: Norton.

Berns, G. S., Chappelow, J., Zink, C. F., Pagnoni, G., Martin-Skurski, M. E., & Richards, J. (2005). Neurobiological correlates of social conformity and independence during mental rotation. *Biological Psychiatry, 58*(3): 245–253.

Burger, J. M. (2009). Replicating Milgram: would people still obey today? *American Psychologist, 64*(1): 1–11.

Canli, T., Desmond, J. E., Zhao, Z., Glover, G., & Gabrieli, J. D. E. (1998). Hemispheric asymmetry for emotional stimuli detected with fRMI. *NeuroReport, 9*(14): 3233–3239.

Chartrand, T. L., & Bargh, J. A. (1999). The chameleon effect: the perception-behavior link and social interaction. *Journal of Personality and Social Psychology, 76*(6): 893–910.

Cohn, J. F., & Tronick, E. (1989). Specificity of infants' response to mothers' affective behavior. *Journal of the American Academy of Child & Adolescent Psychiatry, 28*(2): 242–248.

Cozolino, L. (2006). *The Neuroscience of Human Relationships: Attachment and the Developing Social Brain*. New York: Norton.

Cozolino, L. (2012). *The Neuroscience of Psychotherapy: Building and Rebuilding the Human Brain* (2nd edn). New York: Norton.

de Maré, P. B., Piper, R., & Thompson, S. (Eds.) (1991). *Koinonia: From Hate Through Dialogue to Culture in the Larger Group*. London: Karnac.

Durkheim, E. (1966). *Suicide*, J. A. Spaulding & G. Simpson (Trans.). New York: Free Press.

Ferrari, P. F., Gallese, V., Rizzolatti, G., & Fogassi, L. (2003). Mirror neurons responding to the observation of ingestive and communicative mouth actions in the monkey ventral premotor cortex. *European Journal of Neuroscience, 17*(8): 1703–1714.

Gage, F. H. (2002). Neurogenesis in the adult brain. *Journal of Neuroscience, 22*(3): 612–613.

Gantt, S. P., & Agazarian, Y. M. (2004). Systems-centered emotional intelligence: Beyond individual systems to organizational systems. *Organizational Analysis, 12*(2): 147–169 [doi: 10.1108/eb028990].

Goleman, D. (1995). *Emotional Intelligence*. New York: Bantam.

Greenberg, L. S. (2007). Emotion coming of age. *Clinical Psychology Science and Practice, 14*(4): 414–421.

Haney, C., Banks, W. C., & Zimbardo, P. G. (1973). Study of prisoners and guards in a simulated prison. *Naval Research Reviews, 9*: 1–17.

Hawkins, J., & Blakeslee, S. (2004). *On Intelligence: How a New Understanding of the Brain Will Lead to the Creation of Truly Intelligent Machines*. New York: Times Books.

Heard, D., & Lake, B. (1986). The attachment dynamics in adult life. *British Journal of Psychiatry, 149*: 430–439.

Heard, D., & Lake, B. (1997). *The Challenge of Attachment for Caregiving*. London: Routledge, Chapman, & Hall.

Hebb, D. O. (1949). *The Organization of Behavior*. New York: Wiley.

Horwitz, L. (1983). Projective identification in dyads and groups. *International Journal of Group Psychotherapy, 33*(3): 259–279.

Iacoboni, M. (2007). Face to face: the neural basis of social mirroring and empathy. *Psychiatric Annals, 37*(4): 236–241.

Iacoboni, M. (2008). *Mirroring People: The New Science of How We Connect With Others*. New York: Farrar, Straus, & Giroux.

Iacoboni, M. (2009). Imitation, empathy, and mirror neurons. *Annual Review of Psychology, 60*: 653–670.

Janis, I. L. (1972). *Victims of Groupthink: A Psychological Study of Foreign-Policy Decisions and Fiascoes*. Boston, MA: Houghton Mifflin.

Kandel, E. R. (2006). *In Search of Memory: The Emergence of a New Science of Mind*. New York: Norton.

Kossmann, M. R., & Bullrich, S. (1997). Systematic chaos: self-organizing systems and the process of change. In: F. Masterpasqua & P. A. Perna (Eds.), *The Psychological Meaning of Chaos* (pp. 199–224). Washington, DC: American Psychological Association.

Lazar, S., Kerr, C., Wasserman, R., Gray, J., Greve, D., Treadway, M. T., McGarvey, M., Quinn, B. T., Dusek, J. A., Benson, H., Rauch, S. L., Moore, C. I., & Fischl, B. (2005). Meditation experience is associated with increased cortical thickness. *NeuroReport, 16*(17): 1893–1897.

Le Bon, G. (1896). *The Crowd: A Study of the Popular Mind*. London: Fisher Unwin.

LeDoux, J. (1996). *The Emotional Brain*. New York: Simon & Schuster.

McCluskey, U. (2002). The dynamics of attachment and systems-centered group psychotherapy. *Group Dynamics: Theory, Research, and Practice, 6*(2): 131–142.

McDougall, W. (1920). *The Group Mind: A Sketch of the Principles of Collective Psychology With Some Attempt to Apply Them to the Interpretation of National Life and Character* (2nd edn, revised). New York: Putnam.

McGilchrist, I. (2009). *The Master and His Emissary: The Divided Brain and the Making of the Western World*. New Haven, CT & London: Yale University Press.

Menning, H., Roberts, L. E., & Pantev, C. (2000). Plastic changes in the auditory cortex induced by intensive frequency discrimination training. *NeuroReport: Auditory and Vestibular Systems, 11*(4): 817–822.

Milgram, S. (1963). Behavioral study of obedience. *Journal of Abnormal and Social Psychology, 67*: 371–378.

Moreno, J. K. (2007). Scapegoating in group psychotherapy. *International Journal of Group Psychotherapy, 57*(1): 93–104 [doi: 10.1521/ijgp.2007.57.1.93].

Ogden, P., Pain, C., & Minton, K. (2006). *Trauma and the Body: A Sensorimotor Approach to Psychotherapy* (Norton series on interpersonal neurobiology). New York: Norton.

Panksepp, J. (2001). The long-term psychobiological consequences of infant emotions: prescriptions for the twenty-first century. *Infant Mental Health Journal, 22*(1–2): 132–173.

Panksepp, J. (2008). Carving "natural" emotions: "kindly" from bottom-up but not top-down. *Journal of Theoretical and Philosophical Psychology, 28*(2): 395–422.

Porges, S. W. (1995). Orienting in a defensive world: mammalian modifications of our evolutionary heritage: a polyvagal theory. *Psychophysiology, 32*(4): 301–318.

Porges, S. W. (1998). Love: an emergent property of the mammalian autonomic nervous system. *Psychoneuroendocrinology, 23*(8): 837–861.

Porges, S. W. (2007). The polyvagal perspective. *Biological Psychology, 74*(2): 116–143.

Schore, A. N. (2003a). *Affect Dysregulation and Disorders of the Self.* New York: Norton.

Schore, A. N. (2003b). *Affect Regulation and the Repair of the Self.* New York: Norton.

Schore, A. N. (2010). The right brain implicit self: a central mechanism of the psychotherapy change process. In: J. Petrucelli (Ed.), *Knowing, Not-knowing and Sort-of-knowing: Psychoanalysis and the Experience of Uncertainty* (pp. 177–202). London: Karnac.

Schore, A. N. (2012). *The Science of the Art of Psychotherapy.* New York: Norton.

Shannon, C. E., & Weaver, W. (1964). *The Mathematical Theory of Communication.* Urbana, IL: University of Illinois Press.

Shin, L. M., Orr, S. P., Carson, M. A., Rauch, S. L., Macklin, M. L., Lasko, N. B., Peters, P. M., Metzger, L. J., Dougherty, D. D., Cannistraro, P. A., Alpert, N. M., Fischman, A. J., & Pitman, R. K. (2004). Regional cerebral blood flow in amygdala and medial prefrontal cortex during traumatic imagery in male and female Vietnam veterans with PTSD. *Archives of General Psychiatry, 61*(2): 168–176.

Shin, L. M., Wright, C. I., Cannistraro, P. A., Wedig, M. M., McMullin, K., Martis, B., Macklin, M. L., Lasko, N. B., Cavanagh, S. R., Krangel, T. S., Orr, S. P., Pitman, R. K., Whalen, P. J., & Rauch, S. L. (2005). A functional magnetic resonance imaging study of amygdala and medial prefrontal cortex responses to overtly presented fearful faces in post-traumatic stress disorder. *Archives of General Psychiatry, 62*(3): 273–281.

Siegel, D. J. (1999). *The Developing Mind: Toward a Neurobiology of Interpersonal Experience*. New York: Guilford Press.

Siegel, D. J. (2006). An interpersonal neurobiology approach to psychotherapy: awareness, mirror neurons, and neural plasticity in the development of well-being. *Psychiatric Annals*, 36(4): 247–258.

Siegel, D. J. (2007). *The Mindful Brain*. New York: Norton.

Siegel, D. J. (2012). *The Developing Mind: How Relationships and the Brain Interact to Shape Who We Are* (2nd edn). New York: Guilford Press.

Siegel, D. J., & Hartzell, M. (2003). *Parenting From the Inside Out: How a Deeper Self-understanding Can Help You Raise Children Who Thrive*. New York: Tarcher/Putnam.

Simon, A., & Agazarian, Y. M. (2000). The system for analyzing verbal interaction. In: A. Beck & C. Lewis (Eds.), *The Process of Group Psychotherapy: Systems For Analyzing Change*. Washington, DC: American Psychological Association.

Song, H., Stevens, C. E., & Gage, F. H. (2002). Neural stem cells from adult hippocampus develop essential properties of functional CNS neurons. *Nature Neuroscience*, 5(5): 438–445.

Terrazas, A., & McNaughton B. L. (2000). Brain growth and the cognitive map. *Proceedings of the National Academy of Sciences*, 97(9): 4414–4416.

Tronick, E. (2006). The stress of normal development and interaction leads to the development of resilience and variation. In: B. Lester, A. Masten, & B. McEwen (Eds.), *Resilience in Children* (pp. 83–104), Annals of the New York Academy of Sciences, Vol. 1094. New York: Wiley.

Tronick, E. (2007). *The Neurobehavioral and Social-emotional Development of Infants and Children*. New York: Norton.

CHAPTER FIVE

Introducing couples to group therapy: pursuing passion through the neo-cortex*

Don Ferguson

Introduction

The necessity for cost-effective couples treatments is clear and yet the treatment literature offers only a very few examples of couples groups. This is in spite of, alas limited, research showing group treatment for couples to be as effective as couples therapy and more cost effective (Marett, 1988). Spitz (1979) describes a "structured interactional" group approach with couples that focused attention on one couple each session, with group interaction surrounding that couple's presentation. Framo (1982) described a model of couples group therapy that focused on family-of-origin formulations, which has influenced the educational program presented later in this article. Coché and Coché (1990) provide the only comprehensive model of group interventions with couples and suggest that what is needed is "a school for couples, a place where people could learn basic interactive skills". Feld (2003) describes relational couples group therapy and notes that group also addresses the social isolation that exacerbates the distress that many troubled couples experience. While all of these

---

* First published in *International Journal of Group Psychotherapy*, 60(4): 572–594.

writers acknowledge the challenge of recruiting couples for groups, the limited literature available suggests that such treatment is effective and efficient in treating even very challenging couples.

These group approaches to couples therapy developed alongside the growing body of research into marriage and the treatment of troubled relationships (Gottman, 1999; Jacobson & Gurman, 1995). Object relations theory (Scharff & Scharff, 1991), behavioural/social learning theory (Stuart, 1980), and the pioneers in sex therapy (LoPiccolo & LoPiccolo, 1978; Schnarch, 1997) to name but a few, have provided rich formulations of marital interactions.

In spite of these contributions, many common techniques practiced in couples therapy have been found lacking. For example, active-listening has been extensively taught but there is little evidence that such practice leads to lasting change between the partners (Gottman, 1999). Similarly a focus on establishing marital reciprocity which suggests that marriages are stable when partners feel that they are receiving in equal proportion to what they are offering in the marriage, has not been supported by research.

There is significant support for the efficacy of marital treatment but there is also much that can go wrong. Often novice therapists or therapists untrained in couples therapy (Doherty, 2002) become preoccupied with problem-solving discussions or encouraging angry, overstimulated couples to be nicer to each other, and withdrawn, shut down couples to get more activated. An angry couple, challenged to be nicer, often experiences hopelessness and responds with heightened anger and withdrawal. A disengaged couple may be just as overwhelmed physiologically as an angry couple. They may describe having grown apart or lacking similar interests, or even report feeling numb. Importantly, numbing may result from overstimulation (van der Kolk, 1994) rather than lack of interest. Such disconnected partners do not need encouragement to date, talk more, or have more sex. If a couple is struggling with profound feelings of disappointment, disengagement, or fear, pressure towards intimacy results in increased negative arousal and may do more harm than good (Atkinson, 2005; Gottman, 1999). The couple in such a state is ill-suited for the curiosity, openness to experience, and prefrontal skills necessary for them to experience themselves and their partner in a new way (Panksepp, 1998).

From a neurobiological perspective, both angry and disengaged couples need to first learn to lower their physiological arousal before they can consider re-engagement (Ferguson, 2006, 2008). Atkinson (2005), Gottman (1999), and Johnson (2004) all utilise a neurobiological view of relationship problems in their work with couples. Johnson's emotionally focused therapy (EFT) ties attachment theory and neurobiology to the study and treatment of intimate relationships resulting in the most empirically validated couples' treatment approach to date, with over twenty years of outcome and process research support (Johnson, 2004). Gottman (1999) has demonstrated the connection of physiological arousal (flooding) to an inability of the partners to remain engaged and curious about each other. Atkinson's (2005) pragmatic/experiential treatment for couples (PET-C) is designed to "increase levels of neuronal integration in each partner". The couples group approach presented here draws from the work of these therapists in their application of neurobiological research to couples therapy.

Neurobiology and couples therapy

Panksepp (1998) has described discrete neurocircuitry contributing to seven "special purpose" mood states, described as executive operating systems (EOS). This conceptualisation has gained increasing acceptance as evidence accumulates that indeed different systems in the brain become involved with particular responses to arousing stimuli. For example, he discusses curiosity, what he terms as seeking, as being virtually impossible to access when the EOSs of panic or of rage are activated, such as during separation distress so common to insecurely attached couples. Asking the partners to shift then from rage or panic states to a "seeking" frame of mind is necessary but not easy, as it is a neurologically complicated process that requires practiced steps and considerable focus, based on an assumption of good will that most partners find difficult to achieve without training or education.

Gottman (1999) has documented the contribution of defensive manoeuvres, such as stonewalling, as a reliable prediction of divorce. He also has shown that it is not the actual themes or perceived betrayals between partners that predict divorce, but rather how they treat each other during conflict. Whether they can self-soothe, and respect, listen to, and soothe the other predicts emotional regulation in the moment and their ability to remain connected. Gottman also has described curiosity between the partners as a significant predictor of marital success.

Atkinson (2005) prescribes systematic reprocessing of communications to enable the partners to interact predictably with more positive impact and maintain connection with each other. In his work, he asks probing questions about where the pain or unmet needs lie in the relationship and has each partner practice, restating his or her needs such that the other can really hear and offer a response rather than just attack and defend. This is practiced repeatedly, in more than once per week sessions, and with practice between sessions, using recordings of the exercise developed by the therapist and client during the previous session. It is with this frequency of practice that the behavioural change becomes deeply embedded and habitual.

These models have oriented our focus on listening to how partners experience moments of threat at subtle physiological levels. The couple often wants to focus on "who did what to whom" questions, whereas the more important clinical data is found in the examination of what they experience as they begin to flood, that is, become stimulated to the point of a primitive fight-or-flight reaction.

Adding an attachment perspective

Attachment theory (Bowlby, 1988; Johnson, 2004) suggests that people who are "securely attached" are better able to cope with narcissistic injuries or threatening situations, and are able to explore and take chances with each other. Only if couples feel secure with one another can they take risks, experience doubt or fear, be apart, or suffer disappointments without feeling traumatised. Attachment experiences are largely predicated on early relational learning, developed from infancy through implicit memories, or in emotionally laden or traumatic events, and are not usually available to conscious recognition. In fact, the seeking, curiosity, and exploration that Panksepp discusses (1998) is most possible when a secure bond is present. Insecurely attached people, when threatened, are more likely to push the partner away or to shut down. Fight-or-flight as experienced by couples can then be understood as a failure of attachment and treatment critically involves aiding the partners in soothing self and other and facilitating a sense of safety to reconnect. To this end they must learn about their bodies' reactions to threat and the ways in which they might soothe themselves as they face perceived dangers, such as the loss of attachment with the other. They can then also learn to help soothe the partner and to ask for help from each other in an effective manner. They will need to practice these new responses extensively (Atkinson, 2005) to instil predictability of success, and to allow for errors and relapse without reverting to primitive self-protective but self-defeating responses.

Johnson (2002), writing on the treatment of trauma, emphasised the power of couples therapy in its ability to impact the most immediate and sustained bond with the intimate partner and to encourage partnering against the symptoms of trauma. She reviews the literature supporting that a secure bond with a significant other increases trauma survivors' ability to deal with trauma related symptoms (Simpson & Rholes, 1994; van der Kolk, Perry, & Herman, 1991). Also the threatened loss of the partner often further exacerbates the survivor's traumatic experience, particularly when the trauma is grounded in loss or in betrayal by a significant attachment figure. A cycle ensues of the traumatised person pushing the partner away or shutting down in order to protect against the feared intrusion, arousal, and loss of control. The partner then responds from his or her own abandonment fears and presses for reassurance, which in turn heightens the anxiety of the trauma survivor who must resist even more strongly so as to protect against being abandoned or overwhelmed. This cycle is not limited to couples affected by trauma but is seen in all insecurely attached couples, described by Johnson (2002) as the attachment dance.

Applying neurobiology in a psychoeducational model for couples

This chapter describes the use of psychoeducational programming focused on the neurobiological challenges for couples both as an end in itself and as an introduction to couples therapy. In this process, the couple identifies treatment goals, and enters a first stage of group experience (Feld, 2003). Clinical material from a couples group is presented below illustrating the relationships between brain functioning, attachment theory, and personal relationships.

By the time a couple first enters treatment they are likely to be flooded. This effect is particularly evident in the initial session in which they are doubly stressed, awaiting condemnation by their partner and the feared judgment of the clinician. At this time their heart rates are likely increased and cognitive abilities impaired: they are less able to learn new information, think abstractly, organise their thoughts, demonstrate empathy, self-observe, or engage curiosity. Flexibility of thinking is unlikely in such a primitive, aroused state (Goleman, 1995; LeDoux, 1996). Although there is no clear threat of physical harm present in the intake session, the couple is experiencing symptoms of the fight-or-flight response.

The fight-or-flight response prepares us to defend ourselves or escape from a perceived threat. This response affects virtually all bodily functions, bringing the body to a state of maximum efficiency and focus for escape or combat (Sapolsky, 2004). All processes, unnecessary in the defence against the immediate threat, are reduced or eliminated. In a moment of perceived physical threat, such as an assault or potential automobile accident, these responses are miraculous. In a state of perceived emotional threat from a loved one, however, these same responses reduce our ability to communicate effectively. In the language of attachment theory when the security of the attachment is perceived as seriously threatened, and the danger of being abandoned or betrayed is sensed, the primitive brain sees only two options, to attack or to escape/stonewall.

Goleman (1995) described the negative impact of stress and worry on problem-solving and other cognitive skills. Conversely, he also described evidence that increased hopefulness can improve performance on cognitive and problem-solving tests. As couples feel locked into repetitive damaging patterns and increasingly hopeless about the possibility of change, the instillation of hope and universality of experience (Yalom, 1985) are key factors in promoting higher level cognitive and emotional functioning. When couples come to conceptualise that their battles or distancing behaviours are types of defences rather than indications of not loving each other, they can quickly relax and calm. This is the first step in recognising that the partner is not trying to be harmful and that there are ways of managing these seemingly overwhelming reactions.

Why group?

From a neurobiological perspective, group psychotherapy provides couples with a distinct advantage over traditional couples therapy.

The initial psychoeducational group offers them the opportunity to listen rather than become reactive or defensive. Learning about the "reptilian brain" (Ferguson, 2006) and fight-or-flight responses, the couple is likely to think, "Boy, he's really describing my partner. I hope s/he is paying attention to this". Still, because they are receiving this information in a neutral and structured format and are not called upon, in that moment, to respond they are more likely to be receptive to new information and perhaps entertain alternative descriptions of their dilemmas.

The couples group, even in these early psychoeducational stages, gains its greatest power in the support of the couples for one another and in individuals discovering how often others in the group share their experience. Men bond with, but also challenge, other men. (Some of the small group activities are accomplished by dividing the group into male and female subgroups.) A person may confirm, join, question, or confront a member of another dyad with far greater impact than if the partner or the therapist made the same intervention. Also the people in these groups often seem to be hungry to talk and to be heard, often having shared their distress with no one prior to the group.

Participants begin to understand the need to lower physiological arousal and to create safety between them. They then learn strategies for doing so and recognise that structures needed for positive communication can be readily available. As opposed to the big changes they might have envisioned, they now begin to experiment with scheduling times to talk, slowing their heart rates, organising their thoughts, and discussing the rules of their communication. In parallel practice they increasingly challenge themselves and each other to explore risky questions or behaviours between them. Increased risk-taking tests trust between the partners and leads to greater intimacy. As they experience successes they become more hopeful and bolder about approaching subjects previously perceived as dangerous. Even couples who have not risked sexual play in quite some time may find that they have new skills, language, and trust with which to engage each other physically. A couple that has fought over sex and describes intense fatalism about ever returning to physical intimacy might begin to sit closer while watching television or be willing to engage in mutual massage once trust is developed. They may also be able to talk about their reactions to sexual discussion without reverting immediately to hopelessness and blaming

The first group experience: education

As preparation and orientation to the program, we initially explore with the couple their reasons for being in treatment and offer a biological view of couples issues and the tasks and goals of group participation. We examine their physical reactions during stressful events and how they think about their conflicts. Finally we discuss the efficacy of group therapy as it pertains to couple treatment and the framework of how this group will help them in identifying and avoiding repetitive, destructive fighting.

Many participants are initially quite reluctant due to the common fears that confronting their relationship issues may actually exacerbate their troubles, and fears that they will be exposed and shamed in front of strangers. Couples often feel tremendously alone, ashamed, and perplexed by their problems and behaviours and fearful that these will be highlighted in a group setting. If these fears are not examined and allayed, the partners will remain in an aroused state unable to take in critical new information or to see their partner and their relationship in different ways. Each participant is informed during the preparation session, and again at the first group session, that no one is going to be singled out for discussion and that some participants may opt to remain relatively silent throughout the course of the group. I suggest that open discussion will further their learning but that whether they speak or not is not up to me or other group members. Each can participate at his or her own pace and if he or she becomes uncomfortable with information being revealed by one's partner, I will help to redirect the group.

These kinds of precautions are in place to make the group a safe place where the couples can pay attention and think, without fearing attack or being made unfairly vulnerable. As a result, partners seem more ready to join the group. The following describes the nine teaching modules of the educational program.

Introduction of the theory

The concept of the fight-or-flight response is introduced along with specific examples of how this affects marital communication. In the first session the group is asked to develop a list of their symptoms of stress and to discuss how these impact their marital interactions. We place this in the context of the neurobiological responses to threat, in describing how the body prepares for fight-or-flight and discuss how quickly such reactions occur. It is important that they also understand that we are not usually conscious of moving into the fight-or-flight response until it is too late. They learn that the first goal is not to increase intimacy but rather, to lower the overwhelming physiological arousal they experience in difficult or unexpected interactions. Within this context, they also learn about the concept of neuroplasticity to instil hope that they can change their brains through repetition of new behaviours (Hebb, 1949; LeDoux, 1996).

The material emphasises that successful couples therapy is also successful individual therapy and that they will notice real change as individuals as they begin to focus less on the crimes of their partner and become more curious about their own emotions, needs, and behaviour. This focus on individuation and the psychological health of each partner (Bowen, 1978) is critical to sustained growth in the relationship and overrides problem-solving and negotiation. They are given assessments focusing on their own individual functioning including health, stressors, and stress management styles to complete prior to the next session. These assessments are designed to encourage them to engage their neo-cortical skills, as well as organising and documenting their own reactions to stress. In eliciting self-evaluative statements in the context of early assessment, the partners are already encouraged to look at what they are bringing to the table in terms of stress, bad habits, health issues, and history. This continues with later discussions of family history and cultural issues.

The nature of relationship problems

The group examines the development of relationships, including the initial attraction and arousal, the contributions of biology to attraction, the assumptions that new lovers make about each other, and the turning points in their relationships. Couples have generally tried, in their own ways, to improve their relationship. Unfortunately, due to primitive brain functioning they may approach this in a self-destructive and ineffective manner. Even with the best of intentions, the primitive brain tends to take a black-and-white, all-or-nothing approach, common to flooding (Gottman, 1999) and when something goes wrong with such an attempt partners may feel doubly defeated and hopeless, as demonstrated in studies of intermittent reinforcement and learned helplessness (Sapolsky, 2004). This experience triggers primitive fears of not being competent, or "good enough" or of being betrayed/sabotaged by the partner, which, in turn, can elicit panic or rage (Atkinson, 2005). After such experiences, partners typically report, "I have tried everything and nothing is good enough for him/her", or both might say, "See we've tried to make this better. Maybe there's just no hope". The group is encouraged to experiment and try new things, as well as to evaluate successes and failures throughout this programme and beyond. The couple must understand that a "failed experiment" does not indicate that they are hopeless but rather that they need a new experiment.

Participants are asked to write a brief description of what they think a good marriage would look like but to not yet share this with their partners. This is another step in having them organise their thoughts about what they are looking for and the life they hope to lead. In this way they not only begin to explore fantasy, but also begin goal setting. In response to this exercise we discuss that some of the needs or hopes, on which they have given up with their spouse, are probably negotiable in a renewed relationship. We examine the new ways they have of speaking with each other and how they can now ask for things without an immediate reversion to primitive defensiveness. The essence of this approach is that the partner is *able* to hear their partner in new ways and retain a sense of connection, security, and curiosity. This allows the activation of the seeking mood state (Panksepp, 1998) and is the critical step of de-escalation described by Atkinson, (2005), Gottman, (1999), and Johnson (2004).

The mechanics of poor communications

The mechanics of communications are described, with an emphasis on basic combative or avoidant behaviours. Intimidation, name-calling, sarcasm, one-upmanship, leaving the room, shutting down, or turning up the television, for example, fall within the realm of primitive means to control anxiety. These are described not as ways of hurting the partner but ways of protecting one's self, which is a relief to many who have come to feel that their partner intends to hurt and defeat them. The group creates a list of "stupid fighting techniques" that describes what each of them does when they feel cornered or hurt and respond from their primitive brains. Participants readily identify the fight-or-flight nature of these behaviours. We also review at this time that the primitive brain responses directed by the amygdala are separate from the neo-cortex (LeDoux, 1996) and therefore a partner can be responding to a perceived threat without really thinking at all. We then introduce time-limited, agenda driven, and structured partnership meetings and end with an assignment to plan and execute a brainstorming meeting to list subjects that they hope to discuss successfully. We review the principles of brainstorming in preparation for this and they are asked to list every subject that either of them believes they will eventually need to discuss, which may include tasks, roles, sexuality, money, parenting, extended family, or any number of other issues. They should pay attention to how they respond to this exercise internally and what glitches or successes may occur, including the temptation to self-defend, attack, stonewall, etc.

Partnership meetings

Partners often startle each other, introducing a serious subject without warning, which instantly places the other on guard. They also have usually come to mistrust each other. "Can I talk to you for a minute?", is heard as an invitation to fight for three or four hours, perhaps to be followed by several days of not speaking to each other. That partner's apparent resistance, in turn, invites the initiating partner to feel rejected and hopeless. Also, when operating from a primitive stance of hopelessness, due to repeated disappointments, the initiating partner may introduce a sensitive subject in a manner that predicts failure. "I know you're not going to want to discuss this" or "I guess we won't be having sex again" are fairly typical ways of leading into the fight-or-flight reaction. Gottman and Silver (1999) emphasise practicing "soft start-ups" and we use this in the psychoeducation group as well. However, couples are so aware of each other that they can typically move into battle mode with just a look, gesture, or tone. We explore and identify the earliest triggers for heightened negative physiological arousal and ways in which to slow these reactions.

In order to lower physiological arousal and create some structure and predictability, a series of partnership meetings are proposed with consideration of time limits, meeting place, subject selection, means of taking breaks, and other such rules. The goal here is to establish boundaries and safety in every possible way. The more positive and predictable this experience is, the more the couple will eventually be able to try out riskier behaviours or subjects. The couple is encouraged to limit such meetings to half hour intervals. This limit encourages them to stay focused on one subject and maintain an attitude of exploration and curiosity that is difficult at best in lengthy and disorganised communications. A number of couples have suggested that if they went longer than ten minutes they would lose control and so were encouraged to only meet for ten minutes. Ten minutes of focused, neo-cortical driven interaction is likely to be more productive than hours of their usual attempts. Indeed, in a later exercise, the couples explore one of their complicated subjects in less than ten minutes in order to see how they can quickly learn new things about the issue.

Partnership meetings are a vehicle for exploring problem-solving behaviours but are also about organising the chaos and rubble in their relationship. If they can access executive functioning they are more likely to stay on subject and not become disorganised, and therefore truly feel heard by each other. With practice they build small amounts of trust, and become more hopeful and daring in terms of the topics they are willing to discuss. Couples often report that, with this degree of structure, they quickly tackle subjects in their relationship they had previously viewed as off-limits or feared were hopeless.

Family-of-origin and others outside the couple

Implicit memory dominates the powerful early learning of infants through early childhood (Siegel, 1999), learning at a level of classical conditioning or in response to trauma (Schachter & Graf, 1986; van der Kolk, 1994). Implicit memory includes behavioural, emotional, perceptual, and somatosensory input. As opposed to explicit memory, it requires no recognition that something is being learned and no focal attention for encoding the information. We apply the concept of implicit learning to the ways in which the couple partners have learned to defend themselves and get their needs met. Their earliest learning about how men and women relate is gleaned through observations, from infancy onwards, of their parents and other significant figures. The critical element of this step is to encourage the partners to be curious about their own development as well as that of their partner. We see deeply experienced responses as related to their cultural/familial filters and therefore such responses may not make sense through the cultural filters of the observing partner. Participants grasp this concept quickly and often spontaneously talk about events that have deeply shaped some aspect of their attitudes, behaviours, or beliefs.

For example, picture Rick and Susan who come from distinctly different backgrounds as to the role that alcohol plays in the family. In Rick's family, on a weekend evening, his father would reach for a bottle of wine and soon be more relaxed and jovial. He would be given to storytelling and generally the family would have a very nice evening. In Susan's family, her father would also reach for a bottle and ultimately someone would end up getting hurt. Now they are married and on a weekend evening, Rick reaches for a bottle, anticipating an enjoyable time with Susan. When they were dating, they might have a glass or two of wine, tell stories, laugh, and maybe make love. This time, however, Susan experiences a primitive fear response in which her heart speeds up, her breathing becomes shallower, and she feels suddenly exhausted, at the sight of Rick grabbing for the bottle. She accuses him of resorting to alcohol too frequently. He is stunned because they have never had any problems related to drinking. In his hurt and betrayal, Rick accuses Susan of being boring and never wanting to have any fun. His reaction only reminds her of how dangerous the subject of alcohol can be. Indeed, neither can understand the other's hurt or fear through their own filters. Given that the brain interprets danger signals very rapidly (LeDoux, 1996) and that the fear response to a powerful male drinking alcohol is classically conditioned into Susan, her response is predictable, but completely unwarranted given Rick's perspective. His thoughts on this are filtered through implicit and explicit positive memories of limited, reasonable alcohol use.

The assignments for the family discussions are to fill out a series of assessments to elicit discussion of early learning, family structure, and traditions. These assessments also examine the partners' knowledge of each other's families, including their structures and traditions. The partners are encouraged to fill out these assessments alone and try to learn as much as they can by thinking through the questions. They are then to meet with their partners, discuss what they have learned and to tell family stories.

Managing family-of-origin and other outsider issues

We now expand this discussion of family culture to how the couples respond to their environment. In this context we look at how the partners interact with their respective families as well as with their children, friends, etc. We look at ways in which these people, outside the dyad, may influence or split them from one another. We discuss the importance of building a barrier around the pair against all comers, even their own children. Many struggle with this concept because initially they see it as blocking these important people out of their relationship. "How can you expect me to place my marriage ahead of the needs of my children?" is a common challenge. In fact, although paradoxically, the clearer the boundaries surrounding a healthy marriage, the more welcoming and loving the partners can be to their children, parents, friends, and others. This extends a common theme in this group taken directly from Bowen's (1978) descriptions of individuation and from attachment theory. When the marital bond is secure the partners are better able to care for those around them. This usually requires considerable discussion and multiple examples, because there is very old learning in most of us suggesting that it is wrong and selfish to think of one's own needs and grave danger in a view of separateness from one's love. I have had a number of clients initially react quite angrily or fearfully at the suggestion that they will have a stronger relationship when they have a greater degree of healthy separation from each other as well as from others in their social network.

Defining problems and who has what problem

When struggling, couples are generally not only having the wrong discussion but not even having the same discussion. They have entered a highly charged, distressing arena and their implicit memories, fears, and expectations will override advanced cognitive skills. Their ability to access self-observation and curiosity are minimal at this point, because their need for self-protection trumps such neocortical activities. They will then narrowly focus on some perceived threat (LeDoux, 1996) and miss what is most important to their partner and what might result in relief for both of them. For example, a partner might introduce the topic of worrying about their expenses, and this focus of worry dominates her perception of the discussion they have started. The other quickly but defensively asserts that he is doing his best and is not spending too much. This response may sound related but the initial problem statement is "worry about money" and the response is "I'm a good partner", in which being "good enough" dominates the emotional focus. At the end of a lengthy fight both partners will be able to correctly point out that the other was not listening, because, in fact, they were discussing two separate themes. In fairness, it must be pointed out that the initiating partner may have expressed worry in an aggressive fashion. In this discussion we again review "soft start-ups", efficient ways to introduce a topic accurately and in a way that the partner can actually hear and use.

We illustrate this principle with a brief exercise. The participants, after hearing a common marital conflict story, are asked to generate a list of all the possible issues that might be present between the partners. This exercise is not about solving problems but for the partners to learn to invite their higher brains to be a bit more playful even during conflict. From a simple description of the argument, which is usually about five sentences long, the group quickly creates a lengthy list of possible underlying issues. They are surprised by the number of topics. Each group member has usually identified one or two issues as being clearly the problem, influenced by his or her own filters. We note that, in the story, each partner has locked into a particular focus and is not having a shared discussion. In order for them to engage their neo-cortical skills, they will need to first slow down the old defences and try to hear their partner. We then relate that story to common battles that most couples have experienced.

Discussing sex—applying the strategies to one of the most challenging interactions

In this session we first review some common mythologies about human sexual response and the role the brain plays in the experience of sexual pleasure or disappointment. The information presented is relatively basic; the major teaching is that the same part of the brain that governs sexual response also governs response to anxiety, stress, and fear. Therefore, it is virtually impossible to be simultaneously acutely or chronically stressed and sexually responsive.

Conflicts surrounding sexual response are discussed with an emphasis on the supposition that most of such conflicts are related to the partners "having the wrong discussion". It is noted that most couples will devolve into arguing over frequency and types of sexual acts, deflecting from the core issue of whether they are experiencing pleasure together.

This is primarily a didactic presentation. Couples often appear quiet and uncomfortable during this time and yet many seem to take the information to heart, as evidenced by their bringing back questions later. We review sexual myths (McCarthy & McCarthy, 2003; Zilbergeld, 1999) such as the myth that idealised sexual passion should be spontaneous throughout the relationship and that any dimming of this passion indicates problems in the relationship (Aron et al., 2005). We then discuss how caring partners can revisit the exchange of pleasure with one another as opposed to the common battles over frequency of intercourse, which offers the partners no relief.

Self-contracting for change, inoculation against relapse, and closure of the group

In the final sessions, the group is reminded that the goal is not just for the acquisition of problem-solving skills but also for the partners to actively re-engage in an intimate/romantic relationship. The group explores small ways in which each might pay some form of attention to their partners on a daily basis. We also review the nature of relapse and it is predicted that each partner will make mistakes. It is the combined efforts of the partners to protect against and recover from such errors or slips, which predict success. They are given numerous tips on maintaining a relationship focus, with the emphasis being on tiny changes in behaviours that usually require very little effort, but remind their partners that they are committed and the partner is indeed loved and safe. In the past, they will have attempted to do this through convincing arguments, promises, and demands, which have only functioned to heighten the partner's anxiety. The goals at this step are towards very small joining behaviours. They are then encouraged to fill out a "self-contract for continued improvement" which lists further actions from which to choose their next steps in their continuing relationship efforts.

A case example

In the sixth session of a ten week group, Jack and Brenda arrived separately, both looking very angry. I proceeded cautiously with them particularly as both suggested that they were close to giving up and had considered skipping group altogether. Ultimately however we diagrammed the fight they had been having, which provided the entire group with a living example of the complexities of what initially seemed simple. It had started with Jack forgetting to pick up Brenda's son after school. Brenda did not accept his excuses and saw this as another sign of how little he cared for her and her children. After three days of fighting, Jack had simply not picked Brenda up for the group. They and the group initially wanted to argue about the details of how this happened. It is risky to ignore content completely, lest the partners feel cut off and unheard, as they do with each other, but the specific content is seldom the actual cause for hurt feelings.

As Brenda and Jack explained their views of what had occurred we explored why what appeared to be a simple miscommunication brought out such intense feelings. Jack heard himself attacked as an uncaring or neglectful partner, a familiar feeling that he is bad. He then countered that Brenda's kids are old enough for this not to be such a big deal which she heard as her being too protective and spoiling her kids. It is impossible now for them to get to the real issue or issues. As we diagrammed the various subtopics to this challenge, and indeed there are more, we kept coming back to central questions that they were not asking. "Do you really care for me?" "Do you trust me and can I trust you?". These subjects are perceived as far too dangerous to approach when you are feeling attacked.

From the beginning of the group, participants are encouraged to do a "body scan" to identify their means of escalating as early as possible, with the earliest signs often being physical. They described tension throughout their bodies and Brenda described the onset of a headache. Jack admitted feeling nauseous. As usual, they had already begun to have the argument in their heads before they saw each other, and instantly felt hopeless. Finally, we pulled out the core issues. Brenda feared that Jack resented her children and if he did not want them, did he really want her enough? Jack described always feeling blamed and accused. Since he was a child he felt as though he was always being criticised. We discussed the deep, implicit experience of criticism and how overwhelming this feeling was for him. In a combative, fearful state the level of focus on these core fears is such that our brains resist flexible thinking or taking in new data. The group provided the safety that enabled the couple to lower the arousal and explore this, simply by commiserating and acknowledging that they all had been stuck in similar battles. There was a lot of concern expressed for both Jack and Brenda and admiration that they even came to the group session in spite of this turmoil.

Jack and Brenda entered the group in a physically overstimulated state and were fully prepared for the usual battle. Initially, the presence of the other group members may have heightened their arousal, but the group also imposed some restraint on them. Both wanted to look in-control and reasonable to the other members. Primitively, their need for the other group members to believe and join them against the partner overrode any desire to repair the relationship, the latter requiring neo-cortical functioning. Universality of experience, as well as a focus on the couple's strengths rather than their mistakes, allowed them to look at this in a more flexible fashion. In their normal fight they would meet attack and resistance with attack and resistance with no room for any hint of curiosity or kindness.

Conclusion

The change we are attempting here is not simply a corrective emotional experience but one of actually changing neural pathways through the repetition of new behaviours as described with the axiom, "what fires together, wires together" (Hebb, 1949). Hebbian plasticity, which has gained support with recent brain research (LeDoux, 1996) suggests that as interconnected neurons repeatedly fire together, such as in practicing a new behaviour, the weaker synapse, related to the new behaviour, will gain strength.

Participants in these kinds of groups are typically genuinely surprised and pleased that they were able to sit with other troubled couples and, not only reveal more of themselves than they had expected, but also to be helpful to the other couples. Marital distress is generally isolating. To see other couples struggle and recommit, often in spite of circumstances which may seem more dire than their own, profoundly alters their perspective, and contributes to greater neuroplasticity.

References

Aron, A., Fisher, H., Mashek, D., Strong, G., Li, H., & Brown, L. (2005). Reward, motivation and emotion systems associated with early-stage intense romantic love. *Journal of Neurophysiology, 93*(1): 327–337.

Atkinson, B. (2005). *Emotional Intelligence in Couples Therapy: Advances from Neurobiology and the Science of Intimate Relationships.* New York: Norton.

Bowlby, J. (1988). *A Secure Base* (2nd edn). New York: Basic Books.

Bowen, M. (1978). *Family Therapy in Clinical Practice* (Chapters 21 & 22). New York: Aronson.

Coché, J., & Coché, E. (1990). *Couples Group Psychotherapy: A Clinical Practice Model.* New York: Brunner/Mazel.

Doherty, W. (2002). How therapists harm marriages and what we can do about it. *Journal of Couple and Relationship Therapy, 1*(2): 1–17.

Feld, B. (2003). Phases of couples group therapy: a consideration of therapeutic action. *Group, 27*(1): 5–19.

Ferguson, D. (2006). *Reptiles In Love: Ending Destructive Fights and Evolving Toward More Loving Relationships.* San Francisco: Jossey-Bass.

Ferguson, D. (2008). Case study: suddenly strangers: Iraq war vets, PTSD, and the challenge of relationship. *Psychotherapy Networker* (January/February): 65–68.

Framo, J. (1982). Marriage therapy in a couples group. In: J. Framo (Ed.), *Explorations in Marital and Family Therapy* (pp. 141–151). New York: Springer.

Goleman, D. (1995). *Emotional Intelligence: Why It Can Matter More Than IQ.* New York: Bantam.

Gottman, J. (1999). *The Marriage Clinic: A Scientifically Based Marital Therapy.* New York: Norton.

Gottman. J., & Silver, N. (1999). *The Seven Principles of Making Marriage Work.* New York: Three Rivers.

Hebb, D. (1949). *The Organization of Behavior.* New York: Wiley.

Jacobson, N., & Gurman, A. (1995). *Clinical Handbook of Couple Therapy.* New York: Guilford.

Johnson, S. (2002). *Emotionally Focused Couple Therapy With Trauma Survivors: Strengthening Attachment Bonds.* New York: Guilford.

Johnson, S. (2004). *The Practice of Emotionally Focused Couple Therapy: Creating Connection.* New York: Brunner/Routledge.

LeDoux, J. (1996). *The Emotional Brain: The Mysterious Underpinnings of Emotional Life.* New York: Simon & Schuster.

LoPiccolo, J., & LoPiccolo, L. (Eds.) (1978). *Handbook of Sex Therapy.* New York: Plenum.

Marett, K. (1988). A substantive and methodological review of couples group therapy outcome research. *Group, 12*(4): 241–246.

McCarthy, B., & McCarthy, E. (2003). *Rekindling Desire*. New York: Brunner/Routledge.

Panksepp, J. (1998). *Affective Neuroscience*. New York: Oxford University Press.

Sapolsky, R. (2004). *Why Zebras Don't Get Ulcers*. New York: Holt.

Schachter, D., & Graf, P. (1986). Effects of elaborative processing on implicit and explicit memory for new associations. *Journal of Experimental Psychology: Learning Memory, and Cognition, 12*(3): 432–444.

Schnarch, D. (1997). *Passionate Marriage: Keeping Love and Intimacy Alive in Committed Relationships*. New York: Holt.

Scharff, D., & Scharff, J. (1991). *Object Relations in Couple Therapy*. Northvale, NJ: Aronson.

Siegel, D. J. (1999). *The Developing Mind: How Relationships and the Brain Interact to Shape Who We Are*. New York: Guilford Press.

Simpson, J., & Rholes, W. (1994). Stress and secure base relationships in adult-hood. In: K. Bartholomew, & D. Perlman (Eds.), *Attachment Processes in Adulthood* (pp. 181–204). London: Kingsley.

Spitz, H. (1979). Group approaches to treating marital problems. *Psychiatric Annals, 9*(6): 318–330.

Stuart, R. (1980). *Helping Couples Change: A Social Learning Approach to Marital Therapy*. New York: Guilford Press.

van der Kolk, B. (1994). The body keeps the score: memory and the evolving psychobiology of PTSD. *Harvard Review of Psychiatry, 1*(5): 253–265.

van der Kolk, B., Perry, C., & Herman, J. (1991). Childhood origins of self-destructive behavior. *American Journal of Psychiatry, 148*(12): 1665–1671.

Yalom, I. (1985). *The Theory and Practice of Group Psychotherapy* (3rd edn). New York: Basic Books.

Zilbergeld, B. (1999). *The New Male Sexuality: The Truth About Men, Sex, and Pleasure*. New York: Bantam.

CHAPTER SIX

Sensorimotor psychotherapy as a foundation of group therapy with younger clients

Bonnie Mark-Goldstein and Pat Ogden

I want to know if you belong or feel abandoned, if you can know despair or can see it in others

David Whyte, *Self Portrait*, 1992

Introduction

Sensorimotor psychotherapy (Ogden, Minton, & Pain, 2006) offers a unique lens through which we can enhance the benefits of group therapy by thoughtful engagement with each member's embodied experience. Working "beneath the words", it elucidates ways the body contributes to the challenges of the individual and to the group, including aspects that may not be apparent through the lens of more traditional psychotherapies. The group milieu is an ideal forum in which to uncover, explore, and work with sensorimotor, body-based experience to help members develop awareness of self and other and examine their present moment experience. As the group evolves, the stages of sensorimotor psychotherapy will unfold, from building the therapeutic container, to accessing and framing the presenting issue, to processing experience as group members work together towards transformation and integration. A different, more positive, sense of self emerges, individually and collectively, supported by changes in movement, posture, and physiological regulation that result from attending to each member's somatic experience and how it is interacting with experience of the group-as-a-whole.

Group therapy for our younger clients is particularly beneficial since "development occurs in a psychosocial context. The individual does not grow in isolation, and thus cannot be fully understood in isolation" (J. Schore, 2012, p. 91). It offers a particularly effective format to treat the multifaceted issues of children and adolescents transitioning towards adulthood because the group process enables each member to re-experience the dynamics of their family of origin, change outmoded interpersonal patterns, and establish new implicit relational templates. Group provides an opportunity to revisit early attachment issues, and group members often take on a particular role in the simulated group "family". These roles, visible in the procedural tendencies of the body, are strongly influenced by early attachment relationships and the family milieu, which shapes posture, gestures, and movements in ways designed to adapt to the particular family environment. For example, one teen, Sally, grew up in a traumatic environment with no one to turn to for safety, and her frozen, immobile body reflected the powerless and helpless feelings she had experienced in her early family. Another group member, Patrick, whose family emphasised independence and achievement and offered him little emotional support, had a body that was tense and mobilised for action, which also effectively prevented his more vulnerable emotions and needs from surfacing.

The microcosm of the world that group therapy creates makes it a profound therapeutic setting in which to observe and amend relational problems, examining interpersonal experience as lived in the present moment, as it unfolds, including the physical elements that both reflect and sustain relational dynamics. The group creates a natural, authentic, organic opportunity for members' issues and their physical manifestations to arise in real time: their own life experience recreated on the landscape of a group. The sensations, gestures, tensions, movement patterns, that go along with emotions, thoughts, and perceptions are happening live. The sensorimotor psychotherapist uses "bottom-up" approaches and interventions, teaching group members to observe, follow, and work through issues and relational dynamics starting with the physical experience. Sensorimotor psychotherapy also integrates bottom up approaches that directly address the effects of trauma and relational issues on the body and on emotions with "top-down" approaches that focus on insight and understanding. Bodily experience becomes a primary entry point for intervention, while meaning-making arises out of the subsequent somatic reorganisation of habitual responses.

For example, Sally's group taught her to recognise her frozen body as a necessary and adaptive response to a frightening environment, and to physically experiment with exchanging her immobility for assertive action. Patrick learned in the group context to recognise how he pushed people away, and was supported by group members to gradually depend upon them and relax the tension in his body that went along with "not letting anyone in".

Attunement to the body's actions and reactions can foster curiosity as members reflect upon their bodily experiences and chronic patterns, and come to understand the physical manifestations of their beliefs. As members become aware of their sensorimotor process and skilful at observing and tracking their sometimes-disturbing bodily experiences as they arise, it opens the door for the body itself to lead them into a constructive resolution. For example, Sally, who froze instead of fighting back when her older brother abused her, would later overeat, punch holes in her bedroom wall, and engage in self-harm behaviour. In group therapy, the members discussed the wisdom of freezing and complying with her violent sibling's wishes instead of fighting back (which would have made the abuse worse), thus acknowledging Sally's instinctive survival strategy. Eventually, they transitioned to an exercise that involved pushing against a pillow held by one of the girls, an action Sally first resisted, but with the encouragement of group members, eventually was able to execute with enthusiasm. This therapeutic exercise mitigates freezing by facilitating both the execution of an active, assertive response and social engagement via the support of the group. It provided Sally with the experience of alternative actions to punching the wall and self-harm, and gradually these symptoms resolved as the embodied implicit pattern changed.

Siegel (2010a) writes that mindfulness encompasses "paying attention to the present moment from a stance that is non-judgmental and non-reactive. It teaches self-observation; practitioners are able to describe with words the internal 'tuning in' to oneself that enables people to become 'their own best friend' " (p. 86). Curiosity and mindful attention to the present moment are as important in sensorimotor psychotherapy as the narrative. Throughout the sessions, the therapist encourages members to share their experience rather than only sharing their story. For example, if a group member starts to feel tense and cold, as Sally did when telling her story, the content is suspended while the group therapist and members mindfully explore the inner body sensation together, bringing awareness to the shift and discovering what it represents. Sally began to realise that her tension and sensation spoke of the anger she felt but did not express. Mindfulness in the group milieu, is bringing attention to intention, to intentionally help group members begin to pay attention to present moment experience as it arises, and through reflecting, processing, and integrating these experiences, help the group member learn to understand the reactions of his or her body. In this process, interpersonal support leads to the development of a greater capacity for self-regulating in a more adaptive way. Ogden (2009b) clarifies,

> Through mindfulness, clients shift from being caught up in the story and upset about their reactions to becoming curious and interested in their experience. They discover the difference between "having" an experience and exploring their procedural tendencies in the here and now, days or weeks or years after the event itself. (p. 5)

Sally was relieved and felt supported by the group members as others helped her understand the wisdom in her propensity to freeze, discover her underlying anger, and then receive support in developing her self-assertion and adaptive self-regulation. Presenting these concepts to the group members parallels instruction and modelling of a non-judgmental attitude toward self and other, with compassion serving as the foundation for group cohesion and members' safety. We use the word "modelling" to encompass a beautiful and complex process that involves mirror neurons (Iacoboni, 2009) and resonance circuitry (Siegel, 2007). Through these neural pathways, in the presence of one another, our bodies, emotions, and perceptions resonate with what the other person is experiencing. This gives us the capacity to have a felt sense, often below the level of conscious awareness (but nonetheless influencing our behaviours) of what is happening within the other person. This is likely one basis for empathy and our capacity to attune with one another. These right hemisphere processes often unfold without words but are revealed in non-verbal ways—tone and lilt of voice, quality of eye gaze, body posture, moving toward or away, for example. Because our embodied brains are registering these constant messages from others, they give us a way to stay in ongoing "dance" with those around us at a speed that is not possible through conscious choice (Badenoch, 2011). The learning we do via these right hemisphere-based interpersonal channels is likely more powerful in shaping our relational expectations than the cognitive learning that takes place in our left hemisphere. Under stress, the behavioural, emotional, and perceptual patterns that have changed in the right hemisphere as a result of such interpersonal experiences remain, while left-only learning goes offline. Returning to Sally, we can imagine that she felt the understanding and support of the group around her "freeze", and then had a very different experience from what she experienced with her brother during the abuse. With such sustaining interpersonal connection, her perception of life's possibilities could begin to change and she was more able to begin to explore other emotions and behaviours. The combination of guided mindfulness and relational richness can help Sally gain firm regulatory footing within herself and increase her capacity for responding to others in ways that promote engagement and foster support. Guiding the group in bringing awareness to the present moment supported Sally, and modelled a foundation for using "directed mindfulness" in the group (Ogden, 2009a,b).

Directing mindful attention to particular elements of experience that emerge in the group therapy milieu, both verbally and non-verbally, lays the foundation for individual and group experiential learning. Clients are invited to be curious about focusing their attention, and through directed mindfulness, the sensorimotor psycho-therapist helps expand the client's awareness and non-judgmental acceptance of whatever might arise.

Siegel uses the term "mindsight" to describe the process in the brain that allows for perception of various mental processes, including thoughts, feelings, sensations, memories, hopes, dreams, and beliefs (Siegel, 2010a,b), stating that "[m]indsight is a kind of focused attention that allows us to see the internal workings of our own minds" (Siegel, 2010a, p. xi). In a sensorimotor psychotherapy approach, directed mindfulness is often focused on the body so that group members learn to sense and understand the movement and sensation of their own bodies while receiving support from other members.

Integration of mind and body are informed by advances in our understanding of the psychology and biology of bodily-based emotional states. In particular, the right hemisphere of the brain, rather than the more cognitive and verbal left hemisphere, is primary for emotional and body processing and unconscious affect regulation, and thus represents an unconscious, implicit self-system (A. Schore, 2011). As Schore states, "The right brain implicit self represents the biological substrate of the human unconscious mind and is intimately involved in the processing of bodily based affective information associated with various motivational states" (2009, p. 114). Looking at how the body carries and assimilates one's history provides an essential inroad to the reorganisation of experience (Ogden, Minton, & Pain, 2006) so that more adaptive action becomes possible, as we saw in Sally's case.

Building the container

The first step as the group comes together is to build a therapeutic container in which group members develop the safety to connect and to deepen awareness. For some, just being in the group will push them out of their window of tolerance. However, group members quickly develop neural pathways to modulate their own and each other's arousal, following the therapist's example and/or resonating with the embodied experience of the therapist.

As the therapist skilfully attunes to the members' bodily experience, he or she becomes an "interactive psychobiological regulator" (A. Schore, 1994) for the members' dysregulated nervous systems. A calm and mindful internal state in the therapist offers an invitation to group members to gradually enter a similar calm state through resonance circuitry. In this calm environment, the group members' brains are rewiring the circuitry of regulation in parallel with the neural firing in the therapist's more integrated brain. This deeper kind of right hemisphere learning can make permanent changes in the relational circuitry of the brain. It can be challenging for the group therapist to balance the individual needs of each member with the collective needs of the group while simultaneously tracking everyone's moment-to-moment experience, but group members themselves quickly learn to attend to their own and others' experience. Allan Schore (2001) states that therapists must become "affect regulator[s] of the patient's dysregulated states in order to provide a growth-facilitating environment for the patient's immature affect-regulating structures" (p. 264). These again are primarily right-hemisphere-based communications between the bodily states of the therapist and group members, and secondarily may be supported by words that name and validate each person's emotional and bodily experience. Over time, group members develop the neural circuitry of regulation and can act as affect co-regulators for each other, as well as experience the example and instruction of the group therapist, who names and validates each person's experience, including bodily experience.

For example, one teen group member, Pete, entered the group angry and shut down, having been required to do group therapy by his mother at the recommendation of his school principal who was concerned about Pete's aggressive behaviour. Pete's closed body posture, with arms across his chest, and a sceptical look on his face conveyed the anger he felt about being forced into the group and became a jumping off point for all group members to demonstrate in their own bodies how they felt when they were forced into something they did not want to do. Pete became engaged as empathy and resonance were expressed, not only through words, but also through the body stances of the members. An interesting and illuminating discussion of each person's physical posture, and the others' reactions to it ensued, which the participants could easily relate to situations in their own lives. The therapist and the group members became a community of interactive psychobiological regulators not only for Pete, but for all members.

Following are examples of group therapy to illustrate a sensorimotor psychotherapy approach to create safety and build a therapeutic container.

Patrick

It was a trust exercise that triggered Patrick, age seventeen, disturbing the feeling of safety he had previously experienced in the group.

The group physically explored the issue of trusting one another by forming a tight circle around one group member, who then experimented with "falling" and being caught by the group. Group members verbalised the issues that ensued: "I was afraid no one would catch me, and that you would just let me fall at first! Then I found out you were actually there for me, and it started being fun". "I really liked the feeling of being there for someone. I was hoping everyone would fall toward me so I could catch them. But when I did it, it was scary". Patrick was the only member who had a strong aversion to this exercise, which challenged his most core way of relating—"Depend on yourself, do not trust others to support you, and do not show any need", implicit embodied "truths" he had taken in deeply in a family that offered him little support, leaving him to fend for himself. In response to these repeated experiences, Patrick had adapted by isolating himself, contributing to his poor social skills. "That's it, I'm outta here", he said as the exercise was underway. "Today is a complete waste of time for me. I shouldn't have come". He could barely tolerate being in the room. With his jaw tensed, he hunched his shoulders, while his facial expression fluctuated between distress and disdain, reflecting his discomfort with trusting others to support him, and his fear of showing his own need and vulnerability.

At that point, the group therapist took a break from the exercise, and Patrick's difficulty became a diversionary focus as the group helped to contain him and explore his reaction. The therapist first slowed things down and backtracked to allow for the components of mindful reflection. "Let's go back to right before you had that impulse to get up and leave. What cognitions, emotions, sensations might be happening in your body right now as you remember that moment?" Patrick said his body felt tight and he just wanted to run away. He expressed feeling angry, which he realised was out of proportion to what was taking place in the group.

The group commented on the tightness in his face, the frustration in his brow. "Well yeah, my face is telling you exactly what I feel!" Patrick said. Following the therapist's lead, the group members offered curiosity, openness, acceptance, and love (COAL), aspects of attuned listening and of mindfulness in group practice (Mark-Goldstein & Siegel, in press). They held the space for Patrick to express his emotions, first anger and then sadness. As he expressed them, the tightness in his shoulders and face lifted. In this environment of mindful support and nurturing, the group effectively conveyed to Patrick his importance to them, regulating his arousal enough to continue the trust exercise. Although Patrick never participated in "falling" that day, he did experience the understanding and support of the group, a first step in countering his isolation and felt experience that he was completely on his own.

Helene

For Helene, any group focus on her experience was dysregulating. Her overwhelming anxiety and shame had interfered with her attendance at a small private college. When Helene was asked to speak in class, she could not tolerate the attention; the same anxiety would manifest when she even anticipated coming to therapy.

In order to facilitate Helene's participation, the group agreed to respect her privacy. Through gentle, supportive attunement to Helene's pulled-in body and hunched shoulders, that informed both her and the group of her discomfort, the group helped her develop boundaries that allowed for a sense of safety, paramount for Helene to continue in group therapy. Members demonstrated their own body postures that correlated with trying not to be seen, imitating one another and discussing their experience as they did so. They gently mirrored Helen's hunched shoulders, mindfully exploring together what happened internally. The group therapist listened to and adjusted to Helene's expressed parameters—for example, not calling on her, averting eye gaze, and pulling down the blinds to darken the room when she found the occasional glance of members in her direction to be disturbing. Not wanting to be seen, Helene had found that her past therapy had left her feeling naked, vulnerable, and under-resourced. Helping her create such boundaries in the group environment made the group tolerable and helped her to return, week after week, each week becoming more comfortable, confident, and safe. Additionally, the collective experiments with various postures and stances created an opening to explore all the members' fears of being seen (Helene's expressed main issue), without focusing on her.

Eventually the members, including Helene, embodied the opposite posture that was "big", "upright", and visible, and discussed the emotions that a more obviously open posture stimulated. Members decided to be mindful between group meetings of when they were taking on a posture of hiding, and when they were embodying a more open and visible posture; their discoveries became a jumping off point for the next meeting.

Nate

Nate, aged nine and a half years, came to group with a tear-stained face. He said "Nobody likes me", and then, "All of you don't like me either!". As the group was starting, it was clear his arousal was outside his window of tolerance. He wanted to leave the room, but was encouraged instead to find a space inside the room that was all his own, in which he could feel safe.

He chose a corner of the room that was hidden behind the couch. "This is my corner", he said. "No one can see me, I can't see you", and he made himself a little pillow fortress. This seemed to make him feel safe, so group members helped Nate pile the pillows higher, implicitly conveying through their actions that they would help him feel safe and help him regulate his arousal. He could see out, but it was hard to see in, and the weight and pressure of the pillows, along with the support of his peers, seemed to soothe and calm him.

Nate could overhear the group members (aged between eight and nine) discussing whether any of them had ever had a similar experience of feeling that they did not have friends. Alison said, "When I was six, all my friends left me. My best girlfriend stole my other friend. There were three of us, and then I was alone". Her body showed how dejected she felt, as her head came down and her chest slumped. There was a rustle of pillows from the corner.

Another nine-year-old said he lost his friend after he was picked last for the team, and again his dismay was evident in his physical stance. Then Daryl said he had wanted to run for student council. "My friend didn't even want to run, but then he ran against me, and he won. And now he sits at the table with all the people who are on council and I'm not allowed to be there". Daryl's anger was evident in his tense body and the clenched fists. The therapist gently pointed out each child's physical reaction to the topic, facilitating awareness and curiosity.

As each of the kids shared, the rustling from the pillow pile let them know that Nate was resonating. The physical boundary that he had created let him remain present and attentive while still feeling safe, rather than recreating an experience of aloneness by leaving the room. Over the course of a half hour, he peeked out of the pillow pile and started asking questions. As each member demonstrated in his or her body the feeling of not having friends, Nate became increasingly interested. The tears stopped, the curiosity started, and the camaraderie allowed him to engage in a new way with his group members.

Accessing

When the container is "safe enough", the group explores the second stage of the process, "accessing" during which the group therapist encourages group members to mindfully observe their internal experience and find the words to describe it. Sensorimotor psychotherapy fosters awareness of "building blocks" of present moment experience: inner body sensation, five-sense perception (images, smells, tastes, sounds, touch), and movement, as well as thoughts and emotion (Ogden, Minton, & Pain, 2006). In group, we use directed mindfulness of all of these aspects of experience in order to interrupt the cascade of automatic reactions and make room for unfamiliar or uncompleted actions. For example, Terri, aged 6, tends to distance herself from others, creating a boundary in a home that had none. Growing up with older brothers who fought with each other viciously, she protected herself by creating distance, backing away from conflict, removing herself from engagement of any sort. In group, this manifested when doing an exercise wherein she and another group member who was a few months younger, David, navigated the physical distance between one another. Encouraged to stand on opposite sides of the room, Terri then was guided to slowly invite David to come towards her. She joyfully did so, saying "come close", "come closer", "closer still", until David was quickly approaching her, at which time, she put up her hands quite suddenly and forcefully yelled, "Back, back, back, back", halting David's rapid approach. David, on the other hand, feeling no need for boundaries at that moment, seemed to experience surprise and startle when Terri's distancing hand movements, voice, and instructions directed him backward. While Terri's behaviour stemmed from feeling triggered as her space was encroached upon, David's dejection at the sudden shift was evident with his slumped body, downcast eyes, and diminished energy. Indeed, he was triggered by the sudden reversal in the playful exercise. He then moved in very close to Terri, encroaching upon her space, crunching her against the wall, gleefully seeming to consume her.

In the forum of the group, behavioural patterns that were characteristic of these two children unfolded, and we were able to identify and address them in the moment, while their peers observed. We could help each of them identify the triggers that were causing their behaviour. For Terri, she felt the familiar triggers (her space being encroached upon), and she responded in the manner in which she was accustomed (distancing). These triggers and responses happened so rapidly that there was no space between being triggered and reacting, as her automatic, defensive response arose. Similarly, David was rapidly triggered (feeling surprise, disappointment, or rejection when Terri turned him away), as these were familiar feelings to him. His instinctive, familiar response was to move in even more forcefully, similar to bullying or defiant behaviour, which had proven problematic in prior peer interactions. Helping both group members to become more aware of their sensorimotor experience helped create some space between the trigger and their immediate, procedural, habituated response. Rather than simply thinking about their interaction, psycho-education offered them tools to understand their sensorimotor response to such triggers. They could explore the ways their bodies reacted, in the moments after they reacted. David was able to identify his heart racing and body tensing, saying "I can feel it right here" as he put his hands to his heart. Group members helped him recognise changes in his posture and stance, as he seemed to shift from playful to fierce, his growing intensity apparent to all. Group members also could recognise shifts in Terri, commenting that she was leaning backwards, away, "as if he has cooties". (Cooties are an American idiom for something negative that children do not want to catch through contact.) Their interchange was recreated, much more slowly, with more preparation, as the two children were invited to bring their awareness of their sensorimotor experience into the interchange, thus creating more and more space between the trigger and response. Together, they were able to track their own and each other's response and adjust their own behaviour accordingly. David learned to notice Terri's slight movement backwards when he took a step too close to her, to recognise that she was not rejecting him and thus inhibit his tendency to forcefully encroach upon her boundary, and to then take a step backwards. Terri learned to notice her own reaction to proximity as David walked towards her, and to ask him to stop before she became aggressive, which was her tendency when she became excessively triggered.

Group therapists help to slow the pace down, modelling patience, curiosity, and mindful attention. For example, when conflict arises in the group, there may be multiple reactions: some group members are on the edge of their chairs ready to fight, some want to get out of the room, and some just freeze or shut down and seem to disappear into the couch. The group therapist encourages each member to access and describe his or her own experience. "Let's take a minute, and create a space to just look down and notice what's going on in our bodies with this conflict—what emotions are coming up, what sensations, what does your body want to do, what are we hearing, or seeing".

This kind of mindful awareness offers group members tools for self-reflection, observation, and curiosity about the body's states—the sensations in our chest, our breath (shallow or deep), the rhythm of our breathing, the changes in posture, tilt of the head, angle of the shoulders, muscular tension, and so forth. To foster this understanding and find words to describe bodily experience, group members are introduced to a "menu" or "vocabulary" for sensorimotor experience, offering many options for describing the body (Figure 1).

Learning the language of one's own movement and sensations enhances the ability to form accurate verbal descriptions of these physical experiences. In the group forum, members can better understand their own body sensations and movements as well as learn to better notice those in others. Most children will not have developed a vocabulary for body experience, and the therapist may provide a menu by saying, "I wonder what kind of feeling it is in your tummy— maybe it's tingly, tight, shaky, or warm. Or maybe it feels like butterflies flying around. Or . . .". Providing options in this way will spark the child's own words to describe his or her body (Ogden, Minton, & Pain, 2006). Children will often come up with their own words, like "It feels like noodles that used to be soft but they dried up" or "It feels squishy like a marshmallow".

A child who has difficulty identifying feelings or sensorimotor experiences may prefer a visual menu to a vocabulary list. Facial charts with cartoon characters, such as "How Do You Feel Today"

twitch	radiating	clammy	bloated
dull	shudder	dry	flushed
sharp	numb	jerky	prickly
achy	flaccid	energised	buzzy
pounding	blocked	burning	flutter
airy	goose-bump	damp	pressure
suffocating	congested	electric	jumpy
tremble	heavy	tight skin	tense
shivery	tight	light	wobbly
chills	puffy	fuzzy	stinging
vibrating	bubbly	dense	nauseous
itchy	tingly	cool	spinning
deadened	shaky	throbbing	dizzy
immobile	paralysed	faint	tremulous
frozen	sweaty	quivery	breathless
warm	moist	pulsing	quake

Figure 1: Vocabulary for sensorimotor experience (Ogden, Sensorimotor Psychotherapy Institute, 1996)

(Howdoyoufeeltoday.com) include a wide range of faces with a variety of emotions depicted. Offering each of the members of the group a small flashlight and using a metaphor of "shining the flashlight" to particular areas of the body provides a playful way to turn inward and deepen awareness of both the body and emotions. Handheld mirrors can also add dimension to generating self-reflective insight, while providing visual cues to the group member's inner world. Through the group milieu, members can both lead and follow one another, while responding to one another and/or mirroring behaviours.

Alan

Ten-year-old Alan came to group after witnessing his parents violently fighting in an ongoing complicated and contentious marriage. A self-appointed protector of his mother when his father moved out, he was haunted by their cruel words, profanity, and statements such as "I wish you would die" and "I will kill you if you return here". His mother cried after his father returned to the house, and the fighting continued and escalated until a neighbour called the police. Alan had difficulty discussing these family experiences, and was sullen and moody at school, as well as in individual therapy, showing little ability for self-reflection. He was referred to group therapy and appeared to be relieved to take a break from one-on-one therapy where he reported feeling pressure as he "always needed to talk, talk, talk". Group therapy offered him another way to explore his feelings through the interactions with others, physical exercises and exploration, and the commonality of shared experiences.

During the session where members were offered flashlights and guided through this sensorimotor psychotherapy intervention, Alan was initially playful, shining his flashlight around the room, joyfully aiming it on the ceiling, windows, and at other members. However, when the group therapist attempted to deepen awareness by shining the flashlights toward inner experience of cognitions, emotions, perceptions, body sensations, and memories, he proved to be quite distracted. Alan showed little ability to be self-reflective. Yet, at the same time, he began to discover that observing other members' abilities for self-reflection evoked his curiosity and helped him settle down. In order to foster an environment of reflection and separate this session from previous meetings, the therapist lit a candle in the middle of the room, lowering the room lights so that there was a shift in the environment, effectively quieting the group members. The therapists were able to foster a more mindful, reflective group space by lowering their voices, slowing down their speech and cadence, modelling the change that they wanted to effect in the room. As Alan grew aware of the adjustments in the room, witnessing the mood shift among other group members, he too seemed to settle, eyes wide open with curiosity. As other members took the lead in "shining the flashlight" on different parts of their bodies, becoming aware of how emotions and cognitions were represented in their bodies, where they felt them and naming them, Alan appeared to open up, utilising the others as a model for himself. While this was not an easy exercise for him, as self-reflection was challenging, he was able to shine the flashlight towards his heart, saying, "This is where things feel broken", and "When my dad hits my mom, this area in my heart is where it hurts the most".

The group offered Alan space and time to describe his experiences, acknowledging how hard it must have been for him. This supportive response allowed Alan to further explore his struggles within this safe community. He then shivered and reiterated the words that he heard his mother cry, often, during the fights with his father—"You're breaking my heart". His new insights emerged through the supportive group environment in which this sensorimotor exercise transpired where he was exposed to other members sharing similar pain. As a group, these children grew individually and interpersonally, sewing the seeds for future sessions wherein Alan gained self-awareness and learned from and about others. This group experience of self-reflection was integral to his becoming able to draw upon the community for large and small shifts in self-growth.

Processing and transformation

Processing is the stage in the process that helps group members explore their problems more fully, leading to a transformation or change in cognitive, emotional, and physical patterns. Bottom-up therapeutic interventions can help group members address and transform their relational difficulties and trauma-related issues by implementing physical actions that promote empowerment and success, while challenging old patterns. Physical patterns, such as Helene's hunched shoulders or Patrick's overall tension, develop over time, reflecting and sustaining psychological deficits. Helene hunched her shoulders in an attempt to hide herself; Patrick's tense body effectively kept his own emotions and needs at bay so that he did not have to count on anyone but himself. When attachment figures are unavailable or otherwise fail to respond adequately to a child's needs, he or she may eventually come to depend more upon auto regulation and withdrawal than on seeking help from others. Proximity-seeking behaviours, like reaching out or making eye contact, are invariably abandoned when a child repeatedly experiences that they will not elicit the desired outcome. Ogden (in press) states

> . . .the implicit journey explores what happens when the internal world cannot be seen or understood, but is enacted beneath the words, beyond technique . . .this journey involves the body-to-body conversation between the implicit parts of patient and therapist that takes place unawares.

If a child has experienced trauma, his or her body will reflect dysregulated arousal and truncated or out-of-control subcortical mammalian defences, the telltale signs of interrupted or futile attempts to fend off threat. Exposure to traumatic events of any sort—sexual or physical abuse, medical trauma, accidents, bullying, and so on—elicit subcortical mammalian, or animal, defences that are not mediated by the cortex. Adaptive in the moment of immediate threat, these animal defences tend to become inflexible action sequences in children and teens with post-traumatic stress disorder (PTSD). These defences can be loosely categorised into relational actions that seek the protection of another person: mobilising defences of fight and flight that organise overt action, and immobilising defences of freeze and feigned death that inhibit physical action.

By definition, traumatised children and teens' defensive responses have not worked effectively to ensure that they are safe and protected. However, even though a defensive response may have been unsuccessful or only partially successful in conferring safety, children tend to repeat a defence that was evoked at the time of the original trauma. Addressing defensive responses through bottom up interventions can reinstate the adaptive and flexible functioning of animal defences. And mindful attention to attachment-related procedural habits as well can help mobilise interrupted action sequences that can support relational connection and satisfaction. In the stage of processing and transformation, children and teens learn to become more aware of their procedural tendencies and practice the actions that have been truncated or interrupted to challenge these learned actions, addressing the related traumatic and attachment issues with the support of their group.

Stan

The referring therapist described Stan as a pre-psychotic, dissociative, and extremely at-risk teenager. He had been adopted and there was little biological family information available, but Stan had lived in several foster homes in his early years before being adopted at age five. Stan was the youngest member of his adoptive family, which included an older brother who was abusive to both Stan and his middle brother. His parents were passive and helpless in the face of their oldest son's violence. Stan seemed to live in a state of frozen immobility, described as a "chronic state of hypervigilance, a tendency to startle, and occasionally panic" (Krystal, 1988, p. 161).

Stan froze during the abuse by his big brother and felt extremely relieved when his brother left to join the military and was stationed abroad. In Stan's situation mobilising defences, such as fighting back, were ill advised and would only have provoked more violence from his older brother. Immobilising defences were then the only survival strategies remaining. However, these strategies tend to persist even when the danger is over, and Stan's procedural tendencies were entrenched. He remained passive and "stuck", and his body remained tense and frozen.

In group therapy, Stan was paired with another similarly sized group member, and they were offered a large pillow that might mitigate Stan's habitual immobility. At first, he reluctantly pushed the pillow in a quite helpless and futile manner, reflective of his experiences with his abusive brother when active defences were not effective. However, buoyed by the encouragement of group members, he eventually tried pushing back more firmly, to the cheers of his fellow members. Stan gradually felt the power of his arms increase, as he identified the tingling and slight shaking in his muscles, that he named "waking up". The exercise deepened as the group members utilised the couch as a "safety zone" upon which group members could fall, thereby allowing the person pushing against the pillow to push as hard as he wanted, thus satisfactorily "completing the action". Ogden, Goldstein, and Fisher (2012) state, "This therapeutic exercise mitigates freezing by facilitating both the execution of fight responses and social engagement via the support of the group". At follow-up sessions, Stan practiced this new action with fellow group members, both smaller and larger, using the support of a team-of-teens as they backed each other up physically as well as emotionally. Stan found that he no longer felt so "stuck" in his life, and he began to report taking new actions that he had previously avoided, such as speaking up in class.

Paul

Paul, aged thirteen, had a violent father whom he described as "filled with hot air" who frequently and loudly yelled at Paul's older sister and mother before finding other targets. Paul learned to disappear at home in order to avoid his father's rage. He struggled with depression and spoke of feeling alone, as though he was "on a different planet than his peers and parents".

In the course of an exercise in which members used their arms, legs, and bodies to carve out a space for themselves, Paul began to explore other applications for all that "hot air". He imagined going right to the moment in which his dad was exploding, and pictured himself filling a hot air balloon with the gases. The image of the balloon became a resource for him. He realised that he could utilise all that space around his body—above his head, behind his back, and as far as his arms can reach—to store the hot air in the balloon, instead of letting it get inside and trigger him. The group supported Paul in his exploration, mirroring him, encouraging and supporting him. Initially, Paul seemed a bit hesitant, and another member took on Paul's body, walking around the group room with arms wide open, reaching out and up, checking in with Paul in a supportive manner. This led to each of the members doing a similar exercise, curious about their own experience as they lived more fully in their bodies and explored filling the space around their bodies. Paul went home "armed with tools" and buoyed by the experience he had had in the group.

At our next session, Paul reported, "I used my hot air balloon and it was so cool. Dad didn't even notice, he was so busy screaming . . . but I didn't care as much". The group members responded to Paul's report with encouragement and camaraderie, and others described their own experiences. Paul reported that the most meaningful part of the past session was when everyone went around the room, arms in the air, "trying on his body". As the group processed Paul's experience, it became clearer that through both the explicit and implicit experience in the prior session, profound shifts were occurring within the support of the group. Paul spoke of feeling less alone in the group, "feeling known" by his fellow group members, and of being understood in a new way. Powerful shifts occurred through the body-to-body interchange, as the experience achieved these implied though not plainly expressed objectives within the group milieu. Through the group experience, Paul accessed implicit changes that occur through moment-to-moment attunement and interpersonal support. Parallel to the group interchange through dialogue and exercises lies the profound power of the implicit unfolding interaction between group members.

Ogden (in press) states

> . . . the implicit journey explores what happens when the internal
> world cannot be seen or understood, but is enacted beneath the words,

beyond technique . . . this journey involves the body-to-body conversation between the implicit parts of patient and therapist that takes place unawares.

Similarly, through the group milieu, between member and group therapist, and from member to member, the multifold benefits of what is being articulated implicitly are often unknown until transformation has occurred. Paul's experience of his fellow group members "trying on" his body, as he called the exercise, led to a new sense of awareness of self and other. This resonance and connection alleviated his sense of aloneness, laying the foundation for other reparative work in future group sessions, and helped him tolerate the aspects of his environment that he could not change, such as his father's volatility.

Sheila

Sheila, aged thirteen, learned that the smaller and more invisible she became in her home, the less likely she was to be a victim of her father's abuse when he was drinking, angry, and obstinate. In her teen group, she would shrink into the couch and bow her head down when other members got into conflict. She was already small in stature, and it was as though she wanted to merge with the floor to get away from the conflict.

The group brought that to her attention first by mirroring, to help her see what her body was doing, and then suggested an experiment. "What happens if you try something else on?" She was reluctant to move from her safe retreat. Very gently, the group therapist said, "Let's see if there's any part of your body that might risk coming into the room, any movement or gesture that might want to happen".

Slowly, the left side of her face began to move away from her body, followed by her spine, which elongated. One group member said, "Wow, do you see her getting taller on the couch?" and reached over to help her. Sheila immediately withdrew. We paused, and wondered what could make it safe for that part of Sheila to come back into the room. She said, "If nobody helps me, and nobody tries to pull me faster or tell me how or what to do, that would work". This request reflected her family experience of being pushed and not allowed to go at her own pace, and so the group was instructed to sit back and just create an inviting space.

Everything slowed down for about five minutes. As the group members got comfortable, sitting back in their chairs with their feet on the ground, they were encouraged to notice what was happening for them. Again Sheila lifted her left chin. Her face came into the room, her spine elongated, and she said, "Yeah, this feels good". "It feels good, huh", the group therapist encouraged. "Notice what changes; where in your body does it feel good?" "I feel like there's more space right here", Sheila said, lifting her hand and pointing to her chest. The therapist reflected that motion and encouraged her to take her time. "Just notice what happens in your chest; we can be curious together". Other group members quietly mirrored Sheila's actions such as point-ing to their own chests, wordlessly communicating their attunement and empathy. Conveying the message to Sheila that she could go at her own pace countered her attachment experiences.

Then Sheila took a really deep breath. She smiled a big smile and said, "Yeah, I feel like I can breathe again". For Sheila, this transfor-mation did not come out of any kind of narrative; it emerged through a bottom-up, sensorimotor process that was in sharp contrast to how her body responded to being pushed. Group members also benefitted as the process opened up an exploration of how members respond physically and emotionally when they felt pushed and not given the time to go at their own pace.

Conclusion

Working beneath the words is an essential component of sensorimo-tor psychotherapy. Through the community, group members found that the "missing experience" (Kurtz, 1990) answers the request of a line from David Whyte's poetry (1992): "I want to know if I belong". Our younger clients often lack safety and a sense of feeling grounded. They want to feel okay about themselves with others in family and friendship. Seeking that inner sense of stability is an essential part of the journey where answers can be discovered, not only cognitive answers, but answers in terms of physical posture, gesture, and move-ment. Those answers are not found outside of oneself, in the words or offerings of another, but directly woven into the body of the individ-ual, just waiting to be freed. Outdated physical habits and the cor-relating cognitive distortions that serve to sustain old ways of being are exchanged for new actions, supported by the group milieu and adaptive in that context. Options open up, posture changes, self-regulation capacities increase, and a more positive sense of self emerges, supported by these physical changes experienced in relationship. Within the context of a group that is both supportive and challenging, habits that sustained feelings of not belonging give way to new experiences that speak to a more spontaneous and full way of being and behaving, new competencies, and increased feelings of belonging and satisfaction.

References

Badenoch, B. (2011). *Brain-savvy Therapist's Workbook*. New York: Norton.

Iacoboni, M. (2009). Imitation, empathy, and mirror neurons. *Annual Review of Psychology*, 60: 653–670.

Krystal, H. (1988). *Integration and Self-healing: Affect, Trauma, Aleithymia*. Hillsdale, NJ: Analyic Press.

Kurtz, R. (1990). *Body-Centered Psychotherapy: the Hakomi Method*. Mendocino, CA: LifeRhythm.

Mark-Goldstein, B., & Siegel D. J. (in press). The mindful group. In: M. Solomon & D. J. Siegel (Eds.), *Healing Moments in Psychotherapy: Mindful Awareness, Neural Integration, and Therapeutic Presence*. New York: Norton.

Ogden, P. (2009a). Emotion, mindfulness and movement: expanding the regulatory boundaries of the window of tolerance. In: D. Fosha, D. J. Siegel, & M. Solomon (Eds.), *The Healing Power of Emotion: Perspectives from Affective Neuroscience and Clinical Practice* (pp. 204–231). New York: Norton.

Ogden, P. (2009b). Modulation, mindfulness, and movement in the treatment of trauma-related depression. In: M. Kerman (Ed.), *Clinical Pearls of Wisdom: 21 Leading Therapists Share Their Key Insights* (pp. 1–13). New York: Norton.

Ogden, P. (in press). Technique and beyond: therapeutic enactments and the role of the therapist. In: M. Solomon & D. J. Siegel (Eds.), *Healing Moments in Psychotherapy*. New York: Norton.

Ogden, P., Goldstein, B., & Fisher, J. (2012). Brain-to-brain, body-to-body: a sensorimotor psychotherapy approach for the treatment of children and adolescents. In: R.E. Longo, J. Bergman, K. Creeden, & D. S. Prescott (Eds.), *Current Perspectives and Applications in Neurobiology: Working With Young Persons Who Are Victims and Perpetrators of Sexual Abuse*. Holyoke, MA: NEARI Press.

Ogden, P., Minton, K., & Pain, C. (2006). *Trauma and the Body: A Sensorimotor Approach to Psychotherapy*. New York: Norton.

Schore, A. N. (1994). *Affect Regulation and the Origin of the Self: The Neurobiology of Emotional Development*. Hillsdale, NJ: Lawrence Erlbaum.

Schore, A. N. (2001). The effects of early relational trauma on right brain development, affect regulation, and infant mental health. *Infant Mental Health Journal, 22*(1–2): 201–269.

Schore, A. N. (2009). Right-brain affect regulation: an essential mechanism of development, trauma, dissociation, and psychotherapy. In: D. Fosha, D. J. Siegel, & M. Solomon (Eds.), *The Healing Power of Emotion: Affective Neuroscience, Development and Clinical Practice* (pp. 112–144). New York: Norton.

Schore, A. N. (2011). The right brain implicit self lies at the core of psychoanalysis. *Psychoanalytic Dialogues, 21*: 75–100.

Schore, J. (2012). Using concepts from interpersonal neurobiology in revisiting psychodynamic theory. *Smith College Studies in Social Work, 82*(1): 90–111.

Siegel, D. J. (2007). *The Mindful Brain*. New York: Norton.

Siegel, D. J. (2010a). *Mindsight: The New Science of Personal Transformation*. New York: Bantam.

Siegel, D. J. (2010b). *The Mindful Therapist: A Clinician's Guide to Mindsight and Neural Integration*. New York: Norton.

Whyte, D. (1992). Self portrait. In: *Fire in the Earth*. Langly, WA: Many Rivers.

CHAPTER SEVEN

Hunger and longing: a developmental regulation model for exploring core relational needs

Mitchel Adler

Introduction

As social mammals, we humans are dependent creatures who rely on others throughout our lives. Group psychotherapy offers a contained, yet dynamic social environment to explore the human condition. It provides a rich social field where members can access visceral emotions, spontaneous thoughts, and a wide range of beliefs and implicit memories regarding relationships and intimacy. According to Gantt and Cox (2010), these are ripe conditions for rewiring neural networks and engaging neural plasticity. From early childhood, relationships centrally influence the wiring and structure of our physical brain. The field of interpersonal neurobiology (IPNB) reveals how life experience can be the catalyst to deeper neural integration and healing.

Group therapy serves as a microcosm of life and inevitably triggers fearful subjective experiences for members. When humans perceive danger, limbic arousal, primarily in the amygdala, produces a fight, flight, or freeze response, which prepares us for threats. However, when we are actually safe but perceive danger in our relationships based on old, implicit memories, our anxiety creates "relationship static" (Goleman, 2006). These implicit memories emerge from our visceral, non-conscious, right-hemisphere brain, leaving us unable to recognise that a memory from the past has been activated. Instead, we experience the immediate phenomena as though they are the cause of our current subjective state of distress and dysregulation. This experience can exacerbate difficulties with intimacy and adaptive dependency.

In group therapy, the leader and other members, via empathic right-brain, non-conscious attunement, offer a co-regulatory function for members who become hyper-aroused. For example, members can become more regulated by others through a sympathetic nod or the mirroring of facial expressions that reveal to the distressed member that they are being seen and emotionally held in their subjective emotional state. This co-regulation works implicitly, which is a more non-conscious, somatosensory, non-verbal experience. Members do not have a cognitive, left-hemisphere "knowing" of what is occurring during such co-regulatory moments. However, repeated exposure to positive experiences of implicit attunement (e.g., mirroring, prosody, eye contact, breath synchronisation, etc.) foster affirmative non-conscious, amygdala-based working models concerning interpersonal regulation. Schore (2003) suggests that this increase of complexity in right-hemisphere circuits, even without integration with the left, builds regulatory capacity. Siegel (1999) would add that this subtle re-working of implicit neural networks builds the foundation for the emergence of neural integration where limbic arousal can more adaptively reach left-hemisphere knowing. Eventually, members begin to understand their visceral arousal states and can more intentionally seek the support of others to help with co-regulation. As new neural networks form and neural integration grows, a new implicit mental model and belief can emerge: "When I am in distress, I can rely on others to help me feel more grounded".

The discovery of mirror neurons and resonance circuits provided more evidence to support the importance of relationships and the role of empathic attunement in healing (Cozolino, 2002, 2006; Iacoboni, 2008). Not only does empathy feel nice, it also affects the neuroplasticity of group members' brains. Iacoboni (2008) states that "mirror neurons are the cells in our brain that make our experience . . . more meaningful" (p. 265).

IPNB as a lens for understanding hunger and longing

This chapter will highlight some opportunities for building interpersonal intimacy in groups using a developmental growth model that embraces the experience of hunger and longing. The goal of working with these states is to build mindful intention around how we modulate our core relational needs in order to deepen co-regulation, self-regulation, and intimacy. This model explores different forms of neural integration and how implicit and explicit memory impact neural functioning and neuroplasticity.

Hunger and longing is an eight stage model that clarifies how we identify, express, and satisfy our immediate (i.e., "here and now") core relational needs in group therapy. Through integrating interpersonal neurobiology, developmental theory, and mindfulness, we will explore how individuals co-regulate each other, and how they can learn to use this awareness to support their own regulatory function. By reaching out to others (interpersonal co-regulation), and mindfully attuning to oneself (intrapersonal regulation), group members learn multiple pathways to self-care and connection. This model provides a framework for developing the capacity for meeting core relational needs, which reduces isolation and shame while bolstering self-efficacy, co-regulation, and belonging.

The role of mindfulness in group culture

Creating a group culture of mindfulness, which is a compassionate, non-judgmental observation of the present moment, offers a useful starting point for growth and change (Kabat-Zinn, 1990). It helps group members show up with what I call their six "mind-body domains": thoughts, feelings, physiology, behaviours, relationships, and beliefs/values. Through these six domains, members learn how to pay deep attention to themselves to discover how mind–body sensations emerge and subside. We encourage members to be curious about their judgments, rather than automatically attaching to them as truth. It is through this curiosity and openness that members experience new associative neural links to alternative self- and other-narratives that support neurological and behavioural change. We also work to build self-compassion as a way to quiet negative self-evaluation and shame that block deeper integration of adaptive self-concept.

How self- and other-regulation leads to healing

Attachment theory posits that our earliest relationships implicitly shape and condition our responses to certain relational stimuli in predictable ways (Flores, 2010; Johnson, 2008; Schore, 2003; Schore & Schore, 2008). While adaptive in the family system for survival, particular patterns of interacting may not serve us well later in life. Group members bring to the group non-conscious, embodied, implicit memories of how relationships work based on early relational experience, trauma, and other social learning from families, school, work, culture, etc. Siegel (2006) suggests that memories we have encoded from our past impact our mind–body domains today. When implicit memories get triggered (e.g., feeling rejected or abandoned), members respond in a more visceral, automatic manner, leaving them unable to realise that their responses may be more related to accessing a memory from the past than responding to the present. Instead, they experience their feelings as though they are due fully to the present circumstance, leading them to feel dysregulation. Members might feel emotionally overwhelmed (e.g., sad or panicked), physiologically agitated (e.g., fidgeting or shortness of breath), and behaviourally impulsive (e.g., screaming or leaving). Indeed, these states of arousal make learning and growth challenging in the absence of a co-regulatory function. When we become this unsettled, we lose the capacity to integrate useful feedback and cognitive framing for our experience.

Group therapy provides a setting in which these implicit memories can be identified and worked through based on opportunities for co-regulation with the therapist and other members. Schore and Schore (2008) suggest that it is essential for therapists to help clients regulate their implicit arousal states through the therapeutic relationship. The therapist and other members help in this co-regulation process by offering calming prosody, a caring gaze, empathy, concern, and an intention to understand the other. Research shows that an authentic intention to connect with and understand the other can be non-consciously registered by the receiver's mirror neuron system, thereby regulating the individual, even if the content of the attunement is not completely accurate (Cozolino, 2002; Iacoboni, 2008).

Just as an infant needs the care-giver to regulate somatosensory arousal, our members need us to help regulate them when they become overwhelmed with needs. We want to create what Bowlby

(1988) calls a "secure base" from which our clients can play, individuate, and explore themselves and others more fully, so that new neural networks can be established and reinforced. In this process, the therapist "co-regulates" group members, just as primary care-givers co-regulate their infants (Schore & Schore, 2008). Members' resonance circuits help register the action and intention of the therapist—often without the member's conscious awareness—providing a settling and soothing effect (Iacoboni, 2008). In essence, this authentic interest and care serve a co-regulatory function and set the groundwork for increased capacity for vulnerability and intimacy (Iacoboni, 2008; Schermer, 2010). Throughout each group session, for example, I consistently scan the group with my eyes, attempting to gauge how each member is functioning from moment to moment. When I perceive that a member is unsettled, disconnected, or bored, I might make an effort to have direct eye contact with them to check in concerning their state of being. With a soft look that is appropriate to the group topic and the client's issues, I seek to make meaningful contact that communicates care, interest, and compassion. Such subtle, non-verbal contact serves a regulatory function—as a bridge to the other and a link to themselves. My hope is to help them feel more connected to what they might need in the moment, and/or to how I might support them. Over time, members come to expect my non-verbal check-ins and speak openly about how they help. One member stated, "It means a lot that you check in on me. I feel like I can always come home to your eyes when I feel overwhelmed".

Sometimes my scanning can be stressful to new members because they feel pressure to perform in the moment. One member said, "When you look at me, I feel like I'm supposed to say or do something, and that just doesn't work for me". However, once I shared that my goal was not to get them to do or say anything, but rather to support them in whatever they might need in the moment, this pressure faded away. I encourage members to ignore my gaze when it is not relevant to their needs. I openly admit that I will unintentionally make mistakes and misperceive their needs, perhaps by misinterpreting their processing of a new experience as being "checked out". Therefore, having permission to "use" me as best suits their immediate needs offers group members much comfort and freedom. As one member said, "It's great that I can look at you when I need you and not feel guilty when I don't need you. I didn't have that with my dad.

It's a relief that I don't have to take care of your needs and can just focus on mine". I let members know that if I *need* to make contact with them, I will do so directly by speaking. This seems to settle those who were first put off by my scanning, as they realise that my goal is to make myself available to them as a resource for regulation and support.

In a safe enough group environment, a member's core need expression supports a working through of implicit memory by making unmet needs more explicit. This offers opportunities for other members to support and regulate the member while providing corrective experiences (which become new neural pathways) that counter implicit models for how core needs are experienced. For example, a gay male member (Ed) became unusually quiet and withdrawn in group after hearing a new heterosexual male member (Dave) share the importance of his Catholic faith. Most group members knew that Ed had struggled with his own Catholic upbringing and with deep fears of rejection and abandonment from his family and spiritual community while trying to "come out". Alex, a member who knew Ed's story, commented on Ed's withdrawal and asked if he was having some feelings that he was not sharing. Ed responded, "I'm just not feeling comfortable today. I don't feel safe for some reason". Alex responded with, "I'm invested in helping you feel safe". Several other members also shared their support of Ed's right to feel safe and a desire to help him. Ed began to feel more settled and present as he allowed group members in. However, he was still unclear why he was feeling such discomfort and shame. By helping Ed first with emotional and physical regulation via eye contact, mirroring of affect, and reassurance of care and support, we could then begin building the narrative around what was getting triggered: an implicit memory around shame, rejection, and abandonment. Dave expressed support of Ed's right to feel safe and to express his feelings related to Catholicism. All of this shifted Ed's implicit working model around others' perception of him and his right to exist.

When our clients cannot self-regulate, we must help them via right-brain attunement. According to Schore and Schore (2008), "attachment communications are critical to the development of structural right brain neurobiological systems involved in processing of emotion, modulation of stress, self-regulation, and thereby the functional origins of the bodily-based implicit self" (p. 10).

A model of hunger and longing

Hunger and longing is not only a metaphor that refers to the human need to be fed and nurtured; it also seems to be an expression of an embodied human need that is rooted in our genetic inheritance and includes the push for attachment throughout life (Damasio, 2010). It represents our desires and hopes (longing) for meeting such core needs as love, respect, safety, and belonging. Our hunger and longing represent the human need for food and the way in which our hunger serves as a life force that drives us to seek sustenance. Without hunger, an infant cannot survive, as hunger signals to the mind–body system that food is needed. This hunger propels infants to find ways of expressing that need to others so they can be fed and survive. Therefore, it is this "lack" of something (in this case, food), that drives us to seek satisfaction of a core need for survival (see Lacan, 1991). As adults, we have different ways of letting others know we have needs for care, intimacy, safety, etc. While these needs might not always be conscious, we express them nonetheless. Introducing an eight-stage model of hunger and longing has enabled group therapists to identify various stages that unfold in developing the capacity for more relationally adaptive core need identification, expression, and fulfilment.

Since seeking core need fulfilment is essential for human survival, it is adaptive to be "hungry". Hunger serves as a life force; it motivates us to action so that we get what we need to live. If we do not access our sensation of hunger, we will not eat or thrive. Early in life, hunger and survival are relational. We are totally dependent on others to be fed. As social mammals, we continue to be dependent creatures, as we rely on others in all aspects of our lives: work, family, schools, government, etc. Johnson (2008) states that for humans, there is no such thing as independence from other humans; there is only adaptive and maladaptive dependency. By accepting this, we more fully accept our resources and ourselves.

Hunger and longing: an eight-stage model

Unconscious starvation

In this first stage, there is no conscious awareness of one's own core needs in the present moment. In this stage, members do not recognise they have hunger and longing, and instead experience a non-conscious (implicit) sense of feeling dysregulated (e.g., overwhelmed, numb, disconnected, or disassociated). This is akin to when young children are too hungry or tired to realise why they are so overwhelmed. Group members in this stage are "starving" without knowing they are hungry in the first place.

Group members who have experienced trauma or troubled early relationships are likely to experience what Schore and Schore (2008) call "implicit affective-arousal states" (p. 16). During such implicit states, members have a subjective experience of feeling emotionally dysregulated without awareness of the origins of these emerging feelings. They do not have the regulatory capacity to understand or communicate what they need because they do not even know an unmet need is in play. Instead, they might blame others for their state or think there is something wrong with themselves. Therefore, the group leader becomes a primary source for discerning these states in members based on their relational cues such as body posture, prosody, eye contact, and breathing.

Group leaders might notice "unconscious starvation" in a member because they sense something amiss in their own body associated with that member. Mirror neurons and resonance circuits help us understand the experience of others and reflect it back to them so that they can know themselves more deeply, making the implicit more explicit (Schermer, 2010). Iacoboni (2008) states that mirror neurons "show that we are not alone, but are biologically wired and evolutionarily designed to be deeply connected with one another" (p. 267).

In one session, for example, a member, Jeff, announced that his brother had recently died. Within minutes I noticed tightness in my chest that seemed related to another member, Chris, who had a vacant stare and crossed arms. When I mentioned this tightness in my chest and that I wondered if it had anything to do with how Chris was feeling, he began to weep. His first comment was, "I don't even know why I'm crying". With a warm, inviting posture I said, "That's absolutely OK. You don't have to know anything right now. Just let yourself be here with us and let us hold with you what's coming up". My offering seemed to release Chris's tension, and his tears deepened. In the moment, he did not realise the connection. We later learned that he had lost his only brother, with whom he was very close, when he was eleven years old.

Group leaders help regulate members by mirroring their somatic and emotional cues. When overstimulated by discomfort or an obstruction to getting a need met, members are more likely to be confused by their need, expressing it without awareness that they even have a need. The member is implicitly hijacked and desperately wants something, but is unable to identify what is needed. Mirroring by the leader offers a receptive member access to a deeper under-standing of his/her own self-state.

The role of implicit memory is especially important in this stage, as we are unable to place a time stamp or narrative to our physical and emotional arousal. The left brain system is compromised, as we struggle to access a more logical and linguistic grounding. Therefore, we are dysregulated and controlled by processes outside our conscious awareness. This evokes desperation, without knowing we are desperate, as evidenced by states of confusion, overwhelm, or functioning with extreme rigidity or chaos (Siegel, 1999). Because members cannot articulate their needs directly in this stage, or even know they have a need, others might misinterpret this dysregulation and confusion as resistance, obstinacy, or rebelliousness. It is easier, for example, to sympathise with members who say, "I'm feeling over-whelmed and I need support", than with those who roll their eyes in disapproval, fold their arms and say, "This group sucks". As leaders, patience and understanding of this unconscious starvation stage will aid in developing the "good enough" holding environment needed to move members to the next stage.

Emerging awareness

This stage refers to members acknowledging that hunger and longing exist in the moment. Members realise they need something, but they struggle to identify their specific core need.

Implicit memories foster a repetitive cycle of reinforced expecta-tions. According to Badenoch and Cox (2010), "what we implicitly 'know' is continually confirmed by how we perceive what is happen-ing and how our behavior shapes situations into expected form" (p. 467). To break this cycle, group members need to be exposed to new interpersonal experiences that disconfirm their implicit belief states. These new relational experiences reconfigure the non-conscious right-hemisphere and help adjust implicit models of how relationships can feel. As a viscerally felt shift takes place in the somatic and emotional self, the groundwork is fostered for the emergence of left-hemisphere engagement in which mindful awareness supports the development of narratives about the self. Such changes require safety, openness, intention, and co-regulation.

During emerging awareness, members continue to have difficulty with neural integration. They function with a dysregulated nervous system, despite some emerging sense that something is needed. They experience viscerally felt phenomena as though they were associated with something in the moment, but they are unable to relate them to a triggered implicit memory. Members struggle to recall how these emotional, cognitive and physiological arousal states are connected to a discernible meaning, idea, or need. Members have little "response flexibility" and are unable to link the past, present, and future. When the orbitofrontal cortex is not well integrated with the amygdala, fear might still be an overriding emotion. Members have little ability to interpret physiological stimuli, which limits their use of mind–body data to inform their choices.

In all my groups, I introduce mindfulness meditation training, which offers useful strategies for managing emotional arousal and staying present in one's experience. We discuss the importance of compassion, non-judgement, curiosity, and staying present with our physiological experience. As members learn that feeling overwhelmed and dysregulated are not the totality of themselves, but instead subjective states that come and go, they develop more capacity to be present for co-regulation and settling (Farb et al., 2010). This metacognitive awareness helps members tolerate negative affect states, thereby opening opportunities for more neural integration of cortical areas.

Identification

This stage involves recognising and naming to oneself the actual underlying core need(s). Here members identify and understand their own core needs but are not ready to communicate their needs adaptively. The focus is on the member's identification of his or her own needs rather than on others knowing.

Identifying our needs enables us to make healthy choices around meeting them. Connecting with our hunger and longing allows us to develop a more integrated relationship with our full mind-body system: our thoughts, feelings, physiology, behaviours, relationships, values/beliefs. What we bring to awareness impacts what we experience, as focused attention impacts neural wiring (Siegel, 2007). A chief task for leaders is helping members build mindful awareness of their own intentions. Siegel (2007) states that "mindfulness can be seen as a way of developing a secure attachment with yourself" (p. 180). Therefore, the installation of mindful awareness as a core value in group therapy offers members some key strategies for developing intrapersonal attunement. My group members are primed during their first session to reflect upon an intention to understand their immediate needs in group. Whenever they notice any emotional, cognitive, or somatic arousal, I suggest some questions to consider: "What is going on with me right now?" "What might my immediate sensations be telling me about what I need?". These questions build active attention to our own intention to understand our experience.

Exposing our hunger and longing reveals our vulnerability. This type of exposure might stir a variety of feelings including shame, fear, anger, helplessness, and loss. It might stimulate a sense of insatiable hunger once that need is brought into awareness, or concern that what we might get will not be good enough. Given this, we might try to conceal our hunger and longing from ourselves due to fears of exposing the intensity of our needs, despair in not achieving them, or feeling hopeless about our chances of getting them met. Members might try to disavow their needs because they feel destructive. Some members take as their goal to "not feel" what they want. However, this deepens our disconnection from others and ourselves.

Psychoeducation about the identification process can be a useful intervention at this stage. According to Badenoch and Cox (2010), psychoeducation supports regulation of the neocortex and can help maintain one's emotional regulation within a range that allows for more presence and ability to integrate material. A useful educational intervention involves decreasing focus on left hemisphere processes by normalising the challenge we all face in identifying our immediate needs. To reduce the pressure to "know" and instead compassionately support curiosity and exploration, I might say, "We all have needs that can be overwhelming, scary, or shameful, as well as difficult to identify. This is normal and human. In fact, treating ourselves with compassion and care in that process of discovery is essential to our healing". When members feel free to explore and "not know" without feeling ashamed, they become more flexible and adaptive (Siegel, 1999). I also look for functional subgroups where members share similar needs, as this reduces shameful or disavowed affect, while building universality and co-regulation (Gantt & Agazarian, 2010). Timing, pacing, and attunement are essential factors in maximising integration of both right- and left-hemisphere learning where deeper meaning and co-regulation can be consolidated.

The reduction of shame can free up curiosity and exploration. Siegel (2007) states that "discernment" is the ability of the mind to be aware that activities of the mind are not the totality of the mind. Discernment helps us acknowledge our thoughts and fantasies while accepting that we need not act on them or consider them absolute truths. Therefore, we can open up to exploring our needs without considering our thoughts or fantasies as something to be ashamed of, but rather something to understand more fully. This mindful attention fosters a group culture of curiosity, openness, and exploration, and is built on increasing neural integration in the right hemisphere (Siegel, 2007).

Settling and soothing (self- and co-regulation)

Now that members can identify their core needs, they must learn how to settle and soothe themselves enough to express their needs effectively. The key here is self-regulation and self-soothing, which are built on the capacity for interpersonal co-regulation.

An optimal range of emotional stimulation is needed to integrate new experiences into more adaptive neural pathways. When individuals feel too overwhelmed, they lose their ability to stay relationally engaged, making it difficult for them to participate in co-regulation (Porges, 2007). As leaders, we help members experience what it feels like to be in their optimal range. Logical appeals are likely to fail when members are implicitly activated, as they need more regulation to access the capacity to integrate more middle prefrontal cortex activity. By attuning to the subjective state of the activated member, the potential for regulation emerges.

Group members who do not rely on others for support and regulation, and who have highly dysregulated nervous systems, have difficulty trusting that others can serve a useful regulatory function.

Through non-shaming right-brain to right-brain attunement to implicit arousal, we help such members regulate enough to discover how others can be helpful. As this trust grows, so does help-seeking; this enhances opportunities for new experiences to build healthy neural models of relational intimacy.

Regulation, memory, and attunement play inter-related roles when group members function more from implicit memories where limbic arousal leaves them unsettled and confused about their self-states (Badenoch & Cox, 2010). At times, we need help to regulate ourselves via attachment to others and to ourselves. When members are more neurologically integrated, they can talk about painful feelings without becoming overwhelmed. This occurs when implicit arousal states become soothed based on increased complexity of the right hemisphere and a deepening connection between the orbitofrontal area and the amygdala. According to Badenoch and Cox (2010), this "feeling felt" by the other (i.e., attunement) opens up the possibility of transforming the memory; and "through such living contact, implicit memories become explicit and may now meet experiences in the current world that disconfirm the truth of earlier implicit knowing" (p. 468).

As an intervention for this stage, I tell group members that they will become dysregulated at various points in their group experience. This helps reduce the shock and shame when it occurs. I tell members, "Becoming dysregulated at times is just part of the process of living". I encourage members to pay attention to their own internal signals of overwhelm (e.g., body tightness, shallow breathing, distracted thoughts). We then work together to develop signals that indicate when they are overwhelmed and need support (i.e., co-regulation). I admit I will be misattuned at times because I am human and have limitations. I encourage members to reach out when they are dysregulated (e.g., say, "help" or raise their hands), and to keep reaching out until someone notices. As self-awareness improves, so do members' capacities to reach out and to regulate. Eventually members learn to glean the data of their mind–body system to inform healthy interactions that improve the likelihood that their immediate needs are understood and addressed.

In addition to interpersonal resources, members may also draw on "states of mind" generated within themselves. Siegel (2007) considers mindfulness a form of intrapersonal attunement where we become

compassionate observers of ourselves. Mindfulness may offer a benefit similar to receiving accurate attunement from others. It helps us
self-regulate and feel more stable. Interpersonal and intrapersonal
attunement harness similar neural mechanisms that promote neural
integration and "mutual coherence". Resonance circuits such as the
mirror neuron system and the superior temporal cortex are activated
during mindfulness states (Siegel, 2007).

Useful tools for helping group members settle and soothe include
abdominal breathing, body scans, visualisations, eye contact, feeling
their body in their seat, intentionally perceiving the immediate environment, listening to the voice of the leader or a trusted member, and
reaching out to others for support. By making these tools part of the
group culture early on, members will feel able to access them more
automatically and without shame.

Core need expression

In this stage, group members learn to express their needs in an adaptive way that respects themselves and others. Members stay in dialogue
with others to articulate their needs so the group understands them.

Asserting oneself effectively is a cornerstone of healthy relationships and intimacy. Despite many of us having the wish that others
will "read our minds" and know our needs without telling them, we
increase the potential of having our needs met by directly expressing
them to others. Along with the power of right brain attunement, the
emergence of a left brain narrative helps us express our needs more
clearly and in a particular context, which provides other group
members with useful information to facilitate our need fulfilment.

Group members can take an active role in working with a
member's clearly stated present needs rather than relying on intuition
or guessing. When a member states, "I need to feel more accepted in
this group", others can explore this to see how that need might be
addressed. By directly stating our wishes, desires, or needs, rather
than keeping them private, we open opportunities for having productive and meaningful dialogues. By making needs more explicit and
engaging in active dialogues, we can transform old neural pathways
into more adaptive working models that make use of present moment
relationships for healing. Members also learn that expressing needs
increases the probability of having them met.

Experience from the past shapes what we perceive in the present (Siegel, 2007). Our early mental models are extremely persistent, and we look for evidence that reinforces them. For those who have experienced a lack of success in reaching out to others and receiving attentive responsiveness to stated needs, this stage will pose challenges. Group members need to believe that others have the capacity to be of some assistance, and this might take a "leap of faith" that comes with a good enough holding environment within the group (Winnicott, 1971). This requires vulnerability, an essential ingredient for intimacy (Navaro & Van Wagoner, 2006).

I work tirelessly to promote a group culture where taking risks to assert one's needs is strongly encouraged. My preference is for these self-assertions to be done with respect for oneself and others; however, this can be difficult. My groups know that I would rather a member express a core need imperfectly, where we can openly explore it, than keep it a secret, where no help can be offered. The phrases, "we'll deal with it" or "we'll work it through" often arise when members express caution or fear of asserting themselves. Trusting that the group can work through messy exchanges is essential for the group and the leader. The key is building a group culture where sharing our needs is normalised and expected. This works best when members are willing to look at themselves and their behaviour with curiosity, compassion, and humility so that they can discover more adaptive ways of sharing what matters.

Taking in

This stage refers to group members' receptivity and their ability to process the meaning and intimacy that emerges when they open themselves in an authentic, vulnerable way to get their needs met.

"Taking in" offers an opportunity for new neural connections and pathways, as novel experiences and focused attention promote neuroplasticity. This stage challenges members to face what they most hunger for and what they most fear. Members must be present enough in their minds and bodies to be ready to receive what they seek. If they request support around safety, they will need to attend to the safety messages that come their way; otherwise they will experience others' responses through an old internal working model and not assimilate something new and useful. As focused attention promotes neural wiring, they will need to attend to what can help them change. The interplay of mirror neurons and social context helps us to read the intentions of others (Iacoboni, 2008). Since the present moment is a manifestation of past learning and our immediate perception, members benefit by openly exploring the intention of others based on the social context of the feedback.

Members require support in this "taking in" stage, for finally getting what they want can be quite stimulating. It might activate excessive emotion or a fight or flight response because it contradicts old implicit working models, thereby sending members back to the need for settling and soothing. Accurate tracking and attunement of these members during this stage is essential to keeping them optimally stimulated so that deeper levels of neural integration can occur.

As members authentically take in new experiences of intimacy with others, a refashioning of implicit memory and right-hemisphere "knowing" emerges. One of my group members, Mark, held an implicit belief that women could not find him attractive and worthy if he showed vulnerability. During a session when he openly cried about his father's recent death, he expressed feelings of shame that he was not a "real man". I invited Mark to find out if others shared his perception. Anne, an attractive member with whom Mark had flirted in other sessions, immediately stated, "Your tears bring me much closer to you now than I've ever felt. I think you're more of a man with these tears . . . at least more of a man I'd be interested in". Two other women quickly affirmed this statement. When Mark seemed stunned, I asked him, "Do you believe they are telling you their truth?" After a thoughtful pause, he replied, "Yes". When I encouraged him to take in this truth, Mark wept with relief as he realised he was being embraced for his full self. I encouraged Mark to stay with this feeling and to recognise how it felt in his body. Paying mindful attention to an experience causes neural firing, which changes neural connections, impacting neural pathways and the manner in which we perceive the world (Siegel, 2007).

Savouring

As group members successfully take in the "nutrition" from expressing their core needs and having them met, they develop the capacity to go beyond basic sustenance to the experience of enjoying and savouring the connection and closeness attained while appreciating many of the subtleties of love, intimacy, and belonging. Like enjoying a fine wine, group members in this stage savour the multiple textures that emerge out of having their core needs addressed.

Deeper levels of neural integration typify this stage, where visceral, present-moment experience can emerge without the interference of self-consciousness or dysregulation. Feelings of guilt or shame for having such feelings of peace do not interfere with neural functioning, as feelings of self-acceptance and self-compassion support resiliency and adaptive functioning. Through processes such as interoception—perceiving one's own inner states—group members learn how to enjoy their positive affect states such as joy, calm, engagement, flow, appreciation, love, and connection (Adler & Fagley, 2005; Bryant & Veroff, 2007). These positive self-receptive states emerge out of the internalisation of compassionate others who have modelled such support and compassion for the member. Members are encouraged to pay attention to the mind–body sensations of these positive self-states, as they support the development of memories that increase the chances that such self-states will emerge again in the future (Badenoch, 2008). I might say to members, "Remember this sensation, how it feels in your body, and share it with us so we can hold it with you".

Giving with generosity

In this stage, group members feel they have received what they need and are satiated. From this contentment, members have the capacity to help meet others' needs with an intrinsic generosity that stems from sincere interest in the other's well-being. This stage lasts until the inevitable pangs of hunger and longing (i.e., new core needs) return and members revisit an earlier stage, only to cycle through again.

When our core needs are addressed, our emotional and cognitive resources for supporting others become more available. When group members get their needs met *and* take in and enjoy what they have sought, they experience deeper regulation and neural integration. Resonance circuits (including the mirror neuron system and the insula and middle prefrontal areas) become more flexible and adaptive to contextual factors (Iacoboni, 2007). The generosity stage is akin to Erikson's (1968) developmental stage of generativity, or giving back.

By identifying their needs, settling and co-regulating, expressing their needs appropriately, and taking in feedback that supports them, group members discover opportunities for healthy relational choices that facilitate intimacy. By making group members' implicit needs more explicit, we open the possibility of transforming old implicit working models into more adaptive states of receptive engagement and curiosity about a real-life here-and-now moment. This facilitates more meaningful and authentic contact with others. Indeed, when we feel good about ourselves, we have more to give to others.

Accepting the return of hunger and longing

Hunger and longing never go away for very long. Since hunger and longing guide us to the very core of who we are and what we need, its underlying essence provides us a road map to our authentic self and our intrinsic motivation. Our goal is not to overcome hunger and longing, but to embrace it. We need it to feel alive and to know what we want. We need only to attend to it and discern the mind–body data it offers. The search for our hunger and longing is a search for ourselves, and when we accept it, we accept ourselves.

Case example

A forty-year-old female member in one of my co-ed groups, Lisa, became overwhelmed with fear and dread one session when confronted by another member, Bill, a fifty-five-year-old male, who spoke angrily regarding Lisa's missed sessions and lateness to group. He stated that the last three weeks she was either absent or late, and that he was feeling "disrespected". Within seconds and without her conscious awareness, Lisa went from being a professional woman to a five-year-old girl fearing the anger of her enraged, narcissistic, alcoholic father. In this moment, Lisa had no explicit memory that offered a time stamp or narrative of her past. Instead, she manifested the implicit memory of the experience (increased limbic stimulation and sympathetic arousal), which left her feeling the dreaded physiological and affective sensations of the past as though they were happening now, without an explicit awareness of why it was happening. This trigger of Lisa's implicit memory typifies the hunger and longing stage of "unconscious starvation".

Lisa said she did not know what was going on, but she needed to leave the room and get some air. As is typical for the "emerging awareness" stage, she was aware that some need existed but was unclear what it was. At this moment, I engaged Lisa directly to establish a connection that might help co-regulate her. It was clear she was too stimulated to take in any intellectual interpretation. To make use of this important clinical moment, she needed help to regulate her limbic arousal. By making direct eye contact and using a calm tone with soft facial expressions that conveyed safety and care, I let Lisa know that I was interested in supporting her during this unsettling experience. I expressed confidence that we could work this out together, but that I first wanted to help her feel safer. This immediately settled Lisa into my gaze. Without words, we sat in quiet connection for a moment while I made deep breathing gestures, that she immediately mimicked. This seemed to deepen her into the co-regulation, as evidenced by her shoulders settling and a slower, deeper breathing pattern ("settling and soothing").

Once I sensed she was more physiologically grounded, I empathised with how scary this experience seemed to be for her. She agreed. I suggested that while something made her feel unsafe and scared, it seemed she was not sure what that was. She nodded again and stated, "I don't know what happened. I just needed to get out of here". I offered some psychoeducation about the nature of feeling implicitly overwhelmed and how scary that can feel. I told her I thought she was getting triggered by something from her past history of abuse by her father (which the group was familiar with from Lisa's previous sharing), and I also suggested that this moment of dysregulation was a meaningful opportunity for us to explore and understand something about how she responds to men who are angry with her. I shared, "When we are exposed to trauma, it is harder for us to encode explicit memories that help us develop a narrative about our past. So, when something triggers that implicit memory, we can feel all the mind–body sensations we had during the trauma, even when the present situation is not a real threat like the one in the past. Without consciously knowing it, we experience our feelings and physical sensations from the past and attribute them to the present. This can be a terrifying and disorienting experience for anyone". I then turned to other members, most of whom had similar implicit arousal states at times in the group, and asked if they could relate to this experience. Many members identified with Lisa and her fear, confusion, and dysregulation. By normalising this experience, we reduce the potential shame associated with being implicitly aroused and not acting "rationally."

We then worked together to connect the narrative she had shared about her father to her relationships with other men who had been abusive. Lisa realised that she had a core need to feel safe with others, especially with men with whom she wants to feel close ("identification"). During this process, Lisa told Bill that she experienced his tone as aggressive and it scared her. She shared that a core need of hers was to feel safe with others, even when she disappoints them, and that she would like to feel safe with him ("core need expression").

Bill expressed understanding of how he can sometimes come across as aggressive when he actually feels hurt or disappointed. He explained that his intention of sharing his irritation with her was about enjoying her in the group and wanting more of her there. Bill stated that he really appreciated Lisa's support around his struggles with his wife. He said he felt a loss when she was absent and he sometimes took it personally, as though she did not care about him or the group.

I encouraged Lisa to look at Bill to see if she felt he was sincere. She nodded, tearfully. I also asked if he still felt like a threat. She shook her head and said, "No, not at all" ("taking in"). This served as an opportunity for Lisa to reintegrate him as a safe object and to build a deeper neural connection of men as potentially safe. Lisa expressed great relief at feeling safer with Bill. She shared how important the group had been to her as a support system ("savouring") and she only hoped she could give back, as she had been given ("generosity").

The group therapist stance

Schore and Schore (2008) suggest therapists become sensitively attuned to the nuances of clients' non-verbal, nonconscious, right-brain manifestations of psychobiological arousal. This requires an authentic, engaged, and invested emotional presence on the part of the therapist. Group members pick up on the leader's authenticity and inauthenticity in unconscious, right-brain ways (Iacoboni, 2007; Schore & Schore, 2008). If leaders are irritated but deny it when asked, members will likely feel unsettled by the incongruence they experience based on their resonance circuitry. Members might not know why they feel untrusting, but they will likely sense something does not feel right. This can compromise safety in the group and must be handled with care. Therapists need to attune carefully to more vulnerable group members, and repair any empathic failures (Kohut, 1977). Group leader attunement helps create a secure enough attachment for members to co-regulate and to take appropriate risks to access their core needs.

As group leaders, paying attention to our own hunger, longing, and countertransference will help us engage more authentically and empathically as demands for attention and co-regulation surface. Leaders need to look at their own longing to feed others, as well as their own desire to be a good enough (but not perfect) leader. Members come to us hungry for need fulfilment yet scared to reveal their needs. All the while, they will watch others get fed, which can be painful if they are not getting enough themselves. This can elicit powerful demands on leaders, who also have needs that will emerge in group. Understanding our needs, being in mindful relationship with them, and getting consultation as needed, will help us make informed choices that serve the group.

Summary

The developmental stages of hunger and longing in the emergence of core relational needs offers group leaders a lens through which to experience and move members to deeper levels of regulation, integration, intimacy, and healing. This model guides leaders and participants in learning to identify, understand, manage, and regulate their immediate somatic, emotional, and cognitive experiences related to interpersonal connection and intimacy.

As social mammals, we humans need to connect with others to optimise our functioning, as we are ultimately dependent creatures (Bowlby, 1988; Johnson, 2008). However, this can be a scary endeavour depending on early relational experiences. As group therapists, we instil in our members an openness to sit together at the edge of our relational needs and to be curious about what emerges in our mind–body system: our thoughts, feelings, physiology, behaviours, relationships, and values/beliefs. Mindfulness and right-hemisphere attunement help us work on regulating and connecting more deeply with ourselves and others in a respectful, intentional, and compassionate manner, while making space to explore the entirety of the human condition (Kabat-Zinn, 1990; Siegel, 2007).

Schore and Schore (2008) state that "in relationally-oriented therapeutic contexts that optimise intersubjective communication and interactive regulation, deficits in internal working models of the self and the world are gradually repaired" (p. 13). Clearly, this is the foundation of group psychotherapy. As members' regulatory function improves via right-brain attunement, members begin to shift their implicit relational expectations. This allows for increased self-awareness and more meaningful contact with others. As we develop a safe enough holding environment for group members, we create a space for them to rework old neural networks and form new, more adaptive coping strategies to meet their needs.

We humans are hardwired to connect with others, and these relationships directly affect our neurophysiology. When we feel connected and attuned to ourselves and to others, our brains change in adaptive ways. New synaptic connections and neural networks emerge while others get reinforced and still others lose their strength. In the world of group psychotherapy, the opportunities for new connections and healing, both relationally and neurologically, are astounding.

References

Adler, M. G., & Fagley, N. S. (2005). Appreciation: individual differences in adding value and meaning as a unique predictor of subjective well-being. *Journal of Personality*, 73(1): 79–114.

Badenoch, B. (2008). *Being a Brain-wise Therapist*. New York: Norton.

Badenoch, B., & Cox, P. (2010). Integrating interpersonal neurobiology with group psychotherapy. *International Journal of Group Psychotherapy*, 60(4): 463–481.

Bowlby, J. (1988). *A Secure Base* (2nd edn). New York: Basic.

Bryant, F. B., & Veroff, J. (2007). *Savoring: A New Model of Positive Experience*. Mahwah, NJ: Lawrence Erlbaum.

Cozolino, L. (2002). *The Neuroscience of Psychotherapy: Building and Re-building the Human Brain*. New York: Norton.

Cozolino, L. (2006). *The Neuroscience of Human Relationships: Attachment and the Developing Social Brain*. New York: Norton.

Damasio, A. (2010). *Self Comes to Mind*. New York: Random House.

Erikson, E. H. (1968). *Identity: Youth and Crisis*. New York: Norton.

Farb, N. A. S., Anderson, A. K., Bean, J., McKeon, D., Mayberg, H., & Segal, Z. V. (2010). Minding one's emotions: mindfulness training alters the neural expression of sadness. *Emotion, 10*(1): 25–33.

Flores, P. (2010). Group psychotherapy and neuro-plasticity: an attachment theory perspective. *International Journal of Group Psychotherapy, 60*(4): 547–570.

Gantt, S. P., & Agazarian, Y. M. (2010). Developing the group mind through functional subgrouping: linking systems-centered training (SCT) and interpersonal neurobiology. *International Journal of Group Psychotherapy, 60*(4): 515–544.

Gantt, S. P., & Cox, P. (2010). Introduction to the special issue. *International Journal of Group Psychotherapy, 60*(4): 455–460.

Goleman, D. (2006). *Social Intelligence: The New Science of Human Relationships*. New York: Bantam Dell.

Iacoboni, M. (2007). Face to face: the neural basis of social mirroring and empathy. *Psychiatric Annals, 37*(4): 236–241.

Iacoboni, M. (2008). *Mirroring People: The New Science of How We Connect with Others*. New York: Farrar, Strauss, and Giroux.

Johnson, S. (2008). *Hold Me Tight. Seven Conversations for a Lifetime of Love*. New York: Little, Brown.

Kabat-Zinn, J. (1990). *Full Catastrophe Living*. New York: Dell.

Kohut, H. (1977). *The Restoration of the Self*. New York: International Universities Press.

Lacan, J. (1991). Le seminaire de Jacque Lacan, Livre VIII: Le Transfert (1960–1961). [The seminar of Jacque Lacan, Book VIII: Transference (1960–1961)]. (J. A. Miller, Ed.). Paris: Seuil.

Navaro, L., & Van Wagoner, S. (2006). Competition for intimacy: envy, jealousy and enjoyment. *Presentation at the Annual Meeting of the American Group Psychotherapy Association*, San Francisco, CA.

Porges, S. W. (2007). The polyvagal perspective. *Biological Psychology, 74*(2): 116–143.

Schermer, V. L. (2010). Mirror neurons: their implications for group psychotherapy. *International Journal of Group Psychotherapy, 60*(4): 487–513.

Schore, A. N. (2003). *Affect Regulation and the Repair of the Self*. New York: Norton.

Schore, J. R., & Schore, A. N. (2008). Modern attachment theory: the central role of affect regulation in development and treatment. *Clinical Social Work Journal*, 36: 9–20.

Siegel, D. J. (1999). *The Developing Mind: How Relationships and the Brain Interact to Shape Who We Are*. New York: Guilford Press.

Siegel, D. J. (2006). An interpersonal neurobiology approach to psychotherapy: awareness, mirror neurons, and neural plasticity in the development of well-being. *Psychiatric Annals*, 36(4): 247–258.

Siegel, D. J. (2007). *The Mindful Brain: Reflection and Attunement in the Cultivation of Well-being*. New York: Norton.

Winnicott, D. W. (1971). *Playing and Reality*. New York: Routledge.

Relationship-focused group therapy (RFGT) to mitigate marital instability and neuropsychophysiological dysregulation*

Gloria Batkin Kahn and Darryl B. Feldman

A dvances in the understanding of the neurobiology of attachment, especially the impact of relational trauma, inform us of the need to broaden our framework. This article takes into consideration an appreciation of the recent developments in neurophysiopsychological theory that can aid in clinical formulations.

Based on these theoretical advances, we have broadened the focus of the treatment of couples to include separate relationship-focused therapy groups for each partner and introduced specific techniques to repair attachment wounds, develop individuation, and create empathy for the partner. It is felt that a greater understanding of marital tension and dysregulation and its treatment may best be served through such an integrative approach.

Limitations of couples therapy

The fact that there are some people who cannot work in couples therapy is a problem that is not often openly addressed by couples

---

* First published in *International Journal of Group Psychotherapy*, 61(4): 518–536.

therapists. Hendrix (2006) calls these people "predialogical". Shelley and Wood (1995) spoke of the difficulties of working with couples who were unwilling or unable to listen to each other or to "mirror" using the couples dialogue. Siegel (2008) spoke of the many instances when there is little or no progress in a couple therapy and there is a need to either work with the individuals separately or to refer each of the partners to different therapists.

There are also instances in which couples therapists may have witnessed the capacity for a seemingly well-functioning couple to regress into the throes of intense transferential conflicts right in their office. In fact, it has been postulated that in many rather high-functioning patients, there is the "existence of a subclinical variant of dissociative processes related to attachment trauma" (Adams, 2006). The theory is that there is a blend of strength and vulnerability in some people that goes unnoticed until it is revealed in their most intimate relationships. The etiology of this difficulty is thought to be rooted in lifelong processes of seemingly minor traumatisations, leading to ruptures in attachments that can result in the experience of "chronic shock" (Adams, 2006). This encapsulated, and many times unconscious, chronic apprehension often exists in parallel with more mature functioning that is evidenced in less intimate relationships. In these instances, there would appear to be a relationship between one's capacity towards regression and reactivity and the ability to tolerate intimacy. The pervasiveness and intensity of hypo- or hyperarousal and attendant dysregulation present may be limited to the threat perceived and vulnerability experienced only with more intimate connections.

When the rewounding in the marriage becomes so pervasive as to render the dyad uninhabitable, the couples therapist may indeed be drawn into a vortex of countertransferential reaction (Scharff, 1992). These couple dyads may be unable to effect change together, even with the help of an experienced couples therapist. Distress minimises attachment, and reactivity rather than receptivity may prevail. They may be unable to avoid emotional flooding or prolonged disengagement. Empathic resonance towards each other may be minimal. If one imagines the flow of relationships to encompass a process of rupture and repair, it may be that the repair process is either minimal or absent, leaving prolonged sequences of dysregulation to be the norm in these situations. There is understandably an enormous toll taken on these couple dyads.

Tatkin (2006) sees neurophysiological concomitants of marital instability as a "chronic hyperactivation of hypothalamic-pituitary-adrenal axis (HPA), sympathetic overarousal and/or parasympathetic underarousal". It has been hypothesised that partners rely on one another for regulation of their autonomic nervous systems (Levenson, 2003). When partners have been the object of childhood abuse, neglect, or chaotic and disorganised attachments, responses become automatic and rigidified, and lower cortical mechanisms prevail over higher prefrontal cortical systems. Eye rolling, gaze aversion, tantrum-like outbursts, and stonewalling are behavioural responses often evidenced under these conditions. The couple becomes imprisoned by unconscious early memories that inhibit receptivity—as though they are on automatic pilot, having the same fights over and over again, with minimal understanding of the processes supporting their behaviours.

Couples therapists frequently encounter couples whose capacity for empathy toward one another is almost negligible and who they feel can benefit little from couples work. These couples show such a terror of their differences that losing their sense of self and being annihilated prevents them from having any empathy toward each other. These couples can become stuck in their capacity to recover and are unable to move from a position of fight, flight, or freeze. The themes of feeling victimised and persecuted by one's partner may increase defensiveness to the point that little or no insight or growth seems possible.

Limitations of couples groups

There is literature describing the successful functioning of couples groups where both partners are in the same group (Feld, 2004). However, those groups are composed of couples who agree to be involved in and to tolerate a group experience together. We have found that couples who have difficulty working in couples therapy are often less likely to accept couples group treatment as a viable modality. Because the couple continues to process emotional issues outside the group, Brok (2004) explains that it becomes much harder in a group to achieve the safety and vulnerability necessary for growth. Brok suggests that a separate group for each partner would seem preferable. This model is particularly useful when there is a sense of either member being victimised. The couples therapy would be perceived as similar to an abuse victim being in therapy with the abuser (Buchele, 2000) and may seem like an attempt to collaborate with the enemy present (Coché & Coché, 1990).

The neurobiology of attachment and the impact of early relational trauma

We are only beginning to understand the connection between relationship patterns and neurobiology. We do know that positive early development and interpersonal experiences help form a secure "internal group" which tends to function as a source of affect regulation (Aron et al., 2005). Conversely, the impact of early relational trauma on the neuroplasticity of the brain is probably, in reality, much greater than most previously predicted it to be. We are learning that our experiences can change neurobiology and that the social environment highly impacts the neural circuitry of the developing infant (Siegel, 1999). Traumatic attachments which are imprinted early in life are now seen to have correlates in brain activity as well as behavioural responses to stress. When threatened, our brains tend to function more on automatic pilot, and neural pathways become rigidified. The right brain particularly is seriously affected by early traumatic events. The middle of the prefrontal cortex may suffer in terms of reduced connectivity (Van der Kolk, 1996; Woolley et al., 2004). Disorganised and disoriented insecure attachments form a model that is encoded in implicit memory of the right brain. Recent research implicates the right brain in terms of the responsibility for the development of responses to stress (Schore, 2001, 2002). Small traumas over extended periods of time may have more serious implications than isolated larger traumas. The chronic and cumulative experiencing of stressors tends to lead to long-term patterns of autonomic activity (Siegel, 2007). There may therefore be an over-reliance on more primitive and rigidified brain structures and pathways that result in a lack of capacity for emotional regulation (Schore, 2001). Under these circumstances, mindfulness may give way to impulsivity. Neural firings and pathways tend to rigidify and, as a result, neuroplasticity is compromised: that is, neural integration become minimised (Siegel, 2007). Impulsivity and loss of emotional regulation becomes the norm.

Marital instability and psychophysiological dysregulation

There is a growing understanding of the connection between marital instability, early attachment problems, and psychophysiological dysregulation (Clulow, 2001, 2006; Goldstein & Thau, 2006; Groth, Fehm-Wolfsdorf, & Hahlweg, 2000; Schore, 2003; Siegel, 2003). Just as emotional and physiological attunement can have a positive impact on interpersonal neurobiology, emotional and physiological dysregulation tend to have a deleterious effect. Therefore, it would appear that the process of either attunement or misattunement present in mother–infant interactions may be a familiar template operational in the dynamics of many couple relationships. The predisposition to rigidified toxic couple interactions is viewed as based in childhood attachment difficulties and maladaptive emotional and psychophysiological defensive strategies (Schore, 2003).

During severe marital discord, the hippocampus—the message centre which mediates between both the thinking and the feeling side of the brain—is often in a decreased state of functioning. Thus, memory may become impaired, causing interference with one's perception of an event, leading to a kind of "psychic dyslexia" (Solomon, 2003). This is one reason why couples in a high state of arousal have very different memories about what occurred during an argument. It appears that with impairment in functioning of the hippocampus, a person is left in distress, without much ability to remember circumstances surrounding an actual event.

When couples are in a high state of arousal and emotional dysregulation, a partner may experience a terrible state of almost childlike confusion and fragmentation. In these cases, there is such psychophysiological dysregulation that one or the other shuts down, dissociates, and is unable to remember the situation, and as a result, intentionality becomes impaired. Mindfulness and mentalisation are virtually impossible under these conditions (Siegel, 1999), and it is unlikely that the couple will be able to move toward repair. Siegel (2003) refers to these primitive interactions as "low road" transactions.

Low road transactions occur when feelings of danger are perceived on a subcortical level by structures such as the amygdala. The hypothalamic–pituitary–adrenal axis (HPA), the neuroendocrine stress response system, becomes activated without the aid of orbitofrontal mediation. In these instances, immediate primitive reactivity goes into play with little or no prefrontal cortex intervention. The reaction is similar to that of an animal seeing danger and growling as he jumps to attack. Similar to anger management training, relationship-focused group therapy attempts to teach techniques of stopping, freezing any activity in speech, gaining the time to allow the immediate reactivity to dissipate and for the executive functioning of the prefrontal cortex to come into play and think through a reasonable response.

Although these mature regulatory responses are adapted in the workplace, many individuals continue to function reactively at home. It seems that primitive ego states may coexist alongside seemingly sophisticated, mature functioning. It is quite common for people to function at an exceedingly high level at work and in the community and then to regress into low road functioning (Siegel, 2003) when they are at home. However, secure attachments in the presence of relational attunement may have the capacity to alter brain circuitry. The secure patient–therapist and therapeutic group relationships can positively affect neuronal growth and integration (Siegel, 2007).

Relationship-focused group therapy

Relationship-focused group therapy (RFGT) is conceived by the authors (Feldman & Kahn, 2009; Kahn & Feldman, 2007) as separate psychodynamic therapy for each of the partners, if possible, in conjunction with ongoing couples therapy. RFGT is based on principles of self-psychology, interpersonal group therapy, and object relations theory, and it integrates techniques from imago relationship therapy such as the couples dialogue (Hendrix, 1988; Hendrix & Hunt, 2004). It is a treatment opportunity for work on couples dynamics within a group setting. The thesis is that the ability to metabolise, contain, and empathise leads to safety and mutual growth. However, in less well-functioning couples there are often instances in which growth may be inhibited by the presence of the partner. In these instances, growth may best occur when an opportunity is presented for the working through of marital gridlock difficulties in a safe, separate, relationship-focused group process (Feld, 2003).

Group therapy is basically a psychodynamic process in which imitation, identification, and internalisation are considered primary therapeutic processes (Rutan & Stone, 1993). By adding techniques of imago relationship therapy to the group process (Feldman & Kahn, 2009; Kahn & Feldman, 2007), group members can learn to differentiate between themselves and their partner, thus reducing or eliminating feelings of symbiosis. As the group member individuates, he/she develops feelings of empathy for his/her partner. Each partner becomes better able to create a conscious relationship.

For the therapy group to be felt as safe, each member needs to find at least one (preferably more) person in the group who "gets" them, who is understanding and supportive of them, who is seen as their "twin", and aids in their feelings of connection and safety in the group (Harwood, 1996).

Another important aspect of relationship-focused group therapy is finding a group member who is seen as a twin for their spouse. Almost invariably, each group member finds at least one person in the group who resembles their spouse and then displaces the feelings from that spouse onto the spouse's twin (Livingston, 2004). The member is drawn into re-enacting conflicts with this spousal surrogate. However, working through these tensions with the group is easier because the group affords a dilution of the intensity of the transference distortions. Because this twin is not really the person's spouse, the group member can be led into holding onto his or her observing ego, thereby maintaining his executive functioning and resolving the conflict by utilising Hendrix's (1988) couples dialogue (Kahn & Feldman, 2007).

The couples dialogue

We directly adapt Hendrix's (1988) three-part process known as couples dialogue into the RFGT and apply it to an individual member and the spousal surrogate. The dialogue begins with one person, the sender, who speaks about a complaint, hurt, or wish. The recipient, the listener, mirrors back only what is heard, with no editorial comments. The listener's role is to gain an understanding of how the sender idiosyncratically perceives the world and aspects of the relationship in particular. The listener does not need to approve or agree, but only to "get" what his or her partner experiences.

The second part of the dialogue process is having the listener make a validating non-judgmental statement about what the sender has just said. It is a statement merely saying that "given what you have just said and given what I know of you, I can understand that you might see it that way".

The third part of the dialogue process consists of the listener making an empathic statement to the sender, something along the lines of, "Given what you've said about your experience of this situation, I imagine that you might be feeling sad, frustrated, upset, etc.". This empathic statement by the receiving partner is an attempt to connect to the emotional world of the other partner, but without being pulled into fusion.

Using the structure of the couples dialogue in the group helps the partners contain their mutual projections, lessen their resistances and emotional reactivity, and feel more in control. Increased regulation of neurophysiological systems may develop. Through the use of the new empathy, new response systems better able to contain reactivity are conditioned that can then transfer to their actual marital relationship. The resistances and defences that may have been intractable and interfering with progress in the couples therapy are worked through in the relationship-focused group process, and new response systems conditioned.

Separate relationship-focused group therapy for each partner

These authors postulate that the process in a separate relationship-focused group therapy (RFGT) for each partner can be especially reparative for the couple's functioning. Even if only one of the partners is able to be in a group, the growth in individuation and ability to tolerate differences as well as in self-regulation can be a powerful force toward repair. Separate group therapy for each or one of the partners can be discussed with the couple as an opportunity for either or both of them to be part of a better functioning model of close relationships, which could eventually replace the models they learned from their families. This therapy group can provide the support and connections fostered in a good family and lessen their sense of being alone (Alonso & Rutan, 1990).

The group as a social microcosm often recapitulates the primary family group, and therefore family members are often found transferentially via displacement within a group. These authors have found the same mechanism applies to marital partners; that is, when a group is formed, members will find at least one person who resembles their spouse within the group (Livingston, 2004). Spousal transferences with this spouse twin will abound. When the new "couple" uses couples dialogue and works through their differences in the group, the group dilutes the intensity of transference distortions. Therefore, the intractable resistance that may be interfering with the progress in couples therapy may be ameliorated in the group process. In emotionally interactive groups, transactions of members empathically in tune and serving self-object needs of one another (Stone, 1996) create an experience of well-being and safety. Thus, the group is able to create the safe working space that may not be available in the couple dyad, but is necessary for change and improved prefrontal cortical functioning. Integration can occur and is enhanced only if the environment is safe (Cozolino, 2002).

Scheidlinger (1974) portrayed the well-functioning group as serving to induce superego modifications formed from the incorporation of the image of the "mother group". Especially in couples in which there are symbiotic issues and rampant enmeshment themes, group process enhances individuation and separation, addresses symbiotic needs, and encourages each person to have an empathic focus on the subjective experience of the other (Caligor, Fieldsteel, & Brok, 1984). Because of the variety of possible transferences available, group members can provide support to each member of a dyad in a way that the couples therapist may be unable to. Thus, we hypothesise that relationship-focused group therapy might provide the safety necessary for hippocampal regrowth and functioning.

In separate group settings, partners more readily learn to tolerate disappointments without regressing into splitting. The group affords members the capacity to take a step back and become less dismissive, hypercritical, and judgmental than they might with their actual partner present. There is an opportunity for the re-visioning of one's life story and one's story as a couple in the group. Also, confrontations in group therapy by peers are often difficult for members to dismiss. The group catches on to members acting out their unconscious conflicts in the group process. The members' underlying conflicts may then become more amenable to group exposure and analysis. The false self tends to be quickly spotted in a group, and inauthentic behaviour in general is often not well tolerated.

Therefore, the possibility for empathy for one's partner may be engendered by group interactions (Brok, 2004; Livingston, 2004). The tendency for spousal confusion about their projections is opened up for examination within the group process. The capacity for marital scapegoating may be challenged. It is not so easy to place the internalised projected badness into the partner in a group setting, because the group tends to promote an ability to integrate ambivalence by re-visualising the partner as wounded rather than as an adversary. The multi-transference aspect of the group process provides the group member who has presented as the aggrieved spouse the help and support of "good parents". Group members who feel a twinship connection can provide mirroring and an understanding of the subjective experience of the other that is so necessary for right brain change to occur.

Clinical vignette

Barb: I'm going to be married ten years next week. Sometimes I can't remember why I married him. I walk in from work and I'm greeted with such a terrible mess—coffee cups, stacks of loose paper, clothes on the floor, newspapers, all covering every available space. I want to turn around and walk right out. He doesn't tell me how the job hunt is going, if he has an interview or even a lead. For all I know he did nothing all day but make more mess.

Mary: How terrible for you. No wonder you want to turn around and walk out. When I come home exhausted from my job, I just want to veg, not start cleaning and picking up.

Barb: That's exactly how I feel, Mary, and when Carl was working, how he felt too. That's why we had a cleaning person then, but we can't afford that now. He's home all day; why shouldn't he do it?

Ned: You know, I can really understand Carl. This was me. I lived this. Listen—when I lost my job and I was home those months, there was plenty I could have done around the house, but I felt awful every time I started to clean up. It kind of rubbed my nose in it.

Dr Kahn: Barb, can you mirror?

Barb: Yeah, you felt awful every time you started to clean up.

Dr Kahn: Let's role play. Ned, can you be Carl here?

Ned: Sure. Listen, Barb. When I start to get involved with the clean up stuff, I feel like a loser—like a guy who can't get a job. I feel so bad, I just want to go back to bed.

Dr Kahn: Barb, will you mirror?

Barb: When you start to clean up, you're saying that you just feel like such a loser, you have to go back to bed.

Ned: Yeah, that's it. I can't take it. It's hard enough being at home day after day; but then to have to do the cleaning too, it just makes me feel so bad.

Dr Kahn: Barb, can you mirror?

Barb: Sure. So Ned, you're saying that to do the cleaning makes you feel even worse; is that right?

Ned: Yes.

Dr Kahn: Ned, and cleaning reminds you of . . .?

Ned: My father did the cleaning when he was out of work. He hated it too. He would make me help him, but I never did it good enough. He would scream at me that I was a no-goodnik and would end up being a bum like him. Last year I was out of work. I felt like he was right. It really got me down. I guess that's why I couldn't do work in the house either.

Dr Kahn: Barb, can you mirror and validate what Ned is saying?

Barb: So Ned, let me see if I've got this right. What you're saying is that when your father was out of work, he made you help him clean, he didn't like how you did it, and then he would scream and yell at you that you're a no-goodnik and you would end up a bum like him, and so when you were out of work and you started to do the cleaning, it made you feel really down. Is that right?

Ned: Yes, that's right.

Barb: So I could really understand, then, Ned, why to do the cleaning would feel abhorrent to you.

Ned: Okay, you got it, Barb. Thanks for understanding.

Lester: So you surely didn't need your wife on your back to be cleaning up. Now, when I was out of work, I went and bought a great big motorcycle and I went for long rides on it. It was just wonderful.

Ned: Your wife didn't mind? Every time I spend a few hours playing golf, I get the cold shoulder.

Lester: Well, I don't really know if she minded. She never said anything. I mean, actually, we weren't talking too much back then. She seemed to be out a lot, I think.

Barb: If I were your wife, Les, I wouldn't talk too much either. Imagine, no income and buying a motorcycle.

Ned: Sometimes you're so judgmental, Barb. Why don't you ask him why he bought the motorcycle.

Barb: Okay, Les. Explain to me why, with no income, you go and buy a motorcycle.

Lester: Well, it was my money. I made it. I earned it. And you know, that bike made me feel so good. It cleared my head. It made me feel young and energetic. And then I felt able to be more confident when I networked or I had to make phone calls, speaking to people about a job.

Barb: Actually, you know, that makes sense, Les. What a good idea. Maybe Carl needs some things to pep him up so he can make some job hunting phone calls. Like he can go skiing. I'm really feeling bad that I've been so annoyed at him.

Ned: Now I'm being Carl again. Do you know what upsets me about you, Barb? When you're upset about one thing with me, you forget absolutely everything else about me that's good. It's like you catastrophise. You forget about how I cook all the meals and clean up the kitchen . . .

Mary: Wait. I missed that. Barb, does he really cook the meals and clean up all the meals?

Barb: Well, yes, actually. He does the grocery shopping too. But I forget that, you know. I get flooded with my upset feelings, and I see only the bad things. That's no good. I really have to watch that.

Ned: Well, you know, you really do, because what you forget is how much I need you to see the good parts of me so I can hold on to that image of me.

Lester: Maybe Carl doesn't need to ski. Maybe he needs you to be for him like the motorcycle was for me. Like helping me to remember the bright, energetic guy I am.

Ned: You are so right on the money, Les. Barb, I need you to remember the good things about me; to remember I'm not just a jobless do-nothing. I need you to see me.

Barb: Oh, I do see you, Ned. I see what a caring, good guy you are and how you let yourself be so open and vulnerable so that I would actually hear you. Thank you, thank you. I will really try to stop the negative flooding. Carl will thank you too.

Discussion

The group may be seen here as a vehicle for narrative integration. That is, the possibility of re-visioning one's life story in the presence of empathic others exists in the group setting. One's "movie" (Feldman, 2002) about self and others may take on previously unforeseen aspects. This interpersonal integration is most likely fuelled by concomitant neurophysiological integration. In these instances, it may be hypothesised that the group process allows for mindfulness and increased cortical functionality to replace reactivity. It might be stated that the new group "family" helps to break the more impaired legacy of the family of origin. Therefore, the intergenerational transmission of trauma and psychopathology may be deactivated (Volkan, 2001).

In this example, we saw how a very disturbing situation could create such cognitive flooding that the partner totally forgot important mitigating information. Barb, in her upset about Carl's lack of income and failure to clean the house, totally forgot about everything else he does. However, in the group, she received critically needed support and understanding from Mary so that she was then able to participate in a couples dialogue with Ned and really hear him. Regaining a balanced functioning, she was able to then hear Lester and actively learn from both.

The group provided the twinship allowing for understanding and support. Barb was then able to connect with her feelings and diminish her autonomic reactivity and to interact with her spouse's surrogate in a mature manner. Her verbal responses were clearly more and more tempered by the changes in her right brain subjective understandings and more regulated by her executive functioning. She moved from a position of total disdain and demonising of her spouse to a position of re-visioning him as a wounded person who was really decent and good.

The group therapist was faced with the daunting task of orchestrating optimal detoxifying psychological exchanges between members which would hopefully lead to improved neurophysiological and emotional integration and regulation. Looked at in this light, one might be reminded of Foulkes's (1964) metaphor of the group therapist as a "conductor", creating group therapy experiences that would have the potential of being very powerful right brain exchanges between members. Thus, it might be hypothesised that optimal right-to-right brain exchanges, especially when offered in a relationship-focused group process, modulated in the presence of a safer surrogate twin partner, possess the capacity to enhance emotional as well as neurophysiological regulation.

Conclusion

Hebb (1949) wrote that neurons that fire together, wire together. If the right brain can experience feelings that are safe, secure, and supported, subjective changes can take place and neural integration can proceed. These authors hypothesise that, in many instances, the group may be able to provide an optimal state of neurophysiological arousal that allows for modulation of affective states. This modulation of right hemispheric transactions may not be possible with the partner present, especially in dyads infected with an overabundance of toxicity. In these instances, the promotion of neural integration through the dilution of toxic rigidified transferential reactivity may be possible in a separate relationship-focused group for each partner. The group may allow for self-observation and relaxation of maladaptive defensive operations that are automatic in many couples. The partners may feel less imprisoned by implicit memories that inhibit receptivity and tend to favour reactivity. The possibility of defusing and re-visioning previously hopelessly gridlocked marital exchanges may arise.

This new understanding of the brain is extremely valuable to therapists. It helps to substantiate the hypothesis that left brain analytic understandings are necessary but not always sufficient for change to occur. We now know that a person can analytically understand; but in order for neural integration to be achieved, we need to be attuned to providing therapeutic experiences that address the significant contribution of right brain functions (Doidge, 2007; Schore, 2001; Siegel, 2007; Tatkin, 2009). These authors have found that relationship-focused group therapy (RFGT) tends to encourage the development of a secure, internalised group as a source of affective and concomitant neurophysiological regulation. Internal working models of the relationship may then be revised. In these instances, the hope of having comparatively safer reparative experiences rather than repetitive retraumatisation with one's partner may be rekindled.

References

Adams, K. (2006). Falling forever: the price of chronic shock. *International Journal of Group Psychotherapy, 56*(2): 127–172.

Alonso, A., & Rutan, S. (1990). Common dilemmas in combined individual and group treatment. *Group, 14*(1): 5–12.

Aron, A., Fisher, H., Mashek, D., Strong, G., Li, H., & Brown, L. (2005). Reward, motivation and emotion systems associated with early-stage intense romantic love. *Journal of Neurophysiology, 94*: 327–337.

Brok, A. (2004). Couple dynamics, group dynamics, general dynamics? The impact of group on couples and some thoughts on training for couple therapy. *Group, 28*(2): 127–141.

Buchele, B. (2000). Group psychotherapy for survivors of sexual and physical abuse. In: R. Klein & V. Schermer (Eds.), *Group Psychotherapy for Psychological Trauma* (pp. 170–187). New York: Guilford Press.

Caligor, J., Fieldsteel, N. D., & Brok, A. M. (1984). *Combining Individual and Group Therapy.* New York: Jason Aronson.

Clulow, C. (2001). Attachment theory and the therapeutic frame. In: C. Clulow (Ed.), *Adult Attachment and Couple Psychotherapy* (pp. 85–104). London: Brunner-Routledge.

Clulow, C. (2006). Couple psychotherapy and attachment theory. In: J. Scharff & D. Scharff (Eds.), *New Paradigms for Treating Relationships* (pp. 253–256). New York: Aronson.

Coché, J., & Coché, E. (1990). *Couples Group Psychotherapy: A Clinical Practice Model.* New York: Brunner Mazel.

Cozolino, L. (2002). *The Neuroscience of Psychotherapy: Building and Rebuilding the Human Brain.* New York: Norton.

Doidge, N. (2007). *The Brain That Changes Itself.* New York: Penguin.

Feld, B. (2003). Phases of couples group therapy: a consideration of therapeutic action. *Group, 27*(1): 5–19.

Feld, B. (2004). Using systems thinking to understand attachment in couple and couples group therapy. *Group, 28*(2): 127–141.

Feldman, D. (2002). Whose movie is it anyway? Unscrambling projective processes in our work and in our lives. *NYSPA Notebook, July–August*: 16–17.

Feldman, D., & Kahn, G. (2009). The integration of relationship-focused group therapy with couples treatment. *International Journal of Group Psychotherapy*, *59*(1): 109–126.

Foulkes, S. H. (1964). *Therapeutic Group Analysis*. London: Allen & Unwin.

Goldstein, S., & Thau, S. (2006). Integrating attachment theory and neuroscience in couple therapy. In: J. Scharff & D. Scharff (Eds.), *New Paradigms for Treatment Relationships* (pp. 267–277). New York: Aronson.

Groth, T., Fehm-Wolfsdorf, G., & Hahlweg, K. (2000). Basic research on the psychobiology of intimate relationships. In: K. B. Schmaling & T. G. Sher (Eds.), *The Psychology of Couples and Illness: Theory, Research, and Practice*. Washington, DC: American Psychological Association.

Harwood, I. (1996). Towards optimum group placement from the perspective of self and group experience. *Group Analysis*, *29*(2): 199–218.

Hebb, D. O. (1949). *The Organization of Behavior: A Neuropsychological Theory*. New York: Wiley.

Hendrix, H. (1988). *Getting the Love You Want: A Guide for Couples*. New York: Harper & Row.

Hendrix, H. (2006). Twenty-five years of imago: then and now. *Paper presented at the Annual Conference of Imago Relationship International*, Albuquerque, New Mexico, October 2006.

Hendrix, H., & Hunt, H. (2004). *Receiving Love: Transform Your Relationship by Letting Yourself be Loved*. New York: Atria.

Kahn, G., & Feldman, D. (2007). The utilization of separate group therapy for partners as an adjunctive modality for couples treatment. *Group*, *31*(3): 137–151.

Levenson, R. (2003). Blood, sweat and fears: the autonomic architecture of emotion. *Annals of the New York Academy of Sciences*, *1000*: 348–366.

Livingston, M. (2004). Couples within the group: dyadic interaction in group psychotherapy. *Group*, *28*(2): 87–109.

Rutan, J. S., & Stone, W. N. (1993). *Psychodynamic Group Psychotherapy*. New York: Guilford.

Scharff, J. (1992). *Projective and Introjective Identification and the Use of the Therapist's Self*. Northvale, NJ: Aronson.

Scheidlinger, S. (1974). On the concept of the "Mother Group". *International Journal of Group Psychotherapy*, *24*(4): 417–428.

Schore, A. N. (2001). The effects of relational trauma on right brain development, affect regulation, and infant mental health. *Infant Mental Health Journal*, *22*(1–2): 201–269.

Schore, A. N. (2002). Dysregulation of the right brain: a fundamental mechanism of traumatic attachment and the psychopathogenesis of posttraumatic stress disorder. *Australian & New Zealand Journal of Psychiatry, 36*(1): 9–30.

Schore, A. N. (2003). Early relational trauma, disorganized attachment, and the development of a predisposition to violence. In: M. F. Solomon & D. J. Siegel (Eds.), *Healing Trauma: Attachment, Mind, Body, and Brain* (pp. 107–167). New York: Norton.

Shelley, E., & Wood, B. (1995). Working with difficult couples. *Paper presented at the New York Association for Imago Relationship Therapy.*

Siegel, D. J. (1999). *The Developing Mind.* New York: Guilford.

Siegel, D. J. (2003). An interpersonal neurobiology of psychotherapy. The developing mind and the resolution of trauma. In: M. F. Solomon & D. J. Siegel (Eds.), *Healing Trauma: Attachment, Mind, Body, and Brain* (pp. 1–56). New York: Norton.

Siegel, D. J. (2007). *The Mindful Brain: Reflection and Attunement in the Cultivation of Well-being.* New York: Norton.

Siegel, D. J. (2008). Development, trauma, and treatment of the brain, mind, body. *Lecture presented at Mt. Sinai Medical Center, New York City,* 8–9 November.

Solomon, M. F. (2003). Connection, disruption, and repair: treating the effects of attachment trauma on intimate relationships. In: M. F. Solomon & D. J. Siegel (Eds.), *Healing Trauma: Attachment, Mind, Body, and Brain* (pp. 332–346). New York: Norton.

Stone, W. N. (1996). Self psychology and the higher mental functioning hypothesis: complementary theories. *Group Analysis, 29*(2): 169–181.

Tatkin, S. (2006). *Pseudosecure Couples.* Unpublished manuscript.

Tatkin, S. (2009). A psychobiological approach to couples therapy: integrating attachment and personality theory as interchangeable structured components. *Psychologist-Psychoanalyst* (official publication of Division 39 of the American Psychological Association), *29*(3): 7–15.

Van der Kolk, B. A. (1996). The body keeps the score: approaches to the psychobiology of posttraumatic stress disorder. In: B. A. Van der Kolk, A. C. McFarlane, & L. Weisaeth (Eds.), *Traumatic Stress: The Effects of Over Whelming Experience on Mind, Body, and Society* (pp. 214–221). New York: Guilford.

Volkan, V. D. (2001). Transgenerational transmissions and chosen traumas: an aspect of large-group identity. *Group Analysis, 34*(1): 79–97.

Woolley, J. D., Gorno-Tempini, M. L., Werner, K., Rankin, K. P., Ekman, P., Levenson, R. W., & Miller, B. L. (2004). The autonomic and behavioral profile of emotional dysregulation. *Neurology, 63*: 1740–1743.

CHAPTER NINE

A transformational learning group: inviting the implicit

Bonnie Badenoch

A s I walked into the main room at the retreat centre, about ten of the twenty-four people we were expecting were creating nests on the floor—with back jack chairs, blankets, and pillows. There was a light murmur of voices, as some were talking with one another, while others were more indrawn, awaiting what would come next. I was aware that some of the participants in this interpersonal neurobiology study group knew one another, while others were embarking on this process alone. A small Queen Anne chair stood waiting for me. I felt a moment's hesitation at being "above" the group; then realised that the environment was already supporting ease in a way that would set a tone conveying a felt sense that safety and connection might be possible no matter where I sat. We had each entered through a warm kitchen and were welcomed generously by the woman who had organised this experience. We shed our shoes, and found places for the sand trays and miniatures we had brought. Through the ample windows, we could see mid-summer flowers and the curving green lawns that surrounded our room at this rural retreat. We were going to meet together for a year to sink deeply into interpersonal neurobiology, coming together every other month for a weekend that would include exploration of concepts, always coupled with experiences to help our embodied brains take on the shape and meaning of what we were learning. These people had made quite a commitment and some had come quite a distance as well.

Why do we humans—both as participants and facilitators—move toward group experiences? What is it about our neurobiology that may call us in this way, and what might our embodied brains gain as a result? As interest in right hemisphere-centric processes has grown in the last two decades, we have found scientific roots for the claims of attachment theorists that from before birth until our last breath we are genetically inclined toward seeking connection with others (Cozolino, 2010). In early life, our interactions with those who mother us (regardless of gender or relationship) give the initial shape to the neural circuitry that contains the perceptual templates for how we believe relationships work for us (Schore, 2003; Siegel, 1999). These inner guides are as individual as our fingerprints, and whether they move us in the direction of satisfying relationships or propel us toward a series of painfully familiar encounters, the movement toward making connection is inexorable for most of us.

As we move out of the family into more diverse groups—the neighbourhood, school, circles of friends, eventually work life—this inner knowledge about the potential shapes relationships might take for us forms boundaries around what may be possible. These patterns are active in all the people in the therapeutic or educational encounter, including us, even though we therapists and teachers may not easily welcome our vulnerability into conscious awareness. One of my intentions for our meetings was not just to foster increased awareness of our own relational patterns by learning about interpersonal neurobiology, but to open to the possibility of actual change at the implicit level where our early attachment experiences are held. Because of the way we continually shape one another's neural circuitry, something was sure to happen during our long experience with one another.

Groups can be as much a hideout from vulnerability as an opening into it, especially when there is no structure that requires each person to speak regularly, so it became important to imagine ways that safe vulnerability could be invited into our midst. We began with introductions, asking each person (including me) to share a bit about him or herself (mostly a left hemisphere task), what s/he was wanting from this year (possibly a combination of right and left), any concerns or fears that might be present (potentially more in-the-moment and right-

centric), and one strength s/he brings to offer to the group (if vulnerability is arising, potentially as much a right-brain task as sensing fears).
The first two or three people gave a pretty straight-forward left-centric
offering for all the categories—exactly what is wise when waters are
unknown. However, by the fourth or fifth person, a shift began to
occur—one possibly fuelled by the interpersonal environment that
was beginning to develop. It turned out that the group members had
quite a capacity for attuned listening, and the felt sense of that began to
pervade the room. I was also consciously aware of holding openness,
curiosity, and warmth for all that was happening, making my own
contribution to the environment. How we are present or not present
shows up in our faces, voice tone, posture, gaze (Schore, 2009)—all of
which are communicated to our safety awareness system (mostly
below the level of conscious awareness). When there is this neuroception of safety (Stephen Porges' (2007) term for how we sense safety
before we perceive it), our attachment circuitry becomes available for
neural change. We had very quickly arrived at some degree of safe
vulnerability, held by the group, and my inner delight at this no doubt
expanded this a little more. The dance-like quality of this opening
where each new advance provides the fuel for someone else to take the
next steps is beautiful to experience.

This does not mean that everyone in the room was comfortable,
felt included, or was glad to be there in their heart of hearts because
such increases in vulnerability can also be frightening, especially
when they happen so quickly. By the time we had made our way
around the circle, there had been tears, laughter, people leaning into
one another as well as indrawn energies and downcast eyes—really
an increasingly full spectrum of human emotion being openly
revealed. It was clear we were on our way into the vast expanse of
attachment exploration, being touched in both our joy and sorrow.
One of the most important aspects of this early work was the intention to accept all that was coming into the room without an expecta-
tion that everyone be comfortable. Because of the omnipresent activity
of our resonance circuitry and the power generally given to the group
leader, it was especially important for me to be able to hold both the
comfort and unease with equal regard, not just as a mental exercise,
but in the actuality of my embodied experience.

To support the further opening of this non-judgmental space, we
moved into a two-part practice together. I introduced a particular

sequence of meditative experience that can expand our capacity to be present with our clients (or anyone else) by developing two kinds of neural circuitry. We may begin with a familiar breathing practice by finding ease in our bodies and then focusing our attention on the sensation of the breath in the nostrils, or the rise and fall of chest or belly, wherever our attention can most easily remain that day. When the mind wanders, which it surely will, we may bring it back with gentleness to the breath. This practice develops the circuitry of focused attention, essential for our capacity to stay with our clients and one another.

After several minutes of this practice, taking a slightly deeper breath, we may open our awareness into a bowl of receptivity, kind and non-judgmental, welcoming all that is arising within our thoughts, feelings, and bodily sensations as well as anything coming into our senses from the external world. We might experience something of this state of mind by opening our arms, a gesture that seems to happen spontaneously when I do this practice in groups. Many people report a sensation of warmth and expansion in the chest as they move from the arrow-like focus of the first part of the meditation to the second part. This practice begins to activate the circuitry of compassion as we foster a non-judgmental *relationship* with these various aspects of our experience. This sense of welcome and acceptance has elements of secure attachment within it, and if we are in this state of mind when our clients come to us, we offer them the opportunity to connect with us more quickly than if we are distracted, distant, or on guard. In our group, this practice had a twofold purpose—to develop this non-judgmental capacity on behalf of our clients, and, perhaps more importantly, to nurture a sense of care for our own inner world as a means of creating internal and external safety—one condition for increasing openness and vulnerability within the group. We would practice this along with several other kinds of meditative experience throughout our year together.

While we were going to spend time with many aspects of interpersonal neurobiology, the core for us would be implicit memory, attachment, and the multiple states of mind we could call inner community (Badenoch, 2008, 2011)—all right-centric, relational concerns. Over the last ten years, I have become convinced that this is the heart of therapy. We carry our woundedness mostly in the right hemisphere limbic region, and we heal those wounds in the rich interpersonal environment of right-to-right communication (Badenoch,

2011; Schore, 2009). Yet, left-centric therapies have dominated the last decades, and our training programs have far more of a didactic than nurturant bent to them. They are perhaps following the trend of our society, a world that has largely become dominated by left-hemisphere processes (McGilchrist, 2010). In a left-dominant world, we rely on words and concepts to know where we are, judge people by their behaviours, and find that relational concerns are secondary to the practical issues of how do I get what I want? When left dominance becomes great enough, we are cut off from the resources of empathy, attunement, connection, and presence in the moment. McGilchrist would say that we have arrived at that time as a society. No matter how much we therapists seek to remain in the relational flow, we are all touched by the culture in which we bathe every day. At the same time, if interpersonal neurobiology teaches us anything, it is that these relational qualities are at the heart of how we build one another's brains.

Getting centred in a particular perspective is an important part of the culture of a learning group, so we read McGilchrist in preparation for our first meeting. After discussing the ideas a bit, we focused on their meaning for us. Would it be possible for us to have an intention to cultivate a more right-centric view of how we wish to be in the world, as well as how this particular learning experience might unfold? We agreed that one of our tasks was to move away from the prevailing societal tide. In this group, we would be consciously cultivating right-hemisphere ears in order to truly listen to our own experience (and then the experiences of our clients). The components of implicit memory—bodily sensations, behavioural impulses, emotions, perceptions—all come to us through the gateway of the body, often arriving with a feeling of meaningfulness that is very different from what our left hemisphere guessing mind offers us. So we would be open to listening to our bodies as they whisper to us about our unfolding implicit experience. We might learn to trust that we can drop a question into the right hemisphere and simply wait for an answer to emerge (rather than shovelling around in the left). We would pour ourselves into sand trays and draw with our non-dominant hands to give our right hemispheres a way to speak directly. We might find ourselves feeling tentative, unsure, on unsteady ground, or even floating about in a sea without words—that's what it can be like when we open ourselves to the moment-to-moment processes of the right. So it became particularly important to forge strong bonds to carry us through the potential discomfort of this transition in awareness.

One central piece for this was everyone pairing up into listening partnerships for the year. This is a delicate process that already begins to stir up our attachment circuitry around the issue of chosen/not chosen. Will I play it safe and pair up with someone familiar—or take a chance on someone new? I don't know anyone here—who will want me? We spoke about this, at least bringing the potential discomfort into our group awareness so we could hold it, be with it, no matter what shape it took—and all found partners. I made the suggestion that they communicate with one another during the two-month gaps between our meetings, believing that the variability in being able to follow that suggestion might well reflect emerging attachment patterns. At every turn, we were talking about becoming more aware and holding a non-judgmental space for whatever we notice—including our inclination to be judgmental.

I do not remember a great deal about the content I offered that first day—probably a good sign since what I retained instead is the feeling of being with this deepening group. By the end of the first day, a person came to me and said, "This isn't going to be a typical training, is it?". Having come in with a few intentions and a large amount of uncertainty since I knew hardly anyone in the group, I just smiled and felt grateful. With another group of people, things might have shaped themselves quite differently. There is always a mutual adaptation between the group and the leader, especially when there is less focus on content and a less than clearly defined process in place. I had laid out rough topics for the six meetings, had right-centric aspirations for where we were going, and that was about it. I believe that the maturity and warmth of the woman who gathered this group played a role in how open the participants were, and that the retreat setting created a quiet that let us more easily move away from a left-dominant stance.

The second day of our first weekend was given over to person (as opposed to "case") consultation. I had offered guidelines for people to bring as much of a living sense of their client into our midst as possible. Instead of "fifty-six-year-old Caucasian male . . .", I suggested, "When I meet with Dan, I immediately notice that I feel warm toward him . . .". It helps so much to begin to be able to see, hear, and feel both people in the room. Because I believe that early implicit wiring is almost always at the root of the difficulties that our clients bring

(Toomey & Ecker, 2007), I requested that we hear some history, and beyond that, we would be most interested in experiencing what it is like to sit with this client. Including both therapist and client as a two-person system of equals grants respect for the truth that the implicit attachment experience is present and active in both. After the history, we would all be together with the relationship being shared, expanding the sense of being safely held in whatever might emerge next. So often, consultation has a tendency to back up and take a disinterested stance, focus on interventions and advice, and generally take the right-hemisphere life out of the encounter. Since hopefully this is not what is happening in the counselling room, this kind of consultation really does not offer much support for the actual therapeutic process.

The first person to bring her clients to us decided to sit right next to me on a little stool, and began to share about a father and son who were involved in difficulties with the law. We took a few minutes to understand the history here, both between parent and child, and particularly the father's earlier life circumstances. At an intellectual level, the difficulties made sense in light of the history. However, this particular situation was touching anger and anxiety in this therapist in ways that were difficult for her to tolerate. Seeking to keep equal regard for both father and son, she found herself instead having a great struggle to not openly align with the young man, being aware that she was no doubt telegraphing her dislike to the father. From time to time, I glanced at the group, sensing a deepening connection and intention to hold this emotional intensity for the most part, along with some discomfort shown in eyes and posture. It was a lot to hold at this early juncture.

Shifting away from the father and son, we focused on her embodied experience in this moment, and she found shame at her inability to hold them was the most present emotion. When this depth of feeling flows spontaneously in the room, what is there to do but be present, to honour its arrival? All of us have known these moments in our therapeutic lives, and there was enough strength within this budding group to feel that together and provide a safe space for this moment of deep honesty to be held. I noticed that my breathing had deepened and I was leaning closer to the brave one next to me. After a bit, she said a few more words, straightened, looked out at the room, and let us know she felt much more settled. This significant sense of letting go said to me that we had been able to be present, right hemisphere to right hemisphere, in a way that allowed her system to reorganise itself a bit. We were new at this, so there were a few suggestions about possible interventions, then a quiet voice from someone in the group saying maybe that was not so important right now. We talked a bit about how those suggestions might be more about settling our own internal stirrings than giving guidance to the therapist, and how that is a legitimate need we have at times.

Two more people brought their clients that day, and thanks to what unfolded with the first person, we had a paradigm for working deep in the implicit experience of the therapist. Several who have presented over the months have said that their moments of presentation have changed them in some profound ways. I did not craft this, did not necessarily expect it, was open to it when it arrived, and grateful for it when we were finished each day. Why might it have happened this way? Complexity theory—both our individual brains and groups of brains are complex systems—says that initial conditions and organising principles will create parameters that will influence how the unpredictable chaos unfolds along the way. Even in the introductions, together we had found our way toward deeper seeing, made some sort of agreement that we were setting sail for uncharted right-centric waters, and would explore ways to stick together through it all. As we parted from the first weekend, we each shared a word about where we were in that moment. Words such as grateful, tired, full, and unsettled dropped into the respectful silence as we each held one another right where we were.

I came away from that weekend filled with a quiet sense of something important happening, and returned two months later with even fewer notes for what I might say and a greater sense of following whatever might come into the room. I did have the intention that we would continue to revisit our previous experiences so they might deepen, a rough intention to stay in the territory of attachment the second weekend, and quite a bit of confidence that the group would find its trajectory within that.

I want to offer a few moments from the three weekends that followed, and also say that we have two more meetings in this series before we end in May. I can barely imagine where we will be at that time. At our third gathering, it felt important to focus more directly—from a right-centric place—on what was evolving in the listening partnerships. In our second meeting, we had worked with attachment, exploring at a felt sense level the multiple flows of attachment relationships within ourselves. After I did some traditional teaching about the neurobiology of the different styles, we worked toward deeper awareness using reflection, conversation, and sand tray work— unfolding in both the larger group and between listening partners.

Whatever was touched in this work seemed bound to find some expression also in these burgeoning one-on-one relationships. For some, this might mean less contact/more avoidance. For others, possibly more seeking proximity and reassurance, and likely some push and pull between partners with different styles. We talked about how these attachment echoes might begin to appear so that there was a greater chance of partners being able to reflect on what was emerging in the relationship without judgment, with tenderness, respect, open curiosity, and support.

When we came together for our third meeting, I considered approaching these listening partnerships through conversation, but in opening to receive from the group what it might need, a different plan emerged in my mind. We all brought sand tray miniatures with us (including me), and these were available for all to use. I asked each person to wander about the figures and find two with which they resonated at a bodily, felt sense level without being too concerned about the meaning or how they might be used. Coming back into the room, the partners settled together and allowed their figures to interact. For at least thirty minutes, these scenes unfolded on the floor, shifting, changing—laughter, tears, deep gazing, shyness—such a full spectrum of human responsiveness as the partnerships deepened from the outer manifestation into the meaningful inner layers of their relatedness. I was sitting nearby and had, for the first time, the sense of not being needed, in the good way that a parent might feel as she sees her children flowing in their own unfolding.

The remainder of that weekend was devoted to exploring how we might be more aware of implicit memory in ourselves and our clients. The specifics seem less important to me at this distance than how we arrived at a place where the experience of "rest" became central to our work. As we checked in with one another with a word about where we were in the moment on a regular basis, it became clear that we were working very hard at deep levels within our implicit flow. As important as it is to move into these areas so that we can be as mentally healthy as possible, time for settling and integration is equally needed. To satisfy this growing sense, we began the practice of rest. To say that the group took it up eagerly would be an understatement. It was as though our systems had been just waiting for someone to offer the possibility—to sit restfully together, nowhere to go, nothing to do. As soon as it was clear that we were able to do this, it became part of our between-sessions practice as well. When I returned home, I sent out whatever poetry we might have shared during the weekend, and a reminder to do nothing further with whatever we had explored except allow it to have its own natural path of integration within our broader brains and minds—a period of respectful and delicious rest. Then, about a month before our next meeting, I sent out suggestions for possible reading and reflection for the next time. We had found a rhythm that worked for us.

So now we arrive at the fourth weekend. One of our commitments was to always loop back to prior themes and see how we are integrating them. So far, we had spent a good deal of time with attachment and implicit memory. Early in our day, I asked people to sit for a moment and drop this question into their right hemispheres: What is the attachment style of the parent who was most influential for you? We did not define the term influential, trusting our right hemispheres to sense what was needed. When asking the right to reveal the implicit knowing that it holds, our job is to quiet the left a bit—and wait. When the right arrives with one possible answer to that question, most often it has a quality of meaningfulness that is very different from the guesses made by the left.

Then, using a process known as a spectrogram (Kole, 1967), borrowed from my very good friend who is a psychodrama matriarch, the group placed itself along a line according to the answer heard inside—secure, ambivalent, avoidant, disorganised. The groups sat down together and began a conversation about how it had been for them to grow up with that parent. As I wandered from group to group, I saw a remarkable experience unfold. In relationship with one another, the group manifested the essence of the parental attachment style. Those who identified themselves as secure talked easily, with a broad range of emotions that included laughter and smiles. Those who had experienced ambivalence had some hesitation at the beginning, perhaps unsure about how to begin, about the expectations, but then easily moved into sharing deeply about the quality of their experience. Heads began to nod in agreement as each person spoke, with many leaning forward into a greater closeness. Most striking was the group of those who had experienced the quiet emotional emptiness of avoidance. For a number of minutes, they sat facing one another in silence. I was so touched by the visceral depth of this manifestation of the felt sense essence of their childhoods. When they did begin to talk, there was a great deal of respect for one another's childhood pain. The group who had endured the fragmentation of disorganisation as part of their early lives looked most sombre, but also had smiles of encouragement for one another. As I stood near them, there was a deeper feeling of sorrow, a heaviness. When I asked how they were doing, one member said, "Sobbing or numbing". At the end of this experience, a number of people said they felt they had forged new bonds within the group. A few who were not in the secure group owned feelings of jealousy for "the secures". Then we were reminded that this was not about our own attachment style, but that of our parents, and all in the secure group had had a second parent who had left them with different struggles, too.

As we moved on through the day, it became apparent that we were experiencing a new depth of stillness in our meditations together, and a greater ability to use our right-hemisphere awareness to flow toward our inner world. A number of people shared that their sand tray experience was flowing differently, without so much commentary and questioning from the left. The "people" consultations that weekend brought us experiences along a broad range of how we might be most empathic with one another. For one woman, the best support (in addition to abundant holding of her experience) was the expertise in the room as she faced an agonising and complex situation with a family. The combination of being seen, known, and held in her sense of overwhelm, accompanied by several viewpoints on how to approach the complexity, supported the needs of both her hemispheres—how to be with herself and these families, and how to think about what to do next.

One of the men in the group, who shared his experience with a client whose combination of brain injury and trauma might mean she would never show significant progress, needed most to be held in his implicit sense of sorrow and frustration, as he began to imagine what it might be like to sit with this person for the next five years. Is it possible that sometimes our best gift is to be a source of stability and support each week even when the kind of measurable change we have grown accustomed to expect may never manifest? Can we stay engaged without "progress" as our left hemisphere knows it?

Another of the women in the group chose to bring her own inner world into her presentation time, asking us to sit with her as she explored the depth of activation she experiences with a particular client. This unfolded more as a therapy session, yet clearly related to how she will be able to bring her implicit resources to this client the next time they meet. As this group has become more interwoven, our holding capacity—one clear sign of increasing neural integration—has grown broader and deeper. What I take away from these experiences is the sense that together we have forged an environment in which the core implicit experience emerging in us in relationship with our clients is welcome, held, and to some degree transformed.

Why do we humans—both as participants and facilitators—move toward group experiences? What is it about our neurobiology that may call us in this way, and what might our embodied brains gain as a result? At a core biological level, we are moved toward making connections with others by our hardwired need for the most responsive attachment experiences we can find. At an implicit level, we may sense that we are less vulnerable in a group than in an individual relationship or we may have had the heart-filling and brain-building experience of being held by a group before. In either case, there is at least some possibility of being seen, known, and held in ways that are broad, deep, and substantial. Within the variety of relationships present in any group, much may be called to the surface, and when one of the organising principles is the embodied practice of non-judgmental acceptance, the path toward transformation can open. I place myself within the context of groups regularly because seeing the light of growing awareness spark in one pair of eyes and then spread to another fills me with joy.

As I am writing this, I am aware that I cannot lay out any principles for others to follow about organising learning groups. If I were to do another year-long training, it would probably have more differences than similarities. It would be tempting to try to craft a similar experience since this one is being so rich and useful, but that would violate first principles—what does this new group need? How will it organise itself around the setting, the people, my intentions, the participants' intentions, the way our brains are structured to form relationships and offer empathy? What about the cultural expectations of a different part of the country? So all I will be able to do is show up with my convictions and intentions—and sand tray figures—stay open and willing, stand firm on what I understand about the relational brain, and enter the waters with another group.

References

Badenoch, B. (2008). *Being a Brain-wise Therapist: A Practical Guide to Interpersonal Neurobiology.* New York: Norton.

Badenoch, B. (2011). *The Brain-savvy Therapist's Workbook.* New York: Norton.

Cozolino, L. (2010). *The Neuroscience of Psychotherapy: Healing the Social Brain.* New York: Norton.

Kole, D. M. (1967). The spectrogram in psychodrama. *Group Psychotherapy, XX*(1–2).

McGilchrist, I. (2010). *The Master and His Emissary: The Divided Brain and the Making of the Western World.* London: Yale University Press.

Porges, S. W. (2007). The polyvagal perspective. *Biological Psychology, 74*(2): 116–143.

Schore, A. N. (2003). *Affect Dysregulation and Disorders of the Self.* New York: Norton.

Schore, A. N. (2009). Right brain affect regulation: an essential mechanism of development, trauma, dissociation, and psychotherapy. In: D. Fosha, D. J. Siegel, & M. Solomon (Eds.), *The Healing Power of Emotion: Affective Neuroscience, Development, and Clinical Practice* (pp. 112–144). New York: Norton.

Siegel, D. J. (1999). *The Developing Mind: How Relationship and the Brain Interact to Shape Who We Are.* New York: Guilford Press.

Toomey, B., & Ecker, B. (2007). Of neurons and knowings: constructivism, coherence psychology and their neurodynamic substrates. *Journal of Constructivist Psychology, 20*(3): 201–245 [doi:10.1080/10720530701347860].

INDEX

abuse, 125, 127, 140, 142, 165, 174
  childhood, 173
  physical, 139
  sexual, 139
  substance, 34
Adams, K., 172, 185
Adler, M. G., 163, 168
Adult Attachment Interview (AAI), 57
Agazarian, Y. M., xxiii, 31, 33, 46, 79, 82–83, 85, 88, 92–96, 98–99, 102, 158, 169
Ahola, P., 52, 70
Ainsworth, M. D. S., 53, 68
Alberini, C. M., 11, 21
Alcoholics Anonymous, 40
Alonso, A., 56, 70, 178, 185
Alpert, N. M., 87, 101
Amini, F., 53–54, 58–60, 62, 65, 67, 70
amygdala, xxi, 4–5, 9, 13, 15, 52, 76, 78, 86–88, 91–93, 113, 147–148, 156, 159, 175

Andersen, P., 45–46
Anderson, A. K., 156, 169
Anen, C., 66, 70
anger, 14, 35, 39, 83, 89, 93, 95–96, 104, 119, 126, 129–130, 132, 142, 157, 164–165, 176, 195
Anthony, E. J., 26, 38, 47
anxiety, 8–9, 60, 79–81, 83–88, 91–92, 95–96, 107, 112, 117–118, 131, 147, 195
  chronic, 87
  disorder, 85, 87
Archimedes, 46
Aron, A., 118, 121, 174, 185
Asch, S. E., 81, 98
Atkinson, B., 104–107, 112, 121
attachment, xxi, xxiii, 27, 30, 52–55, 57–59, 62, 65–67, 106–108, 139, 149, 153, 159, 167, 172, 192, 196, 198
  adult, 55
  attuned, 1
  avoidant-, 74, 91

behaviour, 3, 30, 58
bond, 55–56, 59, 65
childhood, 11, 175
circuits, 75, 191, 194
communications, 152
disorganised, 173
early, 53
echoes, 197
emotional, 62
experience, 56, 65, 106, 143, 190, 195, 200
exploration, 191
failure, 90
figures, 55, 107, 138
good-enough, 91
insecure, 53, 105–107, 174
issues, 78, 91, 124, 139
loss of, 107
pattern, 62, 65, 74, 77, 92, 194
perspective, 61, 106
poor, 15
primary, 30
problems, 175
process, 75
relationship, 54, 62, 65, 67, 75, 124, 197
repetitive, 67
role, 91
ruptures, 172
secure, 7, 17, 52, 55–56, 58–60, 157, 176, 192
status, 57
style, 53, 198–199
system, 4, 52, 90
theory, xxiii–xxiv, 3, 52–55, 57–58, 61, 65, 68, 105–108, 116, 150, 190
trauma(tic), 172, 174
wounds, 171

Badenoch, B., xxi–xxii, xx, 2–7, 11, 14, 21, 73–74, 76, 78, 96–98, 127, 144, 155, 157, 159, 163, 168, 192–193, 201
Banks, W. C., 81, 99
Bargh, J. A., 78, 99
Baxter, L. R., 52, 72

Bean, J., 156, 169
behaviour(al), xxiii, 5, 8, 12–13, 17, 25, 29, 31–33, 37, 39, 41, 44, 55, 61, 66, 76, 109–111, 113–115, 118, 120, 125, 127, 133–134, 149, 157, 161, 168, 173, 193 see also: attachment, cognitive
aggressive, 129
avoidant, 112
care-giving, 66
care-seeking, 66
change, 3, 106, 149
chaotic, 20
combative, 112
cooperative, 30
defiant, 134
distancing, 108
immature, 55
impulse, 4–5, 8, 76, 150, 193
inauthentic, 179
input, 114
joining, 118
leadership, 41
mirroring, 136
moral, xxi
overt, 56, 68
patterns, 134
perceived, 25
primary, 52
primate, 30
problem-solving, 114
proximity-seeking, 138
reactivity, 2
response, 173–174
rules of, 61
social, 29–30, 43, 45
theory, 104
transparent, 63
Benson, H., 74, 94, 100
Berns, G. S., 58, 60, 66, 68, 81, 98
Bieling, P., 52, 70
Bion, W. R., xix, xxv, 31–32, 46
Birbaumer, N., 51, 69
Birdwhistell, L., 45–46
Blakeslee, S., 97, 99
Bowen, M., 111, 121

Bowlby, J., 30, 46, 52–55, 61, 67, 69, 106, 121, 151–152, 167–168
Brakefield, T., 11, 23
Braun, C., 51, 69
Brefczynski-Lewis, J., 14, 22
Brody, A. L., 52, 72
Brok, A. M., 173, 179–180, 185, 207
Brown, L., 118, 121, 174, 185
Bruschweilerstern, N., 59–60, 72
Bryant, F. B., 163, 168
Buchele, B., 56, 69, 174, 185
Bullrich, S., 85, 100
Burger, J. M., 81, 99
Burlingame, G. M., xx, xxv

Caligor, J., 179, 207
Camerer, C. F., 66, 70
Canli, T., 85, 99
Cannistraro, P. A., 87, 101
Carr, L. M., 11, 21, 28, 46
Carson, M. A., 87, 101
Cavanagh, S. R., 87, 101
Chappelow, J., 81, 98
Chartrand, T. L., 78, 99
clinical examples
    Alan, 136–138
    Andrew, 57–58
    Barb, 180–183
    Brenda, 119–120
    Helene, 131, 138
    Jack, 119–120
    John, 7–9, 11, 89, 95
    Lester, 181–183
    Lisa, 164–166
    Mark, 63–64, 162
    Mary, 180, 182–183
    Nate, 132–133
    Ned, 180–183
    Patrick, 124–125, 129–131, 138
    Paul, 140–142
    Sheila, 142–143
    Stan, 139–140
Clulow, C., 175, 185
Coché, E., 103, 121, 174, 185
Coché, J., 103, 121, 174, 185

cognitive, xxi, 6, 28, 46, 82, 108, 128, 148, 150, 156–157
    abilities, 108
    answers, 143
    appraisal, 55
    behavioural therapy, 68
    closure, 14
    distortions, 143
    experiences, 167
    flooding, 183
    functioning, 108
    interpretations, 44
    learning, 127
    mapper, 5
    meta-, 156
    patterns, 138
    pre-, 29–30, 32
    process(ing), 57, 76
    psychologist, 30
    resources, 163
    science, 52
    skills, 108, 116
    verbal-, 41
    work, 88
Cohen, B. D., 38, 40, 47
Cohn, J. F., 90, 99
Combs, A., 12, 22
conscious(ness), 3, 6–7, 10, 12, 14, 32, 41, 63, 94, 111, 153, 165, 193
    see also: self, unconscious(ness)
    agent, 32
    choice, 13, 127
    decision, 10
    embodied, 15
    immediate, 41
    integration of, 12–13
    level, 7
    non-, 32, 34, 37, 45, 75, 148, 150, 154–155, 166
    recall, 61
    recognition, 106
    relationship, 177
    awareness, 2, 4, 7–8, 84, 92, 126, 151, 155, 164, 190–191
Cook, E. W. III, 51, 71

Corner, M. A., 12, 23
Cortina, M., 53, 61, 69
countertransference, 41, 167 *see also*:
    transference
    reactions, 39
Cox, P., 147, 155, 157, 159, 163,
    168–169
Cozolino, L., xx–xxi, xxv, 2, 21, 26, 30,
    44, 47, 53, 55, 59, 69, 74–75,
    77–78, 86, 97, 99, 148, 150, 169,
    179, 185, 190, 201
Crago, J., 51, 71
Craighero, L., 28, 48

Damasio, A., 27, 31, 47, 153, 169
Dascola, I., 28, 49
Davidson, R. J., 3, 14, 22
de Maré, P. B., 98–99
Denninger, J. W., 59, 65, 69
Desmond, J. E., 85, 99
development(al), xxiii–xxiv, 30, 33,
    61, 74, 79–80, 83, 91, 94, 97, 114,
    124, 156, 163, 167, 171, 174
    see also: regulation
    achievement, 56
    brain, xix–xxi, 3–4, 6, 74, 152
    child, 53–54
    disorder, 29
    early, 55, 67, 75, 77, 174
    function, 56
    human, 90
    interpersonal, xxii
    natural, 17
    ongoing, xx
    personal, 56
    phenomena, 53, 55
    relationship, 111
    skill, 44
    step, 5
    theory, 53, 149
De Waal, F., 29, 47
Dewey, J., 33, 47
Diamond, N., 54–55, 61, 69
Diego, M., 3, 22
Dilthey, W., 44, 47
disorders *see also*: development

anxiety, 85
    mental, 27
    personality, 43
    psychiatric, 28, 42–43, 45
Doherty, W., 104, 121
Doidge, M., 58, 65, 67, 69, 184–185
Dougherty, D. D., 87, 101
Dubeau, M. C., 11, 21, 28, 46
Durkheim, E., 73, 99
Durkin, H., 33, 47
Durkin, J. E., 33, 47
Dusek, J. A., 74, 94, 100

Ecker, B., 2, 5–7, 11, 16, 21, 23, 195,
    201
Edelman, G., 27, 47
Eisler, R., 66, 69
Ekman, P., 174, 187
Elbert, T., 51, 69
environment(al), 2, 12, 26, 58–59, 66,
    90, 93, 116, 129–130, 137, 142,
    160, 189, 191–192, 200
    accepting, 17
    calm, 128
    controlled, 59
    empathic, 6, 66
    enriched, 58–60
    family, 124
    frightening, 125
    group, 56, 58–59, 82, 84, 131, 138,
        152
    holding, 1, 155, 161, 168
    influences, 65
    interpersonal, 1, 58, 191
    safe, 8, 59, 179
    secure, 92
    social, 147, 174
    therapeutic, 60
    traumatic, 124
Erikson, E. H., 163, 169
Ettin, M. F., 40, 47

FACES (Flexible, Adaptive,
    Coherent, Energised, and
    Stable), 12–13
Fadigia, L., 28, 47

Fagley, N. S., 163, 168
Farb, N. A. S., 156, 169
Fehm-Wolfsdorf, G., 175, 186
Feld, B., 103, 107, 121, 173, 176, 185
Feldman, D. B., 39, 47, 176–177, 183,
    185–186
Ferguson, D., 105, 109, 121
Ferrari, P. F., 78, 99
Ferrett, D. I., 29, 49
Fidler, J. W., 40, 47
Field, T., 3, 22
Fieldsteel, N. D., 179, 207
Fischer, H., 52, 69
Fischl, B., 74, 94, 100
Fischman, A. J., 87, 101
Fisher, H., 118, 121, 174, 185
Fisher, J., 140, 144
Flores, P., 53, 69, 150, 169
Fogassi, L., 28, 47, 78, 99
Fonagy, P., 52, 55–57, 61, 69
Fosshage, J. L., 55, 70
Foulkes, S. H., 26, 31, 38, 47, 184, 186
Framo, J., 103, 121
Fredrikson, M., 52, 69
Freud, S., xix, 30, 33, 47
Friedel, R., 51, 72
functional magnetic resonance
    imaging (fMRI), 26, 28, 44, 52, 81
Furmark, T., 52, 69

Gabrieli, J. D. E., 85, 99
Gage, F. H., 58, 70, 74, 93, 99, 102
Gallese, V., 28–29, 43, 47, 78, 99
Gandhi, M., 41
Gans, J. S., 56, 70
Gantt, S. P., xxiii, 83, 85, 98–99, 147,
    158, 169
Garson, C., 52, 70
Gast, D., 58, 70
Gergely, G., 52, 55–57, 61, 69
Gianino, A., 56, 72
Glover, G., 85, 99
Goldapple, K., 52, 70
Goldman, A., 28, 47
Goldstein, B., 140, 144
Goldstein, S., 175, 186

Goleman, D., 36, 48, 87, 99, 108, 121,
    148, 169
Gorno-Tempini, M. L., 174, 187
Gottman, J., 104–105, 111–113, 121
Graf, P., 114, 122
Gray, J., 74, 94, 100
Greenberg, L. S., 75, 99
Greischar, L. L., 3, 22
Greve, D., 74, 94, 100
Groth, T., 175, 186
Gurman, A., 104, 121

Hahlweg, K., 175, 186
Haney, C., 81, 99
Harrison, A. M., 59–60, 72
Hartzell, M., 4, 7, 17, 23, 75, 77, 102
Harwood, I., 177, 186
Hawkins, J., 97, 99
Heard, D., 90, 99
Hebb, D., 27, 48, 67, 70, 74, 100, 111,
    120–121, 184, 186
Hendrix, H., 172, 176–177, 186
Herman, J., 107, 122
Hernandez-Reif, M., 3, 22
Hesse, E., 53, 71
Higgitt, A., 57, 69
Hintikka, J., 52, 70
hippocampus, xxi, 5, 13, 15–16, 52,
    60, 74, 76–78, 93, 175
Ho, B. S., 52, 72
Hobson, J. A., 11, 23
Horwitz, L., 83, 100
Hume, D., 33, 48
Hunt, H., 176, 186
Huonker, R., 51, 72
Husserl, E., 33, 48

Iacoboni, M., xxi, xxv, 3, 11, 15,
    21–22, 25, 27–29, 33, 40, 42, 46,
    48, 78, 91, 100, 126, 144, 148,
    150–151, 154, 162–163, 167, 169
identification, 26, 29–31, 37–38, 44,
    61, 153, 156, 166, 176
    counter-, 35
    process, 157
Insel, T. R., 51, 70

inter subjectivity, 28–29, 38, 61, 168
interpersonal neurobiology (IPNB),
    xix–xxiii, 2–3, 18–21, 68, 73–74,
    76, 78, 81, 92, 98, 147, 149, 175,
    189–190, 192–193
intervention, 38–40, 109, 124–125,
    139, 157, 159, 195–196
    active, 35
    clinical, 27
    creative, 37
    early, 76
    educational, 157
    group, 103
    helpful, 36
    periodic, 35
    psychological, 52
    psychotherapy, 137
    therapeutic, 138

Jacobson, N., 104, 121
James, W., 33, 48
Janis, I. L., 81, 100
Joensuu, M., 52, 70
Johnson, S., 105–107, 112, 121, 150,
    153, 167, 169
Johnstone, T., 14, 22
Jurist, E. L., 52, 55–57, 61, 69

Kabat-Zinn, J., 149, 168–169
Kahn, G. B., 39, 47, 176–177, 186
Kandel, E. R., 73, 100
Karterud, S., 32, 48
Kasparov, G., 61, 70
Kay, J., 52, 70
Kempermann, G., 58, 70
Kennedy, S., 52, 70
Kerr, C., 74, 94, 100
King, D. B., 33, 48
King, M. L., 41
King-Casas, B., 66, 70
Kohut, H., 38, 48, 54, 67, 70, 167, 169
Kole, D. M., 198, 201
Kossmann, M. R., 85, 100
Krangel, T. S., 87, 101
Krystal, H., 139, 144
Kurtz, R., 143–144

Lacan, J., 153, 169
Lachmann, F. M., 55, 70
LaFrance, M., 29, 48
Lake, B., 90, 99
Langstrom, B., 52, 69
Lannon, R., 53–54, 58–60, 62, 65, 67,
    70
Lasko, N. B., 87, 101
Lau, M., 52, 70
Lawrence, W. G., 40, 48
Lazar, S., 74, 94, 100
LeDoux, J., 9, 22, 86–87, 100, 108, 111,
    113, 115–116, 120–121
Lehto, S. M., 52, 70
Lenzi, G. L., 11, 21, 28, 46
Leszcz, M., 56, 72
Letonen, J., 52, 70
Levenson, R. W., 173–174, 186–187
Levine, D. S., 66, 69
Lewin, K., 31, 33, 48
Lewis, J. M., 55, 70
Lewis, T., 53–54, 58–60, 62, 65, 67,
    70
Li, H., 118, 121, 174, 185
Lichtenberg, J. D., 35, 48, 55, 70
limbic, 9, 75–78, 88, 94
    area, 5, 76–77
    arousal, 147–148, 159, 165
    circuits, 8, 96
    connections, 16, 77
    integration, 88
    level, 61–62
    longing, xxiv
    region, xxi, 2, 4–5, 7, 15–16, 74,
        77–78, 87, 94, 192
    resonance, 62
    response, 93
    stimulation, 164
    system, 4, 9, 40, 52, 62, 86, 91
Livingston, M., 177, 179–180, 186
Locke, J., 33, 48
Lopes DaSilva, F. H., 12, 23
LoPiccolo, J., 104, 121
LoPiccolo, L., 104, 121
Lutz, A., 3, 14, 22
Lyons-Ruth, K., 59–60, 72

MacKenzie, K. R., xx, xxv
Macklin, M. L., 87, 101
Maidment, R. N., 52, 72
Main, M., 53, 57, 71
Mandela, N., 41
Marett, K., 103, 122
Mark-Goldstein, B., 130, 144
Marrone, M., 53–55, 61, 69
Marteinsdottir, I., 52, 69
Martin-Skurski, M. E., 81, 98
Martis, B., 87, 101
Mashek, D., 118, 121, 174, 185
Mayberg, H., 52, 70, 156, 169
Mazziotta, J. C., 11, 21, 28, 46
McCarthy, B., 118, 122
McCarthy, E., 118, 122
McCluskey, U., 66, 71, 90, 100
McDougall, W., 73, 100
McGarvey, M., 74, 94, 100
McGilchrist, I., 77–78, 100, 193, 201
McKeon, D., 156, 169
McMullin, K., 87, 101
McNaughton, B. L., 74, 102
Meade, G. H., 33, 48
Meares, R., 57, 71
Medina, J., 59, 71
memory, 4–6, 9, 11–13, 15–16, 25, 28,
        55, 60–62, 76, 148, 150, 159, 175
    autobiographical, xxii, 3, 5
    coherent, 77
    emotional, 62, 65
    explicit, xxi, 5–7, 13, 15, 77, 114,
        149, 164
    implicit, xxi–xxii, 3–9, 11, 15–16,
        61–62, 76, 94, 114, 152,
        155–156, 162, 164–165, 174,
        192–193, 197–198
    long-term, 1
    procedural, 59
    retrieval, xxi
    rote, 62
Menning, H., 74, 100
Merleau-Ponty, M., 25–26, 32–33, 48
Metzger, L. J., 87, 101
Mikulincer, M., 52–53, 71
Milgram, S., 81, 100

Miller, B. L., 174, 187
Milner, P., 27, 48
Miltner, W. H. R., 51, 72
Minton, K., 74, 101, 123, 128, 133, 135,
        145
mirror
    neurons, xxi–xxiii, 3, 11, 14, 25–46,
        66, 78, 91, 126, 148, 150, 154,
        160, 162–163
    reflecting, 26
    systems, 26–27, 31, 35, 39
mirroring, 26, 30–31, 35–40, 42, 44, 46,
        93, 131, 141–143, 148, 152, 155,
        172, 177, 180
    behaviours, 136
    game, 36
    healthy, 38
    human, 26
    non-verbal, 36
    pre-verbal, 37
    process, 37, 44–45
    properties, 26
    response, 36
    techniques, 44
Mitra, M., 12, 23
Molnar, M., 12, 23
Montague, P. R., 66, 70
Moore, C. I., 74, 94, 100
Moreno, J. K., 83, 100
Morgan, A. C., 59–60, 72
Morris, D., 51, 71
mother, 3–4, 15–18, 29, 38, 59, 129,
        136, 138, 140, 190
    attunement, 38
    group, 179
    harsh, 15
    –infant
        interactions, 29, 175
        research, 38
Muran, J. C., 54, 56, 71

Nader, K., 11, 22
Navaro, L., 161, 169
Neff, K. D., 14, 22
neuroplasticity, 2–3, 68, 73–74, 76, 82,
        111, 120, 148–149, 161, 174

Niskanen, L., 52, 70
Norcross, J. C., 54, 56, 59, 71
Nuhum, J. P., 59–60, 72

object, 173 *see also*: self
    lesson, 43
    relations, 54, 104, 176
    representations, 55–56
    safe, 166
objective/objectivity, 34, 37, 41, 141
    information, 38
Ogden, P., 74, 101, 123, 126–128, 133,
    135, 138, 140–141, 144–145
Olds, J., 27, 48
Oossiota, A., 52, 69
Ormont, L., 56, 71
Orr, S. P., 87, 101

Pagnoni, G., 81, 98
Pain, C., 74, 101, 123, 128, 133, 135,
    145
Panksepp, J., 74, 101, 104–106, 112,
    122
Pantev, C., 74, 100
Pavlov, I. P., 27, 33, 48
Pearlman, L. A., 42, 48
Perry, C., 107, 122
Peters, P. M., 87, 101
Peters, R., 31, 46
Pines, M., 26, 48
Piper, R., 98–99
Pitman, R. K., 87, 101
Porges, S. W., xxi, xxv, 10, 22, 74,
    84–86, 101, 158, 169, 191, 201
post-traumatic stress disorder
    (PTSD), 7–8, 43, 87, 139
Prigogine, I., 12, 22

Quartz, S. R., 66, 70–71
Quinn, B. T., 74, 94, 100
Quirion, R., 51, 70

Rankin, K. P., 174, 187
Ratey, J. J., 53, 58–60, 62, 65, 71
Rauch, S. L., 74, 87, 94, 100–101
Rawlings, N. B., 3, 22

relationship-focused group therapy
    (RFGT), 171, 176–179, 184
Rholes, W., 107, 122
Ricard, M., 3, 22
Richards, J., 81, 98
Riggio, L., 28, 49
Rizzolatti, G., 28, 47–49, 51, 66, 71, 78,
    99
Roberts, L. E., 74, 100
Robertson, R., 12, 22
Rouchy, J. C., 30, 49
Rutan, J. S., 56, 60, 71, 176, 178,
    185–186

Saakvitne, K. W., 42, 48
Saarinen, P. I., 52, 70
Sabbatini, R., 45, 49
Safran, J. D., 54, 56, 71
Sander, L. W., 59–60, 72
Sapolsky, R., 59–60, 66–67, 71, 108,
    112, 122
Saxena, S., 52, 72
Schachter, D., 114, 122
Scharff, D., 104, 122
Scharff, J., 104, 122, 172, 186
Scheidlinger, S., 38, 49, 179, 186
Schermer, V. L., 151, 154, 169
Schmidt, L., 51, 72
Schnarch, D., 104, 122
Schore, A. N., xx–xxi, xxv, 1–2, 4, 6–7,
    22, 27, 49, 53–54, 56, 72, 74–75,
    77–78, 89, 92, 97, 101, 128–129,
    145, 148, 150–152, 154, 166–168,
    170, 174–175, 184, 186–187,
    190–191, 193, 201
Schore, J. R., 124, 145, 150–152, 154,
    166–168, 170
Schweizer, R., 51, 69
Segal, Z. V., 156, 169
Sejnowski, T. J., 66, 71
self, 5, 13–14, 21, 29, 31, 33–36, 38, 41,
    44, 56–57, 82, 91, 93, 106, 112,
    123–124, 126, 142, 156, 162, 168,
    173, 183
    -acceptance, 163
    -assertion, 126, 161

authentic, 164
-awareness, 14, 45, 96, 138, 159, 168
-care, 149
-compassion, 3, 14, 149, 163
-concept, 149
-conscious(ness), 14, 29, 163
-contract, 118
-defeating, 107
-defend, 113
-destructive, 111
-development, 45
-efficacy, 149
emotional, 156
-esteem, 14, 55
-evaluative, 111, 149
-experience, 45
false, 179
-function, 57
group, 32
-growth, 138
-harm, 125
-hood, 31
-image, 31, 55
implicit, 89, 128, 152
-initiated, 32
-insight, 42
-narrative, 57, 149
-object, 55, 179
-observe, 108, 116, 125, 184
-organisation, 21, 33, 44
-organising, 12
-other, 28, 31
-perpetuating, 53
-preoccupied, 37
-protective, 107, 116
-psychological, 38
-psychology, 54, 176
-receptive, 163
-reflective, 56, 135–138
-regulation, 16, 75, 126, 144, 149,
    152, 158, 160, 178
-righteous, 64
-rumination, 14
sense of, 31, 144
-soothe, 105, 158
-state, 155, 159, 163

-systems, 35, 128
-understanding, 38
-worth, 14
shame, xx, 3, 7–8, 17, 110, 131, 149,
    152, 157–160, 162–163, 166, 195
Shannon, C. E., 94, 101
Shaver, P. R., 52–53, 71
Shelley, E., 172, 187
Shin, L. M., 87, 101
Siegel, D. J., xx–xxii, xxv, 1–5, 7,
    11–15, 17, 19–23, 27, 49, 53–56,
    59, 65, 72, 74–75, 77–78, 80, 86,
    89, 94, 97, 102, 114, 122, 125–128,
    130, 144–145, 148, 150, 155,
    157–162, 168, 170, 172, 174–176,
    184, 187, 190, 201
Silver, N., 113, 121
Simon, A., 94, 102
Simpson, J., 107, 122
Sinigaglia, C., 51, 66, 71
Skinner, J. E., 12, 23
Solomon, M. F., 175, 187
Song, H., 74, 102
Spitz, H., 103, 122
splitting, 7–8, 92, 96, 116, 179
Spotnitz, H., 35, 49
Sroufe, L. A., 53, 72
Stacey, R., 31, 49
Steele, H., 57, 69
Steele, M., 57, 69
Stengers, I., 12, 22
Stern, D. N., 38, 49, 53–54, 59–60, 72
Stevens, C. E., 74, 102
Stickgold, R., 11, 23
Stone, W. N., 32, 38, 48–49, 56, 71,
    176, 179, 186–187
Strauss, B., xx, xxv
Strong, G., 118, 121, 174, 185
Stuart, R., 104, 122
subject(s), 33, 52, 60, 66, 109
    depressed, 52
subjective see also: inter-subjectivity
    change, 184
    experience, 3, 12, 147, 154, 179–180
    feeling, 21
    sense, 17

state, 29, 148, 156, 158
understanding, 183
Suddendorf, T., 29, 49
Sulloway, F. G., 45, 49
Symington, J., 32, 49
Symington, N., 32, 49

Target, M., 52, 55–57, 61, 69
Tatkin, S., 173, 184, 187
Taub, E., 51, 69, 71–72
Taylor, J. G., 12, 23
Terrazas, A., 74, 102
Thau, S., 175, 186
Thompson, S., 98–99
Tihonen, J., 52, 70
Tillfors, M., 52, 69
Tomasello, M., 6, 23
Tomlin, D., 66, 70
Toomey, B., 2, 5–7, 11, 16, 21, 23, 195, 201
transference, 179 see also: countertransference
distortions, 177, 179
multi-, 180
resistance, 35
spousal, 178
transferential, 178
conflicts, 172
counter-, 172
reactivity, 184
trauma(tic), 6, 11, 15, 93, 106–107, 125, 138–139, 150, 154, 165, 174, 183, 185, 199 see also: attachment, post-traumatic stress disorder
brain, 43
collective, 42
environment, 124
events, 106, 139, 174
experience, 107
-focus, 8
group, 9
medical, 138
memories, 8, 11
mini-, 42
minor, 172
original, 139

overt, 11
psychological, 43
reactions, 42
related, 107, 139
relational, 171, 174
survivors, 107
symptoms of, 107
therapy, 7
vicarious, 42
war, 8
Treadway, M. T., 74, 94, 100
Tronick, E. Z., 56, 59–60, 72, 74, 90, 99, 102
Turquet, P. M., 32, 49

Umilta, C., 28, 49
unconscious(ness), 32, 75, 128, 166, 172–173 see also: conscious(ness)
conflict, 179
human, 89, 128
starvation, 154–155, 165
Uswatte, G., 51, 71–72
Uylings, H. B. M., 12, 23

Valkonen-Korhonen, M., 52, 70
Van der Kolk, B. A., 104, 107, 114, 122
Van Pelt, J., 12, 23
Van Wagoner, S., 161, 169
Vanninen, R., 52, 70
Veroff, J., 163, 168
violence, 59, 125, 136, 139–140
Volkan, V. D., 183, 187
Vonk, R., 14, 22
Vybiral, T., 12, 23

Walker, M. P., 11, 23
Warneken, F., 6, 23
Wasserman, R., 74, 94, 100
Weaver, W., 94, 101
Wedig, M. M., 87, 101
Weis, T., 51, 72
Werner, K., 174, 187
Wertheimer, M., 33, 48
Whalen, P. J., 87, 101
Whitten, A., 29, 49

Whyte, D., 143, 145
Williams, J. H., 29, 49
Winnicott, D. W., 34, 40, 49, 161, 170
Witte, J. M., 59, 65, 69
Wolf, S., 51, 71
Wood, B., 172, 187
Woolley, J. D., 174, 187
Wright, C. I., 87, 101

Yalom, I. D., 56, 72, 108, 122
Young, L. J., 60, 72

Zhao, Z., 85, 99
Zilbergeld, B., 118, 122
Zimbardo, P. G., 81, 99
Zindel, S., 52, 70
Zink, C. F., 81, 98
Zohrabi, B. S., 52, 72